AFTER NATURE

AFTER NATURE

A Politics for the Anthropocene

JEDEDIAH PURDY

HARVARD UNIVERSITY PRESS
CAMBRIDGE, MASSACHUSETTS
LONDON, ENGLAND

First Harvard University Press paperback edition, 2018

Fourth printing

LIBRARY OF CONGRESS CATALOGING-IN-PUBLICATION DATA

Purdy, Jedediah.

  After nature : a politics for the anthropocene / Jedediah Purdy.

    pages cm

  Includes bibliographical references and index.

  ISBN 978-0-674-36822-4 (cloth : alk. paper)

  ISBN 978-0-674-97986-4 (pbk.)

  1. Nature—Effect of human beings on. 2. Human beings—

Effect of environment on. 3. Human ecology. 4. Philosophical

anthropology. I. Title.

  GF75.P87 2015

  320.580973—dc23

                       2015003588

For everyone who goes walking with me

CONTENTS

AFTER NATURE

PROLOGUE

OFFICIALLY, FOR THE PAST 11,700 YEARS we have been living in the Holocene epoch. The Holocene, which takes its name from the Greek for "totally new," is an eye-blink in geological time. During its nearly 12,000 years, plate tectonics has driven the continents a little more than half a mile: a reasonably fit person could cover the scale of planetary change in a brisk eight-minute walk. It has been a warm time, when temperature has mattered as much as tectonics: sea levels rose 115 feet as ice melted, and northern landscapes rose almost 600 feet, rebounding from the weight of now-melted glaciers. But the real news in the Holocene has been people. Estimates put the global human population between 1 million and 10 million at the start of the Holocene, and keep it in that range until after the agricultural revolution, some 5,000 years ago. Since then, we have made the world our anthill: the geological layers we are now laying down on the earth's surface are marked by our chemicals and other industrial emissions, the pollens of our crops, and the absence of the many species we have driven to extinction. Rising sea levels are now our doing. As a driver of global change, humanity has outstripped geology.

This is why more and more voices in a great range of fields, from the earth sciences to English departments, propose that we live in a new era: the Anthropocene—the age of humans. The term was coined by ecologist Eugene Stoermer in the 1980s and has gained prominence since 2000, when Paul Crutzen, a Nobel-winning atmospheric scientist, urged scientists to adopt it. In 2008, the Stratigraphy Commission of the Geological Society of London—the people who set and enforce the boundaries of eras, the Pleistocene Police—took up a proposal to add the Anthropocene to the official timeline of earth's epochs. (It is still pending: stratigraphers are well acquainted with geological rates of motion.) The proposal suggests that we have entered a new era of the earth's history, when humans are a force, maybe *the* force, shaping the planet.

The scientific debate about geological eras, supposedly rooted in hard facts, ironically reveals that the Anthropocene is not a simple question of fact at all. The classic way to delineate geological eras is via breaks in the fossil record. It's true that the extinctions we're causing will change the mix of future fossils; but that doesn't tell us how to define the Anthropocene. The Anthropocene is, in important ways, a slogan for the age of climate change. Some scientists, accordingly, date it to the Industrial Revolution, when the spike in carbon emissions began. Others look back as much as 5,000 years, to a time when methane levels rose sharply, maybe because of rice cultivation in Asia—a way of saying that farming, not factories, marked the great change in the relationship between humans and nature.

To define the Anthropocene is to emphasize what we think is most important in that relationship. We have to know which critical balance has shifted. Saying we live in the Anthropocene is not like saying the earth is 4.5 billion years old rather than 6,000. It's more like saying the United States is a secular country, or a religious one. It's not a statement of fact as much as a way of organizing facts to highlight a certain importance that they carry.

What has changed, then? How is this time different from all times before it? The Anthropocene finds its most radical expression in our acknowledgment that the familiar divide between people and the natural world is no longer useful or accurate. Because we shape everything, from the upper atmosphere to the deep seas, there is no more nature that stands apart from human beings. There is no place or living thing that we haven't changed. Our mark is on the cycle of weather and seasons, the global map of bioregions, and the DNA that organizes matter into life. It makes no sense now to honor and preserve a nature that is defined by being not human, that is purest in wilderness, rain forests, and the ocean. Instead, in a world we can't help shaping, the question is what we will shape.

The Anthropocene marks the last of three revolutions. Three kinds of order once thought to be natural and self-sustaining have shown themselves to be artificial, fragile, and potentially self-immolating. The first to fall was politics: long seen as part of divine design, with kings serving as the human equivalents of lions in the desert and eagles in the sky, politics proved instead a dangerous but inescapable form of architecture—a blueprint for peaceful coexistence, built with crooked materials. Second came economics: once presented as a gift of providence or an outgrowth of human nature, economic life, like politics, turned out to be a deliberate and artificial achievement, and vulnerable to its own kinds of crises. Now, in the Anthropocene, we have to add nature itself to the list of things that are not natural. In every respect, the world we inhabit will henceforth be the world we have made. This is not reassuring: politics, economics, and ecology are all in near-perpetual crisis.

The revolution in ideas that the Anthropocene represents—the end of the division between people and nature—is rooted in hundreds of eminently practical problems. The conversation about climate change has shifted from whether we can keep green-house-gas concentrations below key thresholds to how we are going to adapt when they cross those thresholds—and change everything from global weather to the acidity of the oceans. Geo-engineering, deliberate intervention in planetary systems, which used to be the unspeakable proposal, is in the mix of responses and almost sure to grow more prominent. As climate change shifts ecological boundaries, problems like habitat preservation come to resemble landscape architecture. We can't just pen in animals to save them; we need to secure migration corridors and help species move as their habitats lurch across a changing map. There is open talk in law-and-policy circles about triage in species preservation—asking what we can save, and what we most want to save. We can call the sum of these changes, the vast and irreversible human impact on the planet, the Anthropocene Condition.

Using the portmanteau term "Anthropocene" for all these phenomena is willful, an effort to meld them into a single situation, gathered under a single name. In this way, talking about "the Anthropocene" is an attempt to do what the concept of "the environment" did in the 1960s and early 1970s: join problems as disparate as extinction, sprawl, litter, national-parks policy, and atomic fallout into a single challenge called "the environmental crisis." Such a term is pragmatic: it tries to help people to act by gathering the elements of their predicament together in a tractable way. The environment had to be named before people could join together to try to save it. The Anthropocene has to be named before people can try to take responsibility for it.

Talking about the Anthropocene, then, can be a call to take responsibility for a changing planet. In this use, the idea of the Anthropocene is simultaneously at its strongest and at its weakest. The language of responsibility-taking easily becomes merely high-minded and sermonizing. It can mistake serious thinking, the earnest naming of problems, and heroic intentions for a high form of action in themselves. The appeal of the language of responsibility is often a delusion: the instinct that talking that way, all by itself, will help to call into being the agent of responsibility—a person or community that can *do something*.

Unfortunately, talk of the Anthropocene has attracted such self-important pronouncements as "this civilization is *already dead*" (emphasis in the original *New York Times* essay) and "if we want to learn to live in the Anthropocene, we must first learn how to die." This is just the sort of suggestive but, upon scrutiny, meaningless gesture that makes talk of "responsibility" feel self-important and ineffective. It manages to suggest that composing one's feelings into the proper existential attitude is the nub of what the *Times* writer calls "get[ting] down to the hard work" of the Anthropocene.[1]

This is just the sort of thing I want to avoid; I want this book to be worth reading. Nonetheless, this book is also, in part, a call to responsibility. In it, I ask which ways of looking at, encountering, and inhabiting the (post-)natural world might help to meet the challenges of the Anthropocene. I try not to moralize or sermonize. I freely admit that no "we" that could grapple with the crises of the Anthropocene exists yet, and that nothing I say here will call one into being. So a call to responsibility is inevitably disappointing: it highlights the ways that taking responsibility for the world remains beyond the reach of anyone who might read this book, and of all of us humans together—for now.

I want to encourage readers to recognize and insist on the seriousness of the Anthropocene challenge. Already there is a complacent response on offer from figures as prominent as the Nature Conservancy's lead scientist, who has seized on the "no more nature" slogan to denounce traditional environmentalists as philosophically naïve and insist that, in the future, conservation should serve human interests, plain and simple. This complacency, which embraces the Anthropocene as "the new normal" and proceeds as if all were business as usual, is just as inadequate as the sermon that converts the Anthropocene into a personal existential crisis. To the complacency-mongers, one needs to say: yes, the Anthropocene will feel normal; it already does; whatever is not actively killing you does. The loss of coral reefs and other ocean diversity, accelerating extinctions, ubiquitous toxicity: these will all feel normal, most of the time, without an active effort to see them differently. The slivers of nature that the wealthy preserve for themselves and stitch into their proudly Anthropocene neighborhoods will feel normal, and may come to feel sufficient. None of this should be comforting.

The natural disasters of the Anthropocene—coastal flooding, deaths from expanding tropical diseases, and crises of food and water shortage—are all but certain to be the catastrophes of the poor. Already, a global landscape of Anthropocene inequality is coming into being, as wealthy countries and the companies that serve them lock up access to farmland in Africa and Latin America and water in the Middle East and other dry regions. It will come to seem normal that rising seas wipe out whole regions in Bangladesh while they meet seawalls and adaptive architecture in Denmark and the Netherlands. The human propensity to naturalize inequality will not recede in a post-natural age, for if nothing is natural, nothing is exactly unnatural, either; nothing about a post-natural world requires an attitude of responsibility, or even makes such an attitude easier to take. Turning Anthropocene crises into occasions of common responsibility will require a politics that finds a way to merge, or at least hold together, certain questions that we have called ecological and others that we have called humanitarian, questions of conservation and questions of justice. The only contribution I can make here is in how we might think about those questions in a way that does indeed hold them together.

So this book is meant to help readers find their footing in the Anthropocene. Much of it is a history of how Americans have shaped their landscape, and how ideas and practices around the natural world have shaped American politics and culture. It is an intellectual history of the natural world in America, and also a political history of American ideas. The concept that unifies these themes is *environmental imagination*. Imagination means how we see and how we learn to see, how we suppose the world works, how we suppose that it matters, and what we feel we have at stake in it. It is an implicit, everyday metaphysics, the bold speculations buried in our ordinary lives. Through this matrix, some facts stand out as essential while others recede into the background. For example, imagination led early Massachusetts settlers to see their new landscape through biblical eyes and to call it a "wilderness" in the sense found in Exodus: a barren place full of heathens, a testing-ground for a people's faith.[2] Imagination was at work when utilitarian foresters in the early twentieth century looked at America's new national forests as if surveying a storehouse of resources: they saw commercial timber but overlooked the many noncommercial species and other interconnections that a later, ecological eye would discern in the same woods. Imagination was in effect when John Muir and early members of his Sierra Club hiked into California's mountains and found overwhelming joy and inspiration in places they trained Americans to think of as secular cathedrals—rather than the frightening, dangerous, and worthless places that high mountains had been for most people through the ages.

It should be clear that, far from being frivolous make-believe, imagination is intensely practical. What we become conscious of, how we see it, and what we believe it means—and everything we leave out—are keys to navigating the world, whether to manage forests for Teddy Roosevelt's Forest Service, to understand ecological connections as conservation biologists, or to survive in a harsh new place while seeking Christian salvation. Imagination also enables us to do things together politically: a new way of seeing the world can be a way of valuing it—a map of things worth saving, or of a future worth creating. This book details that connection: the link between ways of seeing, encountering, and valuing the world— that is, imagination—and ways of acting, personally, politically, and legally, that have shaped the world in concrete ways.

Four versions of environmental imagination are at the center of this history, because they have contributed the most to shaping

American terrain. These are (1) a providential vision, in which the natural world has a purpose, to serve human needs richly, but only if people do their part by filling it up with labor and development; (2) a Romantic vision, in which a key part of the world's value is aesthetic and spiritual, found in the inspiration of mountain peaks, sheer canyon walls, and deep forests; (3) a utilitarian picture, in which nature is a storehouse of resources requiring expert management, especially by scientists and public officials; and (4) an ecological view of the world as being formed of complex and interpenetrating systems, in which both sustenance and poison may travel through air, water, and soil, and in and out of flesh, as each thing becomes something else. Each one defined an era of political action and lawmaking and left its mark on vast landscapes. They all coexist today, in those landscapes, in political constituencies and laws, and in the fractious identities of environmental politics and everyday life.

Each image came alive in laws that channeled human energy to shape the world. Nearly every American landscape is, in part, a meditation on what people have valued in nature and what they have scorned or ignored. Take just one example. The agricultural terrain of the Midwest—that patchwork-quilt geometry of crops that comes into focus from airplane windows—is an artifact of how the federal government drew on the providential vision of nature in turning public land, which had recently been Indian land, into private property. The survey system of squares-within-squares was a model of how a free republic should live on the land—each family with its own sufficient plot, tied together by schools, townships, and county seats.

The survey system was just one part of a legal architecture that channeled human energy into clearing, settling, and planting the continent—laws granting land in exchange for cultivating the ground, planting or clearing trees, draining wetlands or irrigating drylands, mining gold or silver, and gathering stone. During its first one hundred years, U.S. law shaped Americans into forest-clearers and farmers, forests and grasslands into fields. The 1872 Mining Law established a you-dig-it-you-own-it policy to encourage private mining for minerals on public lands. Laws governing irrigation development (tellingly called "reclamation") were mainly designed to support midsized farms and independent farmers on what had been desert. Working the land, which Europeans had long seen as a degraded activity, gained dignity in American culture. The pioneer and the yeoman were model Americans in the rhetoric and imagination of the time. And their version of environmental imagination worked just as surely to push out and erase Native American claims to the land as it did to secure the settlers' claims.

This is a history of a country whose environmental politics has always been Anthropocene, though often not self-consciously so. From the beginning—unmistakably from the time of the first indigenous settlement, and overwhelmingly from the time of European colonization—the human presence in North America has been ecologically revolutionary, wiping out species, changing soils and plant mixes, and reshaping the surface of the earth. At least since Europeans conquered the continent, that ecological revolution has been deeply involved in contests over imagination, over the meaning of the world and the right way to live in it. These are the questions that the Anthropocene finally makes explicit and inescapable: how to live in a world that we cannot help transforming, again and again.

The point of this history is to orient readers on their own terrain—both literal and imaginative. Everyone living today is involved, intentionally or inadvertently, in deciding what to do with a complicated legacy of environmental imagination and practice, now that all simple ideas of nature are irretrievably gone. Losing nature need not mean losing the value of the living world, but it will mean engaging it differently. It may mean learning to find beauty in ordinary places, not just wonder in wild ones. It may mean treasuring places that are irremediably damaged, learning to prize what is neither pure nor natural, but just is—the always imperfect joint product of human powers and the natural world. All of this will require a vocabulary, an ethics, an aesthetics, and a politics, for a time when the meaning of nature is ultimately a human question. And since it is a question we must answer together, it should—but not necessarily will—receive a democratic answer.

I feel a little thrill of reverence whenever I see an image of the earth from space. I remember that the little horizon around me, often so uncharismatic and narrow that I could—and would— throw a stone to its edge, is set on the face of this beautiful sphere. Then I recall some of what the globe contains: acidifying seas, climate refugees, resource wars, and, alongside these human harms, hundreds of reminders that nature does not love us or want us to be happy: Lyme disease, birth defects, and the everyday theater of wild suffering, from the housecat hunting birds in the backyard to coyotes bringing down a terrified deer, to the thousands of ticks that can immiserate and exhaust an unlucky moose in the Rocky Mountain summer. There is no harmony waiting for us in that globe, at least none on a scale that fits our lives, our pleasures and pains and passions. But the blue marble on the infinite black background is still the only possible home of everything we can love. This book asks what we will make of that.

INTRODUCTION

"Come forth into the light of things," wrote William Wordsworth in 1798. "Let nature be your teacher." To his mind, the woods in springtime revealed more about good and evil than the teachings of all religions. "A heart that watches and receives" would know more than the "barren leaves" of science and art could disclose. "Spontaneous wisdom" was all. It entered through the eye that admired a green field, the ear that heard a finch's song. "Quit your books," the poet urged, "or surely you'll grow double": fat from sitting at a desk, but also divided against yourself by too many doubts, too much confusing learning, too many theories.[1]

"Observe nature and follow the path it maps out for you," Jean-Jacques Rousseau had advised in *Emile,* his treatise on education and moral development.[2] The book was a guide to preserving the natural goodness and temperance of humanity against the vanity, excess, and anxiety that infected social life. "Everything is good as it leaves the hands of the Author," Rousseau wrote; it was good just "as nature made it," and to force it into some other form was corruption.[3] Though Rousseau did not live to see the French Revolution, whose early days Wordsworth called "very heaven," his phrases made him a touchstone for many who did and who imagined it would rejoin human virtue to its taproot in a harmonious nature.

Yet for every claim that nature supported a revolutionary vision of human freedom, someone was prepared to testify to the contrary: that nature was the guarantor of hierarchy and tradition. A century before Rousseau, John Evelyn, the English forester and author of the first tract on air pollution (*Fumifugium*, 1661), praised nature for being terrifying. Terror, he wrote, was a lesson in obedience. Even atheists shuddered when they heard thunder. Crashing storms were reminders that people were sinners in the hands of an unrelenting God. John Ray, a pioneering naturalist a generation after Evelyn, argued that insect swarms were nature's scourges, reminders that divine order dealt harshly with rebels. The locusts were sure to come for atheists and democrats, delivering nature's judgment on their deranged ideas. Where Rousseau and Wordsworth saw a proto-democratic nature, pregnant with harmonious equality, Evelyn and Ray portrayed a nature made for piety and monarchy. The natural order taught discipline, obedience, and "mutual subserviency."[4]

Nature turns out to be flexible like that. It has been the handmaiden of revolutions and the underwriter of kings, proof of divine design and of atheistic materialism, from Athens and Rome down to the age of democracy. It has proved and disproved the justice of slavery. The most "natural" of peoples, Native Americans (as Europeans imagined them) stood as a rebuke to decadent civilization—except when the study of nature revealed, as it did to John Locke, that the indolent tribes must give way to "the industrious and rational" Europeans.[5] No wonder Edmund Burke, attacking certain theories of natural rights, announced, "Art is man's nature"—that is, as social beings, we are what we make ourselves through collective action, not the splendid products of any blueprint.[6]

Burke did not deny the existence of natural rights but regarded those rights as seeds that yielded different forms in the diverse soils of culture and politics, the art that is human nature. Others were much harsher in attacking Wordsworth's idea that nature should be a teacher. John Stuart Mill called all political appeals to nature nasty and obscuring: they superstitiously projected human values onto a mute and violent natural world, usually to defend a narrow and reactionary interest like the subjection of women, the preservation of slavery, or the glory of the monarchy. "The doctrine that man ought to follow nature," he wrote, "is equally irrational and immoral."[7] For Mill, the human duty was instead to struggle against "nature": to drain swamps, channel rivers, and overcome our own natural barbarism—our love of power, our cruelty toward the weak, and our subservience to authority, all of which distorted personality and society. Our purpose was to replace nature with art.

This brief view of nature's political, ethical, and cultural uses is a reminder of why Wordsworth's invitation—let nature be your teacher—can seem so quaint today. Most of us know, or suspect, what history bears out: that "nature" has been a vessel for many inconsistent ideas, whether one claims to be following it or overcoming it. When we hear opponents of gay rights denounce "unnatural" sexuality, we may agree with Mill that "nature" in politics is an honorific for prejudice; but we also know that Mill's humanist program to master and reform nature is not innocent, and fostered its own kinds of moral blindness. Mill's rationalism and faith in progress nourished his enthusiasm for British empire in India, which he saw as an unregenerate mass of all-too-natural humanity that must be reformed. Americans who followed Mill's call to transform nature were sometimes imperialists, too, spinning administrative schemes for Native American resettlement, and military expeditions to Cuba and the Philippines. Some were enthusiastic eugenicists—sure that, if nature needed to be overcome and perfected, human nature was the place to begin. These agendas were integrally related to their ideas of nature, which might give one pause about harboring any idea of nature at all. Maybe "nature" is one of those ideas, like "race," that confuses more than it illuminates and does more harm than good.

At the same time, Wordsworth's picture of a deeply felt response to the natural world still resonates. I'd guess that most readers of this book have known some of the following experiences. You might have identified with, felt uniquely at home in, some landscape, whether the one where you grew up, the one you moved to as soon as adulthood allowed, or the one that you've only visited or glimpsed but that has always had a special claim on you. You might have walked into the mountains and, after a few hours, felt clearer, more alive, vividly aware of what matters to you and what is just distraction and time-wasting; or you might have woken up on a farm and felt intensely the nearness of living things, the ways that plants, animals, and soil are linked in growth, eating, and decay.

But we know, too, that these encounters with nature are themselves not natural; they are cultural. Wordsworth is the teacher who taught us to meet nature as a teacher—Wordsworth, John Muir, Annie Dillard, Edward Abbey, and the many friends, parents, and in-the-flesh teachers who inducted us into their ways of seeing and feeling. These heirs of Wordsworth are one side of a culture war over the meaning of "nature." Ranged against them are those who believe the world was made to be used—to be mined, grazed, harvested, and planted. The same Appalachian terrain that, in *Pilgrim at Tinker Creek,* taught Annie Dillard about the mystical power of ordinary places teaches other pilgrims contrary and no less obvious lessons: that coal is there to be dug and burned, that slopes are to be leveled for development.

And many of the most intense encounters with the nonhuman world are strange and disruptive, not lessons in any kind of harmony. You might have felt the macabre fascination of stumbling across a decaying carcass and feeling your eye focus on a seething layer of maggots, or held a cut of meat and sensed the spooky familiarity of the joints where it was cleaved, which correspond all too neatly to those of your own body. Maybe you helped to slaughter something, a chicken or a lamb, and felt its brief struggle and spasms transmit a terror to your nerves that took hours or days to seep back out, and left you wondering about the boundaries of species and feeling. Maybe you have been terrified—caught in a strong current, separated from a friend on a windy ridge, intoxicated in a dark forest—and found yourself, half-panicked, superstitiously bargaining with higher powers for survival, only to toss aside the superstition with amusement and disgust when you were safe again. The nature that Wordsworth portrayed as harmonious in his carefully formed lines is all of these things, too, and so is the human mind that receives and answers it.

Come forth into the light of things? More like the cacophony of things, including many irresolvable contests over the meaning of "nature." We know too much, and have felt too many things, to learn in good conscience from the natural world.

Another reason Wordsworth's invitation is hard to take up today has, ironically, everything to do with "the light of things." What things reveal today is that they are neither natural nor artificial. And neither are we. The contrast between what is nature and what is not no longer makes sense.

The natural and the artificial have merged at every scale. Climate change makes the global atmosphere, its chemistry and weather systems, into Frankenstein's monster—part natural, part made. The same is true of the seas, as carbon absorption turns the oceans acidic and threatens everything that lives in them. The planet's landscapes, its forests and fields, along with the species that inhabit them, are a mélange of those we have created, those we have cultivated and introduced, and those we let live—or, in only the deepest jungles, have not yet reached. Even wilderness, that emblem of untouched nature, persists where lawmaking and management create it, artificial testament to the value of natural things.

The plants and animals that some people eat and others keep for company are human creations, through selective breeding (which now seems almost artisanal) and pruning and grafting of the genome. The human body, seat of Wordsworth's mutually counseling head and heart, is no more purely natural than our grains and cattle. Tuned with vaccines, kept up with antibiotics, patched with surgery, every function extended by engines, screens, and data streams, we are cyborgs in artificial worlds, whether we are the paralyzed child who acts through his robot extension or just a bicyclist with black-rimmed glasses and a smartphone. If Nature were a place, we could not find it. If Nature were a state of mind, we could not attain it. We are something else, and so is the world.

Post-natural as we are, we have not advanced far toward Mill's ideal of emancipated mastery over nature. Instead, the more we understand and the more our power increases, the more our control over nature seems a precarious fantasy. We brew the storms, bring the droughts, and raise the seas, but we do not command our genies. Climate change unleashes forces like those of the ancient pagan imagination, in which nature was filled with arbitrary, violent gods—one for the thunderbolts, one for the sea—who warred with one another and made human lives their playthings. With technological mastery, we have remade that unmastered world. In our own bodies, there are ecosystems, colonies of bacteria that make their home in us, and whose health is as important to ours as our lives are to the future of the planet. Whether we look to the globe or to our own navels, we are imperfect, destabilizing, and vulnerable governors, apprentices without a master sorcerer.

Because the human impact on the planet has grown enormously over the past two hundred years, and especially the past fifty, scientists, as noted above, are discussing whether the earth has entered a new geological era: the Anthropocene, the age of humanity, when our actions are transforming the world. The idea of the Anthropocene is useful, but it needs to be seen in the right light. Despite its scientific trappings, it is mainly a cultural idea, and its potential is political and ethical. Most important, the Anthropocene is a call to take responsibility for what we make, as well as for what we destroy. It is the starting place for a new politics of nature, a politics more encompassing and imaginative than what we have come to know as environmentalism.

Three Crises

The Anthropocene begins amid a threefold crisis—of ecology, economics, and politics. These are the three great modes in which humans make a home. (It is not just chance that the first two words derive from the Greek for "household," *oikos,* and the last from *polis,* "city.") The three crises share a starting point: the recognition that a system believed, or at least imagined and hoped, to be stable and self-correcting has turned out to be unstable and even prone to collapse.

Ecology first. The urgency of the Anthropocene begins with the realization that, after nearly ten thousand years of relatively stable climate and burgeoning human wealth, ecological systems are intensely stressed, and that their health or collapse, as well as the shape in which they will survive (if they do), is substantially down to human choices. Ideas about natural ecological equilibrium are gone. So are older fantasies, also rooted in ideas of nature, to the effect that the world was made to foster economic wealth and development.

Economics next. Modern economics rests on an image of inherent equilibrium: billions of decisions merge into a spontaneous harmony through the invisible hand of a pricing system that puts supply and demand into balance. When everyone is free to choose, efficiency reigns and all are better off. These are the premises of economics, the dominant social science of the age, and also the premises of a form of life: the market societies in which most of us live.

Our ecological crisis begins, in part, with the failure of economic harmony. The first lesson of environmental economics is that the invisible hand is (to mix metaphors) blind to so-called externalities. That is, the discipline of economic efficiency does not apply to actions whose effects we can offload onto others while avoiding all responsibility for ourselves. Greenhouse gases are a perfect global externality: mostly free for those who release them, they are soon perfectly dispersed through the global atmosphere, which distributes their harms around the planet.

The economists' term "externality" suggests an aberration, the incidental exception to a system that otherwise works—but here, that is the reverse of the truth. What economic analysis treats as an externality, what is invisible in market transactions, is the globe that houses all economic activity. Needless to say, everything is inside *that* "externality." The harms that are invisible to the economy may overwhelm the system itself.

That is one economic crisis. Here is a second. Even when markets work normally, two hundred years of evidence suggests that they produce accelerating levels of inequality, levels so high that they are quite likely to become politically intolerable.[8] This finding disrupts a familiar picture of the economy as a self-stabilizing system—a picture long associated with the "Kuznets curve," which showed economic inequality stabilizing at (arguably) moderate levels in wealthy economies. Ironically, this influential curve counted among its offspring an "environmental Kuznets curve," which showed pollution rising during industrialization, then falling in wealthy societies. Both versions now look like unwarranted extensions of the relatively favorable conditions of the mid-twentieth century. Today, greenhouse emissions continue rising with wealth, and so does inequality.

Both families of crisis, economic and ecological, reflect the same predicament: if we want a self-sustaining world, both social and natural, we must build and preserve it. Nothing inherent in the physical world or social life will produce that stability by itself. What humans get will be no better or worse than what they have made.

The only way to build a shared living place deliberately is through politics. Collective, binding decisions are how people can give the world a shape that we intend. But here lies the third great crisis.

Of the major realms we inhabit—ecology, economy, and politics—politics was the first to be recognized as unavoidably artificial. The authors of the U.S. Constitution were already, in their own minds, drafters and framers, not servants of a natural order of authority. More than a century earlier, Thomas Hobbes had argued decisively that political power can only be artificial, and that in creating it, people take on the responsibility that theology and superstition assigned to gods: the task of creating an orderly world. The recognition that both economy and ecology are also created orders means that both are also partly political; they are political to the same degree that their shape is intentional, and inasmuch as they are not political, the shape that humans give them is inadvertent. The choice is between politics on the one hand and accidental world-making on the other.

This is an uncomfortable truth. Politics suggests instability, arbitrary power, intrusions on personal liberty and on local harmonies. It is politics that authorizes strip-mining and produces mass surveillance in the United States, takes Chinese peasants' farmland for development, leases African communal lands to Chinese agribusiness, and sets off wars in Iraq, Afghanistan, and Ukraine. Shouldn't we avoid rather than celebrate it, and find some other, more harmonious order—economy or ecology, say—to lean on instead?

The attraction of getting away from politics is potent and perennial. The problem is that it is merely a fantasy. No order that grows spontaneously will stabilize and preserve the world. The alternative to spontaneous order is deliberate creation, and its source must be politics. Since we cannot have spontaneous order in ecology or in economics, all that remains is to create order deliberately through politics. It is perfectly possible, of course, to foster a *political* embrace of spontaneity, local harmonies, and markets, and in many cases that may be just what we should do. But the embrace must be political: it depends on deliberately adopting rules and institutions in which spontaneity can emerge. We lack those now—at least in any form that can match our ecological and economic crises.

But back to the crisis of politics. As with the economy, part of the political crisis is that familiar approaches are failing to match new problems. All serious responses to global climate change—and to inequality in global capitalism—face the same basic problem: there is no political body that could adopt and enforce them. Breakdown in a global system outruns the reach of any national government. Serious climate-stabilizing policies impose costs on domestic economies in order to benefit the world population and future generations. Although national constituencies in the rich countries will stand for, even urge, some such policies, they have not been nearly enough to slow the rate of climate change. National self-interest breeds weak responses and failure to cooperate. The discovery that politics is the necessary source of a solution to global problems turns into a troubling meditation on the barriers to a political solution.

This unhappy situation coincides with a larger crisis of faith in the possibility of political order. It was only in the twentieth century that democracy, long a radical rallying cry and, before that, a term of abuse and a synonym for anarchy, became instead the sole standard of political legitimacy. Since the start of the twenty-first century, short-lived confidence in a global democratic tide has receded to reveal a landscape littered with doubts. The United States recently launched a pair of destructive and wasteful wars on demagogic grounds; in both, an optimistic version of "exporting democracy" came to ruin. At the time of writing, Europe's democracies seem to have put themselves in an ungovernable corner in the poorly coordinated, unpopular, and not-very-democratic European Union, and openly nondemocratic governments such as China's are enjoying a new self-confidence.

Be that as it may, there is no alternative to political engagement with our three interlinked dwelling places—ecology, economy, and politics itself. Recognizing this turns the idea of nature on its head. "Nature" has had many political meanings and alliances, as diverse as democracy and monarchy or hierarchy and equality, but it has always had one defining characteristic. In a purblindness that has marked all of human history before today, nature has been the thing without politics, the home of the principles that come before politics, whether those are the divine right of kings or the equality of all persons. That purblindness is coming to an end with the Anthropocene. The next politics of nature will be something different and more intense: an effort at active responsibility for the world we make and for the ways of life that world fosters or destroys.

Nature as Politics and Anti-Politics

Why talk about an intensified politics of nature, rather than a politics without nature? Why not say that "nature," that all-too-flexible argument stopper which never quite succeeds in ending the argument, is just an archaic way of talking and thinking, best overcome and discarded? There are several reasons that I don't think this is either possible or desirable. The most telling is that ideas about nature have been much more than rhetorical flourish or metaphysical gloss. They have deeply shaped the landscapes, economies, and social practices in which we continue to live. The material world—so-called natural and so-called artificial—that we inhabit is in many ways a memorial to a long-running legacy of contested ideas about nature: how it works, how we fit into it, and what we have at stake in doing right by it.

What does it mean to say that ideas have shaped landscapes? Is this "idealist history," which imagines that concepts create events? No, but it is history that takes ideas seriously in quite a specific way.

We shape the world by living. Our lives knit into a kind of collective landscape architecture. By the ways we eat, move around, stay warm or cool, and amuse ourselves, we create the subsystems of a vast metabolism tying us at every point to our environment. We call these subsystems the energy economy, the food economy, the transportation system, and shelter—cities and suburbs.

We do not act blindly, though we often see only a part of the whole system. From the beginning, as noted in the Prologue, there has been a link between how Americans have acted toward the natural world and how they have imagined it—as a wilderness designed by God to become a garden, as a piece of symbolic art with the power to bring spiritual insight, as a storehouse of essential resources for national wealth. *Imagination* is less precise, less worked-out, more inclusive than *ideas,* and it belongs to people in their lives, not to philosophers working out doctrines. Imagination is a way of seeing, a pattern of supposing how things must be.

Law is a circuit between imagination and the material world. Laws choreograph human action in a thousand ways: governing the construction of highways and the electricity grid, allowing and regulating mining and drilling, setting the price of gasoline and carbon emissions (if the latter have a price), guiding and limiting the growth of cities and suburbs, shaping the use of farmland. Such legal strictures channel our lives, providing the implicit blueprints of the landscape architecture that we impose on the world.

Laws have various sources, among them economic self-interest and political partisanship. Imagination, too, is part of what makes law. Laws play out the logic of competing versions of environmental imagination. American environmental laws may be sorted according to the four pictures of the natural world that were delineated in the Prologue: the *providential,* the *Romantic,* the *utilitarian,* and the *ecological.* Each image contributed to forming a landscape, as well as to shaping a mode of identity, activity, and experience on that land.

Consider the pro-development laws, infused with the providential vision, that turned early Americans into an army of settlers. Under their aegis, pioneers treated the world as conditionally bountiful, the way providential imagination drew it. The Jeffersonian surveyors' grid and the statutes creating private farms produced an American geography where these providential attitudes made sense as a human relation to nature. This was true even to the point of making settlers blind to the inconvenient facts of weather and geography. The repeating rectangles of the settlement grid galloped over streams and wetlands and mounted the high plains, where rainfall was too scant to support farming. After a few unusually wet summers and warm winters, the seasons returned to normal and threw back the settlers, who became the first modern ecological refugees in North America. The fact that the land itself curtailed settlement in this case only highlights by contrast how successful the project of continental settlement otherwise was. The ecological transformation and the cultural developments around it were world-historical, yet Americans often discussed them as if they were the most natural things in the world, the expected upshot of a people meeting a continent. Soon another wave of settlers returned to the Great Plains, armed with technology to extend the grid westward, its lines now framing the crop circles of center-pivot irrigation.

A vision suffused these clearing and settlement efforts, a picture of nature with religious and philosophical sources. The world was a potential garden that existed to serve human needs, but only if people developed it with labor and settlement. This vision was the keystone of an idea of national mission: turning the continent into private property. It linked economic development to a cosmology and a sense of planetary purpose. It helped to underwrite the dignity of labor in a democratic culture that increasingly embraced the equal dignity of all its white, male members.

The second great American picture of nature, the Romantic one, has also relied on law to anchor experience and activity that, in turn, made real a way of encountering nature. Seen in a Romantic light, the most extreme and dramatic places inspire epiphany: flashes of insight into the order of things and one's place in it. One encounters divinity and one's own self on a mountain peak, in the rainbow-laced spray of a crashing waterfall, or at the lip of a deep crevasse. John Muir called Yosemite Valley's South Dome "full of thought, clothed with living light, no sense of dead stone about it, all spiritualized . . . steadfast in serene strength like a god." It was a landscape "singing with the stars the eternal song of creation."[9] Drawing on literary sources such as Wordsworth and Ralph Waldo Emerson, early Romantic social movements, especially the Sierra Club, wove these themes into the landscapes of California's Sierra Nevada and other Western high country. Soon they were working to ensure that American law dedicated large tracts of ground, such as Yosemite Valley, to visual delight and inspiration. Although many of the national parks were founded on the non-Romantic theory that they would nurture public health and civic spirit, by the 1920s the Park Service itself was calling them shrines to nature and the human spirit it trained.[10]

Parks made the Romantic way of meeting nature into real and widespread experience. Public wild lands were dedicated by congressional action to a picture of nature as a spiritual destination, a site for pilgrimage. In turn, those lands make that cultural idea of nature a physical reality for sojourners. Their material landscape brings alive a cultural practice of aesthetics and spirituality. These landscapes were inspired by ideas; but the ideas can enter lived experience only because the landscapes exist. So humans spell out their imagination in the landscapes they shape, and the landscapes write their forms on human experience and the imagination it fosters.

The protected public lands soon became testing grounds for radical ideas about nature. Starting in the 1920s, a new movement arose, dedicated to "wilderness." This word historically referred to unproductive land, and in the providential vocabulary it was closely linked to the derogatory term "waste." Wilderness advocates instead made wildness a virtue, insisting that the solitude of wild places edifyingly revealed a human being's smallness and dependence on the vast and ancient natural world. They went into the wild to be strangers and to learn from that strangeness.

The 1964 Wilderness Act, the fruit of decades of advocacy, gave legal standing to the new concept of wilderness; the act now protects more than 107 million acres of public land from development. Crafting their arguments, wilderness advocates found words for their own experience and made it more fully available to others. Both their practical reform and their rhetorical innovation rested on platforms their Romantic predecessors had built: on the one hand, a public language of the moral weight and aesthetic power of wild places; on the other, big tracts of public lands dedicated to aesthetic perfection. They used law and politics to shape landscapes—both molding a physical terrain and developing a cultural lexicon for encountering it, a way of seeing, feeling, and describing the big place and the many small places that it contains. In shaping landscapes, law also shapes modes of experience, enshrining and amplifying some and shunting aside others. The land that law shapes is a geography of experience, as much as of landforms and things.

This is an unequal landscape. The four pictures of the natural world that have most markedly shaped American law, and so American geography, are imperial conquerors. They have covered the continent like Jefferson's grid. Many other landscapes and experiences remain peripheral in this American geography, or are foreclosed outright. Native American farming practices are gone, now glimpsed only in traces such as the deep-red "Indian corn," called Bloody Butcher, that is still grown in the folds of central Appalachia where I grew up. Hunting and gathering as a way of life is gone too, though echoed in country foraging traditions and their urban revivals. The gardens that enslaved people kept on plantations and that some of their descendants brought north generations later in the Great Migration are mostly forgotten now, and there has been room only on the margins for the plots cultivated by immigrants from Latin America, East Asia, and elsewhere.

There are many rich stories to tell about these experiences, some of them centered on violence and injustice, some on solidarity and pleasure seized in places that remain mostly invisible to those who do not live there. I come from a marginal American landscape, one that does not fit the big pictures and grand stories so well. I know that there is no equality among American landscapes: some are treated as sacred, some guided into many generations of habitation and use, and others sacrificed in just a few years. And so, there is no equality among Americans who care about their landscapes and wish to imagine that their children and grandchildren might live there as they have. If you live in a wooded suburb of Boston and treasure the preserved lands next door, if you live in the dense neighborhoods of Boulder, Colorado, and like to go to Rocky Mountain National Park for your summer hikes, your relation to the land is secure, a privilege enshrined in law. But if you love the hills of southern West Virginia or eastern Kentucky, if they form your idea of beauty and rest, your native or chosen image of home, then your love has prepared your heart for breaking.

The styles of environmental imagination I am describing are, among other things, ideologies. They organize the world by simplifying it, highlighting some realities and casting shadow on others. They enable people to see themselves in convenient ways—as nature's allies or as the servants of divine order. They "justify" people in doing things to one another, such as clearing Native Americans from the land to further providential settlement. Approaching North America in a providential light encouraged people to see the continent as a potentially democratic nature, a terrain where each competent man might have enough land to live by, a terrain that, unlike the scarce and unequally distributed lands of Europe, did not impose a hierarchy between lords and commoners. The same view made nature complicit in genocide by treating clearing and development—European land-use patterns, which whites tended to assume were uniquely theirs even after Native Americans such as the Cherokee adopted them—as human obligations written into the world itself. Even as it shut out the first peoples of the continent, the providential view also screened out ecological nuance, such as the dry land, swamps, and inconvenient species that did not fit easily into the agenda of development.

Why give pride of place to these already privileged accounts of nature, with all the crimes they abetted? For one thing, they have contributed to the shape of the continent. To live in North America today means living in their legacy. Overcoming their limitations, redressing their crimes, and improving on their past requires understanding the politics of nature that they informed at so many points. Moreover, emphasizing their crimes and omissions tells only half the story. Like American democracy itself, American environmental imagination contains charismatic practices and ideas, but is also fraught with violence and exclusions. Both aspects deserve attention.

Speaking for myself, I feel all four versions of American nature alive in me. The providential view came to me through my grandfather, a fifth-generation Pennsylvania farmer whose great-great-great grandfather was deeded a piece of land for service in a revolution that was one part democratic insurgency, one part an elite land-grab with crumbs for the soldiers (but what crumbs, compared to what he could have farmed in Ulster or the Scottish borderlands!). It comes in the feeling I take from him that there is no better praise than being recognized for working hard all day outside. It comes, too, in the political and constitutional legacy of Free Labor, the idea that American citizenship means economic dignity, freedom from fear of bosses or masters, a claim on the good things of the world. Half myth, often used disingenuously, this idea is the reworked version of the democratic landscape of mobility and self-reliance that the providential vision celebrated and made real for some of those it favored.

I carry the Romantic view in the part of me that has been drawn to mountains, to their highest places and steepest defiles, for as long as I can remember. It was in my rapt stare when, at seventeen, I watched through a train window as the foothills of the Swiss Alps approached, and for the first time saw a peak that was not gradual and rounded like the topography I knew, but abrupt, angular, even jagged. It was in my racing along the crest of a volcanic ridge on Kaua'i, my hiking boots thudding on the dirt and stones of a wooded pasture that narrowed into a promontory perched fatally, commandingly high over an emerald jungle clinging to land eroded into the shape of a mad Bavarian castle, whose every line plummeted into the Pacific Ocean. It was in my shouting to no one, as I ran, that I, never a religious person, had come there to talk to God. Each of these is also a moment of tourism, a visit to a place whose everyday life I had no part in, where I had no thought of staying, and to which only my money—not much for an American, in those years of my life, but more than most people ever have—had brought me.

The ecological view of nature describes what I professionally do: teach the laws that govern strip-mining, farming, and the treatment of endangered species and their habitat. Thinking about these problems carries me into an attitude that is both scientific and aesthetic. Complexity and interdependence are the keystones of practical management (how much of a river's biological richness comes from the headwater streams that mountaintop removal buries? how much of a chemical spill in the Elk River will reach Louisville, on the Ohio?), but also the keys to fascination—the love of the world and the wish to understand it that motivate all of us who do this work. Its aesthetic speaks in the way I, like so many readers, can spend an afternoon following Michael Pollan through the life cycle of a meal because it carries me into so many interwoven systems. It speaks to me in the feeling that I participate in some of those life cycles when I eat a tomato I have grown, or return from a walk with a basketful of chanterelle mushrooms or a bag of young milkweed for the table.

The utilitarian attitude is on my tongue when I admit that, no matter how I am drawn to the idyll of a neotraditional farm, agricultural policy is foremost about feeding billions of people safely, a vast and technical problem that we can get hold of only by weighing calories, units of fertilizer and fossil fuel, the lifespans of aquifers, and the incentive structures of commodities markets. It is present when I say that, to pivot the energy economy in an appropriate direction, we need a pricing system that captures the harms of greenhouse-gas emissions, even if this can only be a false exactitude that conceals many political and ethical judgments. These are the techniques of social rationality—developed in the national forestry regimes of Europe and the United States and since extended to all useful things—that reflect the realization that everything we need is too scarce and fragile for us to use it casually, without an eye to the needs of others and to the future. They are the stock-in-trade of people who study law and policy, even those like me, for whom they hold no poetry.

I doubt that any reader comes to these inheritances in quite the way I do, and some will not regard them as inheritances at all, or at least not welcome ones. For some readers, one or more of what I call inheritances will probably feel lifeless or hostile. Many will come from their own marginal landscapes, places like my beautiful, wasted and eroded Allegheny Plateau, which no vocabulary of American landscape quite captures. Wherever anyone starts, we are all on this American landscape, all facing this daunting global future.

Regulating nature has never been a narrow, specialized task, or at least not for long, and ideas about nature have never remained just literary and aesthetic conceits. The imaginative and practical dimensions, vision and action, have been like the spirals in a double helix. The history of law, politics, and power is also the history of imagination. Landscapes, natural and human, bear the shape of both. History reveals the present as the joint creation of power and imagination, including the political power—sometimes but not always democratic—that imagination makes possible.

Understanding these shaping legacies can be a way of taking their measure in order to change them, to go forward in a different way. The landscapes that law shapes have ideological meaning. They resonate—or they do not—at the level of identity as well as that of policy. They also make articulate what people might rather not admit. They make priorities explicit. When mountaintop-removal mining dynamites hills and hollows into a flat, treeless terrain and buries many hundreds of miles of Appalachian streams, that wrecked landscape bespeaks the values of the energy economy as clearly as anything could. It is no surprise that coal companies make it as hard to see a mountaintop-removal mine in action as it is to look inside a slaughterhouse. The effort that goes into concealing these places is unintended testament to how precisely they express the value that American law ascribes to nature, and how poorly that fact sits with what some Americans would rather believe of themselves.

Four Versions of Anti-Politics

American uses of nature have always been both political and anti-political. Each form of American environmental imagination has called on the natural world to underwrite, to "naturalize," one version of politics while excluding others from serious debate. Each version has in some ways powered political imagination and mobilization by enlisting nature in support of political agendas; at the same time, each version has evaded politics, tried to shut down imagination and mobilization, by claiming that certain collective questions must be decided by nature, not by human judgment.

Consider one of the shaping political narratives of American nature, a pivot between the providential vision and the managerial one. Frederick Jackson Turner's "Frontier Thesis" diagnosed American democracy as the product of a fast-passing ecological moment and proposed to lay the ground for the managerial state of the twentieth century.

Turner, a University of Wisconsin professor who later taught at Harvard, announced his thesis at a meeting of the American Historical Association in Chicago on July 12, 1893. He argued that the frontier had created American democracy and indelibly shaped national culture. The free land of the frontier was a safety valve: both malcontents and the ambitious could head west. Their constant emigration from eastern cities saved the country from being divided into European-style permanent classes of property-holding elites and low-wage workers. The practical-minded equality of the frontier was a wind from the West, blowing east demands for voting rights and democratic constitutions, as well as resistance to faraway government. But that era had ended. The report of the 1890 Census had found settlement everywhere, merging the westward line of settlement with the Pacific Ocean, and so "the frontier has gone, and with its going has closed the first period of American history."[11]

Chicago in 1893 was the site of the Columbian Exposition, the World's Fair marking four hundred years of European presence in the Americas and celebrating the cult of progress. The fairgrounds were rife with displays of a future perfected by technology and planning, all centering on the famous White City, stucco-coated, lighted by electricity, and meticulously designed. It was both a monument to optimism and expanding human powers and an unintended reminder of the fragility of all designs for the future, from its ephemeral architecture to its unplanned closing event, the assassination of the popular mayor by an angry and delusional patronage seeker.

Turner's thesis had an ascent-of-man linearity that would have suited an exhibition in the White City. He claimed that the whole outline of human history displayed itself in condensed panoramas on the opened continent, as it had in the longer and more meandering ascent of older societies. Turner issued an invitation to his readers: "Stand at Cumberland Gap and watch the procession of civilization, marching single file—the buffalo following the trail to the salt springs, the Indian, the fur trader and hunter, the cattle-raiser, the pioneer farmer—and the frontier has passed by. Stand at South Pass in the Rockies a century later and see the same procession with wider intervals between."[12]

There was a shadow in Turner's account of progress. He delivered his thesis at the moment when remaining a frontier people became impossible. With the end of abundant land, a nation of individualists faced the interdependence of people who were stuck with one another; a culture built on the expectation of effectively limitless resources confronted scarcity and class conflict; and a democratic community, accustomed to self-governance, met a world too complicated for prompt, shared decisions, a world that only experts and planners could navigate. Americans had lost their original nature, and they would now have to produce a chosen second nature, in some ways as artificial as the White City.

So, when Turner wrote that "American democracy . . . came out of the American forest, and it gained new strength each time it touched a new frontier," he was also saying that democracy's time had passed, at least in the version that the frontier had shaped. The country was now "looking with shock upon a changed world." The national task was no longer to cut and burn the western forests but to preserve timber, not just to spur settlement but to nourish scientific agriculture. The age of conservation and management had come.[13]

Nature now needed to be managed collectively and by experts. New social conflicts demanded the same. Turner believed the spirit of American democracy had been acutely individualist and mistrustful of organized power. Yet, as he lectured about the frontier, the country was torn by labor strife, that most collective of conflicts—organized workers gathered against massed capital. His beloved West was producing the most radical, which is to the say the most collectivist, of the American unions, among the miners of Montana and Colorado. Turner concluded that a new synthesis was needed, preserving a version of the old individualism in very different circumstances, when its simple form had become impossible.

So Turner wrote in 1903 that American politics seemed to divide mainly on "the question of Socialism"—the question of how far economic life should be subject to collective control, and for what purposes.[14] In an address delivered late in 1910, he aligned himself with Theodore Roosevelt's "New Nationalism," a program of strong government that Roosevelt imagined would preserve the virtues of individualism and civic spirit through—perhaps paradoxically—intelligent management.[15] Like Roosevelt, Turner contrasted this management-for-individualism with the simple, laissez-faire individualism of conservatives like the railroad baron E. H. Harriman, whose rejection of government was a throwback to a lost frontier.[16] Turner and Roosevelt proposed instead that intelligent regulation could preserve the individualist spirit of the frontier even as it annulled the frontier's libertarian mode of governance.

Losing the frontier, then, meant losing political innocence. Turner wrote that American democracy had taken shape in historically unique exemption from the basic problem of modern and democratic politics: the problem of managing conflicting interests and values in a world of relative scarcity. There is not enough of all the good things in life—land, wealth, leisure—and conflict over those determines whose wishes come true, and whose lives end up as the compromised instruments of others' comfort. Because one of the easiest ways to live comfortably is to exploit others, one of the basic political problems is what Turner identified as the political theme of his time: the relation between capital and labor, the social terms of work and cooperation. The frontier had eased the pressure of these problems, making expansion an alternative to political conflict, exit an alternative to exploitation. When (white) Americans felt trapped in poverty or exploitation, they could (in principle) leave for open land, reverting to what Turner imagined as an earlier stage of social development and giving themselves a second chance at history's casino. This was an individualist safety valve to release social conflict, not a collective means of resolving it. By reducing the force of clashing interests, as much as by cultivating settler self-reliance, the frontier gave American politics the individualist stamp that Turner called democratic.

No doubt one reason the Frontier Thesis captured Americans' imagination is that Turner's claims were the opposite of original. He was recasting the tenets of a civic religion, often summarized as Manifest Destiny: the belief that it was Americans' mission to redeem and shape the untamed continent with their agrarian virtues and civic institutions. Thomas Jefferson had promised in his first inaugural address that frontier land would enable Americans to live a rural, egalitarian life for a thousand generations. Two years before the Civil War, Abraham Lincoln had argued that open land created unique social mobility, so that the Old World division of labor and capital did not apply in the New World.[17] William Gilpin, Colorado's first governor and a great rhetorician of Manifest Destiny, announced that geography formed America's destiny—the destiny of a continental empire of liberty.[18] These were only some of the most prominent expressions of a whole world of American rhetoric.

Turner's claim that the frontier had closed and thus had changed the terms of American life was not altogether new, either. Already in the early nineteenth century, the philosopher G. W. F. Hegel had argued that because the American frontier was an escape hatch from the conflicts of politics, the United States would not develop a genuine political life until it ran out of land and Americans had to turn and face one another. Until then, its politics would be a gloss on escapist expansion, and would hardly confront scarcity, exploitation, or conflicts in social vision. This was, of course, the conclusion Turner reached decades later, when events seemed to have caught up with Hegel's thought.

The idea of a closing frontier was hardly restricted to speculation in the universities. Five years before Turner announced the Frontier Thesis, Theodore Roosevelt had founded the Boone and Crockett Club, an elite sportsmen's organization devoted to conserving North American big game in the face of commercial hunting and development pressure on wild lands—concerns that would attract Roosevelt, nostalgic "western" novelist Owen Wister (an elite Philadelphian best remembered for *The Virginian*), and other members of the club to Turner's thought, as Turner would later be drawn to Roosevelt's political agenda.

Turner's thesis has been subject to so much academic criticism that it is, itself, more an object of historiographic interest than a contender in theories of American political development. Yet no one can deny that American political culture was formed in constant engagement with, and reflection upon, a rich continent which settlers turned into wave after wave of advancing frontiers. In a broad sense Turner can only have been right, even if he was wrong in many damning particulars.

Turner argued that Americans had been oblivious to the basic problems of politics, enjoying a long national adolescence in which energy and individuality seemed enough to organize the world. They had evaded politics until his time, when Roosevelt and other Progressive reformers squarely faced the problems of social and political order. Nature had long powered a peculiarly American anti-politics.

What Turner left out of this story was just as important as what he included. His own account was an anti-politics, too. Looking backward, he treated the continent's clearing and development as a natural process, the pageant of universal history, when in fact it was a project of war and ethnic cleansing. After all, the continent was rich and "empty" only after it was cleared of its first peoples, in a campaign that Turner effectively concealed when he placed the Indian hunter at the head of a pageant of progress, first to follow the bison, next to fade peaceably away before the dawning future. Turner's ecological determinism also missed the importance of political initiative even in the frontier period: the demands from the West were democratic—not just for ecological reasons, but because much of the country's public culture was staked on the notion of equality among white men, which helped the liberty of the frontier become an emblem of the country in a way that it never was, for instance, in more orderly and persistently imperial Canada. Turner described the character of the providential republic's ideal citizen—alert, practical, and self-reliant—as if it had been molded from prairie soil and fired in the heat of burning midwestern forests, rather than taught in thousands of sermons, campaign speeches, and humbler exercises that tied democratic culture to the labor of grubbing up roots and planting a continent in grain.

But the more momentous anti-politics in Turner's account concerned the nation's present, not its past. He described the utilitarian reforms of the Progressive era as the advent of mature politics; but these reforms had their own anti-democratic uses of nature. They offered another version of nature, with a political and legal agenda implied.

Progressive reformers such as Roosevelt saw nature as existing to serve human purposes, but insisted, contrary to the providential view, that nature did not smoothly support the small-scale clearing and settlement of frontier culture. For them, the American landscape was not precomposed for harmony with the Homestead Act and the Jeffersonian grid. Instead, many natural systems, such as forests, rivers, and soil systems, worked on scales that were too large, and in ways that were too complex, for Jeffersonian settlers to manage them well. Pioneers had cleared timber too quickly, exhausted their fields, and sent eroded soil downstream to clog waterways. The country was using its natural wealth recklessly. What was needed was management at the scale of the complex and interdependent resources themselves—forests, rivers—over nature's time-scale, and in the interest of the whole political community, not just some lucky members of the present generation. Only government could achieve that, a government staffed by people with the scientific training to manage resources well. Where the providential version of nature called out for clearing and settlement, this utilitarian, Progressive version demanded to be administered. Early in the nineteenth century, the continent had seemed to call forth a homesteading, agrarian empire of liberty; now it invited a strong national state, the administrative state of the twentieth century. This was the program that Roosevelt advanced, and Turner praised, as what came after the frontier.

How was this embrace of governance an evasion of politics? The key lies in H. L. Mencken's famous remark about Theodore Roosevelt—that he loved government but did not care for democracy.[19] It is not, of course, just a matter of Roosevelt's personal temperament; rather, his attitude captures something in the politics of his time. Roosevelt once said that his whole program of domestic reform was nothing but widespread application of the principle of conservation. From antitrust to labor law, from city planning to public-health regulation, social and economic life was encountering the same problems that Progressives found in nature: the systems were so large and complex that leaving them up to individual decisions disserved the public good. Like rivers and forests, the streams of commerce and even the lives of citizens had to be managed for the long-term benefit of the whole population. This management was a public-minded project, but not a democratic one. It took its standards not from popular will, but from expert knowledge. It is hardly strange, then, that some of the strongest conservationists, including Roosevelt and his great supporter, Indiana senator Albert Beveridge, were adamant imperialists, confident that the United States could govern the Philippines and other far-off places for the benefit of local people, since the touchstone of legitimate government was not democracy but, as Beveridge argued in support of Roosevelt's foreign policy, efficient administration. Nor is it strange that many of Roosevelt's closest advisers, such as Gifford Pinchot, who built and led the Forest Service, were committed eugenicists, for whom the human species was itself a kind of resource for rational management.

Many Progressive reformers shared the conviction that there was one right definition of the public good, a utilitarian calculus that would tell the expert manager just where the national interest lay. When Roosevelt and his allies treated natural-resource conservation as the model of all regulation, they implied that the social benefit of a policy was an uncontroversial quantity, not a target of competing values and interests. Managing a forest for timber and erosion control allowed a straightforward accounting of public costs and benefits that a manager could use to schedule logging over decades. Forestry, as a young science of resource management, had little room for disputes about just what the value of a tree was, or whether trees or ecosystems might have their own interests— ideas that Romantics like Sierra Club leader John Muir had begun to sound in public, but that Roosevelt's circle mostly scorned. Taking forest management as a general model meant acting as if the competing demands of labor and management, laissez-faire capitalists and socialists, were open to the same objective accounting. It implied that there was no irresolvable clash of values between antitrust advocates such as Louis Brandeis, who wanted to protect an economy of smallholders, and others, like Roosevelt, who wanted to embrace big business, then regulate it. There was only the question of coming to the right answer.

Conservation, then, was pivotal in the rise of cost-benefit analysis, which today is a touchstone language of American policy and lawmaking. Since the 1980s, when cost-benefit analysis became central to environmental policy, its critics have argued that a would-be objective technique cannot provide a judgment on whether laws are good, or legitimate. Historians of economic and social policy recognize that those debates crystallize broader problems that emerged when American policymakers after World War II began pursuing overall consumer welfare rather than openly distributive politics or other traditional concerns of political economy, such as the quality of work. That shift from the conflicts at the heart of politics to a conflict-smoothing (or -concealing) focus on consumer welfare has its roots in the Progressives' technocratic, managerial approach to social policy, which itself rested on their understanding of nature and the human place in it. In a sense, it was the American landscape—the vast tracts of interdependent forests, waterways, and soil systems, many still under public management and ownership when Roosevelt's reforms got underway—that made plausible a managerial, welfare-maximizing approach to social policy at large. This approach remains a leading way of making policy appear nonpolitical, even anti-political, in the name of an objective and technical conception of the common good.

Another politics of nature was also emerging alongside the utilitarian management of Roosevelt and his allies, and it concealed yet another anti-politics. Romantic activists such as John Muir insisted that the landscapes they treasured should be preserved as something like secular cathedrals. Their position was not exactly that these places should be outside the utilitarian calculus of public benefit—the Sierra Club made an early peace with the rhetoric of cost-benefit analysis—but that aesthetic, recreational, and emotional satisfaction should be central to the meaning of public benefit. They defined themselves against "philistinism and commercialism," and all merely material measures of well-being.[20]

Because it was arguing over the values that government should pursue, the Romantic movement had the potential to show that what counts as "public benefit" is an inevitably political matter, not an impartial scientific judgment. Muir and his allies, who clashed loudly with conventionally utilitarian bureaucrats over land-use decisions—famously, over the flooding of the Hetch Hetchy Valley for San Francisco's municipal water supply—did greatly enrich the politics of nature; but they carefully avoided acknowledging that they were opening the horizons of democratic argument. Instead, they had their own ways of evading politics in nature's name. They claimed to call on the real meaning, value, and purposes of nature, which, as its devotees, they had special power to perceive.

The Sierra Club and its allies also limited the radical potential of their claims by making a hasty peace with a consumerist relation to nature, whose paradigm was the vacation. Their call for a new, spiritualized outlook was always focused on defending high-country sanctums while ignoring the environmental politics of everyday life, which belonged to the fallen lowlands. They claimed to rise above politics when they spoke for the places they valued most, while ignoring what might have been the political implications for daily life of their call for a more conscious and humanly enriching relation to the living world. This combination of quasi-religious elitism on one hand and touristic consumerism on the other meant that the Romantic movement produced no political agenda to open wide the human relation to nature as a democratic question.

The fourth major version of American nature, the ecological, has now been at the center of environmental politics, lawmaking, and imagination for roughly fifty years. It took energy from the growing visibility and sophistication of ecological science; from the massive increase in the American and western European resource footprints in the consumer-industrial economies that grew up after World War II, which pressed many natural systems harder than ever before; from a new cultural emphasis on security and cleanliness in the prosperous suburbs of the era; and from growing doubts that technological mastery of nature always meant progress—doubts spurred by, among other things, the atomic threat and the failure of U.S. technology and planning in Vietnam. The heart of ecological nature is interconnection so deep and widespread that boundaries among organisms, places, and systems are neither stable nor secure. Rachel Carson's *Silent Spring* crystallized what this meant for an industrial society: toxins released into air and water ended up in soil, flesh, and DNA. The suburbs were unsafe; even the body was not secure. From the beginning, this ecological image carried a threat—the apocalyptic specter of a "poisoned world."[21] It also brought a comforting, pastoral promise: recognizing oneself as a part of the nonhuman world, as continuous with it, could be a remedy for alienation and discontent. This promise was a version of the restorative unity with nature that the Romantics had sought, but with a basis that was more homely than the "cathedrals" of the high country.

Ecological nature required new scales of regulation: at the level of systems, such as the Clean Air Act and Clean Water Act; cutting across public and private land, as the Endangered Species Act does. Earlier laws had amounted to zoning on a continental scale, with regions of private property implicitly dedicated to economic use, public lands explicitly committed to a mix of managed production and recreation, and wilderness consecrated to solitary contemplation and adventure. The zoning-style approach grew palpably inadequate, once no one could deny that natural systems overrun jurisdictional boundaries. The ecological insight did to the conservationist, zoning-based approach what the conservationists had done to the providential, property-oriented lawmaking that came before: it showed that the artificial boundaries of the zoning approach were too narrow for a deeply interconnected natural world.

There is no separating human beings from ecological nature. Wilderness was the apex of the Romantic view—a nature without people, devoid of production or extraction, set aside for leave-no-trace pilgrims. By contrast, *agriculture* would make a more apt touchstone for ecological nature. Eating is one of the most basic ties between the human body and the rest of the world, a relationship of sustenance and survival. Agriculture shapes landscapes and soil systems, as well as human labor, technology, and culture. Its practices, from plant breeding to pesticides and antibiotics, define the chemistry and bacterial ecosystem of the human body. Another candidate for an ecological emblem is *energy*. The energy economy reworks the chemistry of the global atmosphere and drives change in the world's climates. It forms landscapes through mining and drilling, windmills and solar panels. It shapes human habitation: suburbs and exurbs have grown up around cheap fuel, just as towns and villages once clustered around rivers that drove their mills and carried their goods. In these ways, ecology has deepened the problems and raised the stakes of environmental law and politics. In fact, the intensification is so great that referring to "environmental" questions has become artificially narrow; when we talk about the human relation to the natural world, we sweep in most of what we do and how we live.

Yet ecological nature has inspired its own evasions of politics. Some, to be sure, are not to be taken seriously—to wit, 1970s fantasies that a Green authoritarian state might be the answer to the ecological crisis. Such ideas are instructive more as symptoms of disaffection from stumbling democracies than as prescriptions for a cure. Quite apart from the moral priority of democracy, which is no small thing, the hope for enduringly benign authoritarianism is so absurd as to be a mark of intellectual desperation.

Other evasions are more serious. The most influential ecological anti-politics is the ubiquitous idea that all would be well if only markets were engineered to reflect the "true costs" of economic decisions. On one level, this is a fine idea. Pollution needs to be regulated, and raising prices is one kind of regulation—a kind that has some practical and ethical advantages over more direct control of individual decisions. (It would be complicated and intrusive to tell each person how much fuel to burn; better to raise the price and let people decide how much that big car is really worth to them.) This approach also has the appeal of hard-headed objectivity: forget about moral and aesthetic arguments, and just get the numbers right! Perhaps not surprisingly, environmental advocates and policy types have rushed to put a price on nearly everything, from swamps to oceans to wild plants. This kind of thinking closely resembles the traditional cost-benefit analysis of the early twentieth century, but with an essential difference. Then, the imagined goal was a decision by a public planner, who would schedule a logging concession or require a certain level of cleanliness in water to maximize benefit to the public. The economic bottom line, in that traditional calculation, appeared on an administrator's ledger. In the new version, the ideal is a market, which registers and aggregates the preferences (at least the ones backed by money) of everyone involved. All environmental goods would come into the marketplace, generating a price for the stability of the earth's atmosphere and the diversity of the deep seas, as surely as for phones and shoes.

In this way, market-oriented environmental reform fits the spirit of a time when people are urged to understand themselves as consumers and entrepreneurs, their conversations as sales pitches, even their personalities as brands. These cultural echoes are not random or trivial. They express the widespread assumption that markets are dynamic, intelligent, and effective, while politics—not least democracy—is static, stupid, and bootless. In this image, whenever we can switch a problem over from political governance to market governance, we can expect the market to do the better job.

There are serious problems here. There is no objective way of pricing the environmental values that reformers want to bring into markets. The "price" of biodiversity, climate stability, and wetlands must be a function of how much, and in what ways, they matter to people. This is not much of a problem for, say, shoes: their price reflects how badly consumers want them and how much money buyers have to spend. But market-oriented environmental reforms address externalities, effects that escape ordinary market processes. This means that reformers cannot just wait for a price to bubble up from the play of supply and demand, because they would wait forever—it would be like waiting patiently for the world's gasoline buyers to begin paying a spontaneous surcharge to show their worry about climate change. Instead, reformers must act politically to put a price on the good, either directly (as with a carbon tax that would translate into an extra charge on fuel) or indirectly (for instance, by limiting total carbon emissions so that the price of releasing carbon would rise with its relative scarcity). That means the "market-correcting" price can take hold only when there is a binding political decision to impose it, which includes deciding, through politics, how and how much to value the environmental good. There is no way around politics here. Environmentalists in the United States were rudely reminded of this fact in 2010, when they tried and failed to pass a market-oriented climate-change law whose technical details for regulating greenhouse gases had been many years in the making.

Market reform is not a way around politics. Imagining that it could be dampens the very politics that might produce an adequate response. Widely held, strongly felt ways of valuing nature are sometimes necessary conditions of new laws that govern nature in new ways. Such new ways of valuing nature arise, crystallize, and spread in politics. Running from politics toward a fantasy of an ecologically appropriate market doesn't only put the cart before the horse; it also starves the horse. Our market-oriented anti-politics saps the political and cultural energies that drive new kinds of governance. The effect is to deepen disaffection with politics by increasing its sense of futility, and to amplify the notion that a corrected market would make everything right—if only we could get there. This is a double bind that grows tighter as we struggle with it, unless we can find and undo the knot. Undoing the knot would mean recognizing that we need a renewed environmental politics that can generate both the values and the power to engage our generation of problems.

Prospects

Politics will determine the shape of the Anthropocene. Consider one dystopian prospect. Earlier versions of nature have concealed inequality among people, their landscapes, and their forms of life by naturalizing that inequality, treating it as a simple aspect of the given world. Theories of race and sex, of the inherent direction of history, or of the purpose for which the natural world is designed have all done this work. These are not gone, of course—indeed, their traces are everywhere; but they are greatly weakened. The more distinctive and potent danger today is a naturalized version of post-natural human mastery. That is, the danger is in an approach to the Anthropocene that rhetorically embraces the need for humans to shape the world, but cuts off all avenues of radical and generative politics about how to do that, reducing our Anthropocene choices to a convenient minimum.

As economy, ecology, and politics unite with growing intensity, the natural world itself will enforce unequal economic and political power. Wealth has always meant the power to resist natural shocks and carry on with one's life. Wealth commands vaccines and antibiotics, upland real estate safe from floods, reliable flows of food and water when drought strikes, and muscle and weaponry when the desperate and the opportunistic try to take those things for themselves. In these ways, natural catastrophe amplifies existing inequality. When sea levels rise, malaria spreads, and storms intensify, low-lying and poor regions will see their poverty confirmed by disasters for which no one can quite be blamed, while rich countries, even ones that have started out as haplessly as the United States has on climate change, will build seawalls and innovatively adaptive buildings and cities. The global atmosphere is a great launderer of historical contributions to, and benefits from, inequality. Everything washes out in the weather. The fact that Europeans enjoyed technological and immunological advantages over Native Americans and other indigenous peoples once seemed to show that they were favored by providence or racial destiny; in the same way, the disasters of the Anthropocene near future will seem to confirm the rich countries' resilience, flexibility, entrepreneurial capacity, and that everlasting mark of being touched by the gods, good luck. But luck, of course, is the residue of historical and structural advantage.

It is too anodyne to say that climate change creates hazards for which wealthy countries are better prepared. It is more accurate to say that it creates a global landscape of inequality, one in which the already wealthy peoples who have contributed most to the problem see their advantages multiplied. As human pressure shapes the planet and global inequality inflects that shaping, other landscape-level inequalities will emerge. Already, many millions of acres of rich agricultural land in Africa are under leases of a hundred years or longer to feed burgeoning China as the Middle Kingdom dives into meat eating and obesity and builds cities on its farmland. Once, in a world of scarcity, peasants produced for lords and priests in a landscape that mapped out hierarchical bonds in different claims to the land. Such intense inequality has persisted on the global scale, but has been concealed and made politically avoidable by distance—literal distance, but also social and imaginative distance, the distance of those who do not believe their lives are entangled with the lives of others. Now, as competition for resources gets more severe, we may reproduce by region and continent the landscape of inequality that feudal society enforced field by field and family by family. It was once hard to imagine that the landlords would starve, even when crops failed and spring came late. Will it be hard to imagine that China, let alone the United States, might sacrifice its appetites when other bellies are tight?

The prospect is similar for water, as global demand outstrips total supply. Rich regions will become, to use an American image, the Los Angeles of the world's water, surviving on the rains of other lands, transferred across deserts by technology and wealth. Some places will become uninhabitable so that others can remain ecological exemption zones, where no cities would be possible without massive hydro-engineering. Those exemptions will become increasingly invisible as the engineering becomes more pervasive, just as we seldom think today of skyscrapers and suburbs in the American South as "exemptions" because they rely on air conditioning to keep up year-round business and busyness, or of dense cities in general as exemptions because vaccination and clean water save their residents from epidemics. But the half-hidden logic of a world of scarcity will be a landscape of artificial drought and plenty. We might think of this global water engineering with reference to the West Bank of Israel-Palestine, where Israeli settlements enjoy running water at all times while Palestinians in neighboring villages plan their weeks around some ten hours when water is available. The inequality is vivid there because it falls out along ethno-religious lines at a flashpoint of international politics. We might expect to see the same logic, however, spread out through canals, pipelines, and tankers, without the nearness and the political fire that make it so vivid in a single valley of olive groves, pastures, and militarily fortified exurbs.

I would call this dystopia the *neoliberal Anthropocene*. It is distinguished by free contract within a global market, which launders inequality to the point of invisibility. The hundred-year leases that African governments are entering into with China may look like the extractive imperialism that marred world maps for centuries, but they are agreements entered into with open eyes by governments that, in theory, are equally sovereign. It is another question whether this justifies the inequalities that result, especially considering that the agreements are themselves the products of underlying inequalities. In the neoliberal Anthropocene, that would hardly be a question at all. This version of the Anthropocene does not treat it as a source of new political questions, but simply envisions ever-intensified management of the globe, carried forward by market means, beginning from our vast present inequality. If scarcity and environmental disruption tighten under these conditions, the planet will become a man-made unequal landscape, a dispersed and interconnected version of a feudal manor or an occupied territory, but one constructed out of market materials: free agreements backed by wealth.

The alternative would be a *democratic Anthropocene*. It would begin by extending a famous observation of Amartya Sen's: that although many millions of people have died of starvation in modern times, no democracy has ever suffered a famine. Sen's point is that famines are not natural products of absolute scarcity, but political products of distribution.[22] Famines occur when some, who have enough or more than enough, can ignore others who do not. By tying together the fates of rich and poor, rulers and ruled, democracy puts a limit on such indifference. It is, alas, a broad limit that does not guarantee anything like equality or even decent treatment, but it is a limit nonetheless. Extending Sen's point would mean accepting that, in the Anthropocene, landscapes of inequality are human creations, and our decisions whether to create, tolerate, or change them are all political. The neoliberal Anthropocene would be a politics of the Anthropocene, but a self-straitened one, implicitly committed to man-made ecologies that amplify existing inequality.

A democratic Anthropocene would mean a few things. First is Sen's point, that the world of scarcity and plenty, comfort and desperation, is not just where we live; it is also what we make. Second is a premise of equality: if Anthropocene ecologies are a political question, then no one should be left out of the decisions that shape them. In a world with no political institutions that can grapple meaningfully with global ecology, this principle is more a demand—a standard of legitimacy that will call all arrangements into question until it begins to be met—than it is a scheme of governance. It is a way of saying that global ecology is everyone's: not just because it affects everyone, not just because everyone has a part in shaping it materially, but because, for these reasons, it should be everyone's authorship politically. As long as it is not, those who are committed to a democratic Anthropocene should work to imagine it so, and to insist on it.

Saying that the question of global ecology should be answered by everyone's authorship has three meanings, each of them tied to one of the things that democratic politics does. One of these is *sovereign:* it draws everyone's vote into a single decision about what will happen, what the world will be. That the world can pivot on that decision is the sovereign power of democracy, the most vivid and direct sense in which people can be, together, the authors of their world. The second is *discursive:* everyone's voice is in the often cacophonous scrum as the argument (too exact and orderly a world) unfolds over What We Should Do Together, a question that has grown into What the World Should Become. Third is *exemplary,* or prophetic. People may display and prefigure a way of living in and valuing the world that, though it would once have been impossible or even unimaginable, becomes a living question because someone embodies it in his or her life. The prophetic strand has been important in the long history of environmental politics, and one of the reasons to insist on a democratic Anthropocene is the circuit it maintains between the wildest creations of ecological imagination and the sovereign decision that makes a world.

The discursive and exemplary aspects of democracy are especially important because the Anthropocene is not anthropocentric in the narrow sense of treating the world as a storehouse of resources for human interests, or even in the somewhat broader sense of assuming that the only perspectives that should count in politics are human perspectives. The history of environmental imagination shows recurrent aliveness to the ways in which the world is full of consciousness, experience, and pattern that are distinct from ours but, in imperfect ways, available to us. How to behave in relation to the vital opacity of other life and of nonhuman order is one of the basic questions for a politics of the Anthropocene. The world we make expresses our alertness or insensibility to these things, and, in turn, shapes us for greater sensitivity or blunts us into indifference. Imperfect as democracy still is as a human thing, part of its challenge now is to make space, in the imagination and sympathy of people, for the nonhuman world.

1

AN UNEQUAL TERRAIN

Order and Disorder in Early New England

IN HIS FIRST inaugural address as president, Thomas Jefferson portrayed North America as an open continent with space for a thousand generations of settlement along the surveyors' grids.[1] Half a century later, Colorado's first governor, William Gilpin, forecast an American population "equaling that of the rest of the world combined," the populous fruit of Manifest Destiny.[2] It was a confident century, when "wilderness" and "waste" were things to be "reclaimed," brought back into flourishing order—the century of the federal Bureau of Reclamation, but even more the century when redeeming the continent stood as a national mission.[3] That mission was a keystone in an ideology that treated North America as the naturally deeded property of its white settlers, if only they would claim it.

It was not so clear at the beginning. William Bradford, first governor of the Plymouth Colony, wrote that the new land was "a hideous and desolate wilderness, full of wild beasts and wild men." This passage has become famous for its strangeness to the modern eye: wilderness hideous and desolate, not beautiful or sublime? Bradford's words conveyed the unease of the first European settlers—their feeling that they were living in near-chaos, a land hardly fit for the ordered and holy life that they sought.

The distance from then to now is even greater than it might appear. It is not just that Bradford saw wild land as bad rather than good. It is that he was not much interested in *the land* at all, not in the way that Jefferson and Gilpin would later be. For him, landscapes were the settings of spiritual dramas. *Wilderness* was not an ecological idea for Bradford, but a moral and theological one. The term aligned the Pilgrims with Israelites in the Sinai wilderness, and evoked Jesus' testing in the wilderness where Satan tempted him.[4] It described a place where order and holiness were absent, a desolation that pilgrims passed through on the way to the Promised Land. Indeed, many New England settlers imagined they would return to England and establish a holy government, a vision that flourished as England fell into civil war and Puritans in the old country moved nearer the center of power. It was not until the restoration of Charles II in 1660 that this hope began to fade.

Bradford wrote about land in a way that was less topography than trope, oriented by prospects for salvation, not by surveyors' lines. He approached the land not with a settler's eye, but as a sojourner.

Nor could the first New England colonists assume that the broad continent of North America would be open to them, should they wish to settle it rather than simply sojourn there. The first seventy or so years of English colonization were a hard affair, in which the newcomers were about equally matched with Native Americans, who sometimes traded with them, sometimes attacked them—as the colonists did in equal measure. Even with many of the local populations devastated by European epidemics (sometimes recently enough to leave food caches that the colonists claimed), material experience did not suggest that North America was made to yield to the ax and plow. It was a land that resisted invasion rather than welcome settlement.

Bradford's writing from Plymouth is especially concerned with theological themes, even by the standards of his time and place. The journals of John Winthrop, long-serving governor of the neighboring Massachusetts Bay Colony, give a fuller picture of the colonists' outlook on their new terrain. The nature that Winthrop described was always open to theological interpretation, like Bradford's—but for Winthrop, this was only one of its uses. On July 8, 1632, Winthrop reported "a great combat between a mouse and a snake, and after a long fight, the mouse prevailed and killed the snake: the Pastor of Boston Mr. Wilsson a very sincere holy man hearing of it, gave this interpretation, that, the snake was the devil, the mouse was a poor contemptible people which God had brought hither, which should overcome Satan and dispossess him of his kingdom. Upon the same occasion he told the governor that before he was resolved to come into this country, he dreamed he was here, and that he saw a church arise out of the earth, which grew up and became a marvelous goodly church."[5]

It was a world of signs, where there was no reason to assume that a mouse was just a mouse, and where animals' struggle for survival calls to mind humans' spiritual struggle. Nature expressed God's wishes and judgments. Winthrop often portrayed encounters with dangerous forces, especially the sea, as governed by "God's special providence," a specific and intentional divine act. Special providence carried shipwrecked sailors through dangerous rocks in the winter of 1630–1631, though it did not save their legs from freezing in the water: they had to be cut out of the ice.[6] When servants of one Moody of Roxbury drowned while gathering oysters, "it was an evident judgment of God upon them, for they were wicked persons." One of Moody's servants, in particular, had recently declared that he would rather swelter in hell than serve his master.[7] Nature and nature's God took the side of masters in the Massachusetts Bay Colony.

For all their concern with signs and providence, however, Winthrop's journals are also full of reminders that the colonists had to wrest a living from the Atlantic coast, a region abundant in wild goods. The journals brim with accounts of the patterns of tides, winds, and weather—intense concerns for coastal colonists in a marginal climate. A journey up a local river inspired reflections on access to fur markets, not efforts to divine God's message from the rapids, and a season when worms (rather biblically) beset the colonists' corn drew no religious interpretation from Winthrop. His comments on wolves' slaughter of calves are notably matter-of-fact (and the regularity of these attacks is a reminder of how fragile the transplanted agriculture of England was in wild New England). To the extent that the colonists thought about the new land in economic terms, Winthrop shows them thinking as trappers and traders: farming was part of survival, but it was not destiny in a hard and dangerous place where sojourning, not settling, was the aim.

What comes through above all in Winthrop's journals, with their blend of spiritual and practical attitudes, is a vivid sense of the *discipline* of a people who understood themselves as besieged both by physical nature and by sin. Winthrop shows his people taking the onslaughts of their environment stoically: when a fifteen-year-old boy had his brains dashed out by a tree he was felling in midwinter, his father responded with "prayer, and much patience and honor."[8] Sin was more insidious than fatal accidents, and frequently appeared through sensual irruptions. A prominent settler who had neighbors in to drink and ended up in bed with someone else's wife had to be resettled elsewhere. Discipline was more severe for servants. On June 14, 1631, one was whipped, lost his ears, and was then executed for "foul scandalous invective against our churches and government."[9] The pious applied the same disciplinary scrutiny to themselves, though not the same physical violence: late in the winter of 1634, Winthrop described a young man who felt overwhelmed by sin, manifested in blasphemous thoughts that he could not control (and whose content Winthrop did not record). He languished for months, refusing all comfort, before a renewal of faith relieved him.[10] An outbreak of sin—with its promise of providential punishment—could come anywhere, at any time, in a settlement besieged from outside and menaced by blasphemy and disloyalty within, in the lower orders of the community or the sudden stumbling of an individual soul.

Much of this was general to the pious Protestantism of the North Atlantic, but the American setting presented a special threat: an alliance between the forces of the wilderness outside the community and the compulsions of sin inside. Winthrop reported, without much elaboration, that Thomas Morton, a settler under the Plymouth Colony's jurisdiction but not a co-religionist, was imprisoned until he could be returned to England, while the other colonists burnt down his house. Morton had run an alehouse that served Indians and, it was alleged, had set up a maypole for pagan celebrations.[11]

William Bradford added much more texture to this hint of paganism (which, in his watchful eyes, was never far beneath the surface of the rural Anglicanism in which Morton had been raised). Bradford wrote, "Morton became lord of misrule, and maintained (as it were) a school of Atheism. . . . They also set up a May-pole, drinking and dancing about it for many days together, inviting the Indian women, for their consorts, dancing and frisking together (like so many fairies, or furies, rather) and worse practices. As if they had anew revived and celebrated the feasts of the Roman goddess Flora or the beastly practices of the mad Bacchinalians."[12]

Morton portended an alliance among the forces that threatened the discipline of the settlement. Bradford and Winthrop agreed that he had sold guns to the Indians, whose arming threatened serious consequences for the settlers. Bradford also complained that festivals at the place Morton called Merry-Mount would mean that settlers could "keep no servants, for Morton would entertain any, how vile soever, and all the scum of the country, or any discontents, would flock to him from all places." The especially severe discipline that the colony visited on its servants would collapse, Bradford feared, if rebellious laborers could form their own community. Therefore, "if this nest was not broken . . . [settlers] should stand in more fear of their lives and goods . . . from this wicked and debased crew, than from the savages themselves."[13]

Thoroughly entwined with the threats of native attacks and social insurrection was the spiritual rebellion of a revived paganism, a "school of atheism" and sexual license, conducted with heathens and, according to Bradford, in the carnal and chaotic spirit of classical paganism. When they burnt Morton's house, the colony's governors treated his expulsion as a way of eradicating the "nest," which they renamed Mount Dagon, after a biblical god of the Philistines, whose temple Samson destroyed as his last act, and whose image (in a different temple) was overthrown and dismembered by the power of the Ark of Jehovah.[14] The American land, full of Bradford's "wild beasts and wild men," threatened to align itself with forces hostile to the settlers' rigorous order. Mount Dagon stood as a reminder of the continuing struggle between the discipline of the colonies and the wild lands outside, whose forces could align themselves with the internal impulses to misrule.

In the same decades, a set of English naturalists and "natural theologians," students of divine design, were at work in England. Politically and theologically, they were the people the New England colonists had emigrated to escape. Anglicans and royalists, they abhorred the Puritan and republican forces that had executed Charles I and had brought the first parliamentary government to early-modern Europe. Nonetheless, figures like the naturalist John Evelyn and the theologian Henry More show a deep commonality with their dissenting opponents in Massachusetts. Like Bradford and Winthrop, they saw the natural world as an unequal terrain, one whose harmonies were designed to teach lessons in hierarchy and obedience. Nature was a teacher, often a stern one, that kept people in their place. As in New England, though, nature also contained rebellious impulses that could tear apart the delicate threads of order. In both places, social rebellion, in which the lower orders claimed more than their share of freedom and authority, was the threat that lurked everywhere and demanded special rebuke from both God's nature and those who interpreted his design.

Although parliamentary rule in England lasted just four years—to be followed by the Puritan governorate of Oliver Cromwell and the short, troubled rule of his son, Richard—the period sometimes called the first English Revolution brought enormous social disruption. So, not long after William Bradford expressed concern that a servants' revolution was brewing at pagan Merry-Mount, John Evelyn, a wealthy and genteel Anglican who would have despised Bradford as a fanatic, was voicing his own objections to servants and working people who were suddenly out of place. Evelyn's diaries, which span the years of civil war and restoration of the monarchy, are full of alarm at the king's execution, the rebels' radicalism, and, in particular, the loss of elite control over religious interpretation. In an entry from the early winter of 1653, he reported: "Going this day to our church, I was surprizd to see a mechanic step up." A commoner's preaching was already a kind of insurrection, and soon the "mechanic" was calling for worse. "His text was from 2 Sam. Ch. 23, v. 20: *And Benaiah went downe also and slew a lion in the midst of a pit in time of snow.* The purport was that no danger was to be thought when God call'd for shedding of blood, inferring that now they were called to destroy temporal governments . . . so dangerous a crisis were things grown to."[15] In the hands of commoners, allied to a revolutionary government and without a stake in the old order, biblical interpretation spun out of control and reinforced insurrectionary energy. Evelyn saw the same danger everywhere in a social life turned upside-down: in the spiritually inspired ranting of Quakers ("a new sect of dangerous principles who show no respect to any magistrate or other and seem a melancholy proud sort")[16] and in a general invasion of the churches by "sectaries of all sorts, blasphemous and ignorant mechanics usurping the pulpits."[17]

Evelyn was intensely interested in the natural world. He authored *Sylva*, a study of his island's trees and their care and abuse, whose blend of practical science and vitalism led Thoreau to quote him in the famous passage of *Walden* describing the Concord hermit's bean-field: "the earth, especially if fresh, has a certain magnetism in it, by which it attracts the salt, power, or virtue (call it either) which gives it life, and is the logic of all the labor and stir we keep about it, to contain us."[18] Evelyn's *Fumifugium* urged the planting of sweet-smelling trees to mitigate air pollution in London; he also wrote *Acetaria: A Discourse of Sallets*, about edible plants that could be used in salads. His writings on nature had practical and political stakes. Simon Schama has observed that Evelyn saw the destruction of royal forests after the execution of King Charles I as a symptom of anarchy, a world turned upside-down.

So when John Evelyn sat down to compose *A Rational Account of the True Religion* following the restoration of Charles II to the throne, he set out a vision in which natural and political order were closely entwined, and theology was the key to their unity. He began by describing the contemporary events that he believed demanded his defense of true religion. Authority had collapsed. A king had been executed by process of law ("murdered," as Evelyn put it), and bishops and priests denounced. A proliferation of sects, each claiming a version of truth, had displaced "the old Christian [religion], which taught men obedience to princes, reverence to antiquity, order and discipline in the Church." In this time, "fundamental laws and establishments [were] subverted" and, with human judgment unleashed from authority, "there was no king in Israel, but every one did what was right in his own eyes." These changes produced a "rebellious and disobedient people" who behaved "maliciously and wantonly" in deposing their king and setting themselves up as rulers. Such events, Evelyn suggested, made atheism plausible by driving evidence of divine order out of the world. Moreover, the insurrections Evelyn decried were inspired by the atheistic doctrines that he ascribed to Thomas Hobbes and Baruch Spinoza, who, in Evelyn's words, aimed at "making religion a mere figment and . . . discarding all natural justice, goodness, and charity, and resolve it [sic] into brutish force."[19]

Evelyn claimed that the rebels had recklessly deified nature by making it the only source of moral guidance. To understand this claim, one must appreciate that for Evelyn, as for many of his contemporaries, the word "nature" had two meanings, which were at odds with each other. On the one hand, it could figure "natural goodness, justice, and charity" in the interrelations among its species, places, and forces. These relations were both mutually supporting and hierarchical, like the dominant picture of social and political life at the time. While the natural world was an unequal terrain, it was also a harmonious one, and supportive of the harmonies of an unequal social world. On the other hand, nature could stand for the disorderly appetites that alarmed Evelyn as they did Winthrop and Bradford across the Atlantic—*mere nature,* one might say, or *brute nature,* rather than divinely ordered nature. This was the nature that Evelyn identified with his "atheist" opponents. Brute nature supported a kind of equality, for all people were made of the same matter and had the same life spans and appetites, but it was a disorderly and frightening force. This was the nature that the rebels looked to, according to Evelyn, and he and allies denounced its doctrines as "atheism," "anarchy," and "democracy," three terms that meant much the same thing for them: a

the woods to form their own anarchic societies and leave the orderly plantation isolated and unmanned. It also echoes, almost certainly by design, the most famous image of the "atheist" and philosophical materialist Thomas Hobbes—that of the life of "natural" man: solitary, poor, nasty, brutish, and short. For Evelyn and his allies, abandoning the unequal terrain where nature, divine design, and social and political hierarchy reinforced one another meant descending into this allegorical wasteland.

Evelyn was a political restorationist: with fellow supporters of the Crown, he celebrated the return of Charles II to England's throne. But he was also a restorationist in a different sense. He worked, like More and other natural theologians, to restore and elaborate a harmonious picture of the natural world that underwrote political harmony. He wrote to show divine intelligence at each point in the natural order. He and his allies articulated a picture of a natural world that was deeply interconnected and instructive in its patterns—a picture so resonant with ecological imagery three centuries later that environmental historian Donald Worster has identified Evelyn, More, and the others as progenitors of the ecological idea of "nature's economy," a self-ordering and self-sustaining system.[21] In hindsight, Worster's interpretation holds: Evelyn influenced Henry David Thoreau, and his school helped to inspire more systematic naturalists, such as John Ray, who set some of the foundations of scientific ecology. In their own context, however, Evelyn and his allies are better seen as reaching backward to a very old tradition which took the world's interwoven harmonies as evidence of indwelling intelligence and support for an orderly social hierarchy. This line of argument extended unbroken back to Plato's dialogue *Timaeus* and Cicero's *On the Nature of the Gods*. Its first motivations were inseparably political and theological.

In Evelyn's picture, humans might not understand every aspect of providence, but they could be sure that it ordered the world for mutual benefit.

Though the pregnant clouds dissolve in the most seemingly unnecessary places, they may be the ... originals of those rivers ... which flow from those eminences to refresh the valleys, and give drink ... both to man and beast. In a word, there is not silliest fly, or worm that crawls, not any grain of seed which falls, and becomes lost and scattered on the ground, but is for the food or help of some creature, at some time or other necessary for us; so as there is nothing made for nothing ... but [i.e., except] such ungrateful creatures, who blaspheme upon these accounts, and from their shallow reasonings.

The most abject, vile, and trivial things in nature are admirable, and those creatures which we reckon most defective, the most curious, and completely accommodated to their several functions. Indeed, some are noxious poisons, yet become antidotes; one fierce animal devours another, lest the wild beasts should increase upon us.[22]

Evelyn's account of the world's complex and paradoxical design suggests that all things in nature are admirable—not straightforwardly, but because "the beauty of the world consists not in its separated parts, (which seem imperfect) but united, its order, economy, and concurrence to the end; which shows it to be the work of a wise and voluntary Agent." "The world," wrote Evelyn, "is a poem—the most perfect and consummate piece that ever was made."[23] Read correctly, the poem pointed the way not to democratic Beirah, but to the rule of just kings.

Restorationist nature, the ally of crown and scepter, made short work of rebels. John Ray, a founding English naturalist and fellow of the Royal Society, declared that natural order taught humans "mutual subserviency" and ultimate subservience to God. Ray pointedly argued that noxious insects were God's shock troops, like those of an earthly ruler—unpleasant but "necessary, either to suppress rebellions, or punish rebels, or other disorderly and vicious persons, and keep the world in quiet."[24] These scourges would exact revenge, especially against the "atheists," those "rebels . . . who have made it their business to banish Him out of the world, who is the great creator and governor of it; to undermine his being, and eradicate all notions of him out of their own and other men's minds; to provoke his creatures and vassals to a contempt of him, a slighting of his fear and worship, as being such imaginary chimeras as are fit only to keep fools in awe. Certainly all this is the highest provocation that any man can be capable of, so it shall be punished with the surest vengeance."[25] The worst rebels, therefore, were those who misused their human reason—who employed it not to complete Creation by participating lawfully within it, but to clear the world of God and usurp his place as lawgiver and meaning maker.

For Ray, who traced his thought to the Cambridge natural theologian Ralph Cudworth, nature's God was a subtle landscape architect, a craftsman who set natural forces and living things in complex interdependence. The human role was that of a faithful gardener: to improve Creation in line with its design. To be in harmony with the design revealed by Creation, humans must resist their own "brutal nature," the mere equality of atheists and democrats, and instead maintain the proper subservience.

The fearsomeness of nature was key to these arguments in favor of the unequal terrain. It was not just that insects were scourges. Fear itself, the spontaneous terror at nature's power, made the case for Ray's "subserviency." John Evelyn triumphantly insisted that even atheists felt uncontrollably afraid at the sound of thunder, evidence that their speculative reasoning and hubris could not uproot the deeper recognition of divine mastery in the world. Terror of thunder and lightning was an emblem of human subordination that went back to classical arguments over the authority of the gods. The terror was, so to speak, metaphysically intelligent. It expressed recognition that people were always, as John Edwards would famously put it, spiders in the hands of an angry god, hanging by gossamer over consuming flame.[26]

In 1727, a hot Boston summer was followed by an earthquake that Cotton Mather described as "a horrid rumbling like the sound of many coaches together, driving on the paved stones with a most awful trembling of the earth."[27] Thomas Prince, the Harvard-educated minister of Boston's Old South Church, took the chance to remind his parishioners of the same themes that Ray and Evelyn had sounded: vulnerability and humility before a terrifying nature.

> With God is most terrible majesty; and when he has a mind to show it, he can easily and in a moment do it in such an astonishing manner as to affright the hardiest creature. He can put all nature, even the great and inanimate parts of the world into such a commotion, as to make us see in a most sensible manner, the terrifying actings of his powerful presence, and excite the highest and most awful reverence of him. He can make the heavy and dull earth to tremble, as if it felt the force of those awakened passions that should rise in our minds at the appearance of God, and as if it were moved with the fear of its present destruction. The everlasting mountains are scattered, and the perpetual hills bow down before him.[28]

The seeming permanence of the earth, its apparent stability, was always and everywhere subject to God's sudden action. Even "everlasting" landscapes could shake and change like spilled jelly. This violence was an emblem of human vulnerability, and so a lesson in the fear and reverence that should constantly disrupt complacency, pride, and any sense of personal security. Human vulnerability and fleetingness were much nearer and more palpable than the mountains'. Prince drew this lesson from the earthquake: "Let us then . . . bear in our minds a lively sense of our continual danger.

Let our flesh still tremble for fear of God; and let us be ever afraid of His judgments. Let us stand in the greatest awe of this most glorious being, and not sin against him. He is always present, and as holy, mighty, and terrible, as he appears in the most hideous earthquake."[29]

The nature that Evelyn, Ray, and Prince portrayed was full of grounds for joyful appreciation. The beauty of the world was a great theme in the works of Jonathan Edwards, and the Evelyn who is full of reverent wonder at the benign work of rainclouds is the same who loves to see atheists cower at the thunder. The world they portrayed was not always or everywhere frightening; but it was full of terror for those who defied its hierarchical order. It was and must remain an unequal terrain.

Two Paths toward Democracy

Were atheists and "democrats" really in league against the restorationist nature of John Evelyn and his allies? The question is a tricky one. The natural theologians were reacting against something real in the realm of ideas: the revival of an ancient line of philosophical skepticism, associated with the Greek philosopher Epicurus and the Roman didactic poet Lucretius, that did indeed seek to drive the gods out of both natural and human events. Lucretius, whose great poem, *On the Nature of Things*, was rediscovered in a German monastery in 1417 and reprinted in 1473, argued that the world was matter in motion and nothing more—a position that came to be called "atomism," or materialism.[30] By denying that nature had indwelling purposes or expressed divine judgments, he sought to cure the spontaneous terror—the fear of thunder, earthquakes, and the haunted dark—that figured the world as a storehouse of warnings, portents, and punishments. Thomas Hobbes, the *bête noire* of the natural theologians, was indeed deeply influenced by Lucretius. Both his political philosophy and his account of nature brought into early modernity Lucretius' classical project of mastering the sources of fear, which arose from superstition and disorder. These arguments ran hard against the natural theologians' positions.

The way that the natural theologians described their enemies, though, was more polemical than precise. It is implausible to imagine the eccentric Hobbes, dependent on patronage and often in fear for his freedom or even his life, as a leader in a league of atheist democrats, or to think that such a league was at work in the politics of seventeenth-century England. Although the question of Hobbes's religious belief is obscure, his writings overall suggest he was an unorthodox Christian in a time when England was overrun with heterodox sects. As for democracy, his theory of politics does indeed say that government is founded on the consent of all, and that the form of day-to-day politics—whether monarchical, republican, or democratic—must be decided by a majority vote of those who create the government by their consent. The philosophical elements of a democratic theory of politics are here, but Hobbes never called for organizing real-life government along democratic lines. There were radicals in the English Civil War, most famously the Levellers, who sought something like democracy, notably universal male suffrage; but there is no reason to think that they identified with Hobbes, atomism, or atheism. (Indeed, they would have seen Hobbes as an enemy, or at least untrustworthy, as his patrons were Royalists and he spent some years in exile with Charles II in France before his philosophical radicalism spoiled his welcome there.) The English radicals' vision seems to have faded quickly after the Restoration of 1660. While John Evelyn would have known of them, may even had them in mind in his denunciations of upstart "mechanics," John Ray, writing in the early eighteenth century, would not have had them in view.[31]

But the ideas about nature, God, and politics that we have been tracing were not just debaters' topics or poetic decoration. As explicit systems of thought, they consolidated broader versions of imagination and vision, such as those that William Bradford and John Winthrop voiced in their colonial American version of the unequal terrain. As Max Weber famously wrote, ideas are not generally the engines of history, but they are its switchmen.[32] At inflection points, they can bank events off at one angle or another, with big consequences as time hurtles forward. The engine of the century that elapsed between John Ray and Thomas Jefferson, or the two centuries between John Winthrop and Colorado governor William Gilpin, was the opening of North America for the largest project of clearing and settlement anywhere in the modern world, arguably the largest and most important in world history. Along with that opening came a democratic revolution in American politics—a move from a suffrage restricted to landholders and the wealthy, along the lines that England had long maintained, to voting and full political and civic participation as a basic feature of citizenship.

The irony of this great expansion of democracy was that it drew a hard line between, on the one hand, the white men who were the citizens of the new United States and, on the other, the Native Americans, enslaved people, and free blacks whom the new country shut out. (Women's exclusion is also a key part of the story, but it worked differently, partly because white women were often described as members of the political community, just unsuited to participate in its political life because of their "feminine nature.") Britain, Europe, and their North American colonies had lived in complex gradations of social and political status: royalty, aristocracy, gentry, yeomanry, servants and laborers, and varieties of unfree labor, from indentured servants to serfs and outright slaves. Eligibility to vote, serve in government, appear in court, or enter the professions might depend on such status, or on one's religion. (In Britain, the final stage of Catholic Emancipation, which allowed Roman Catholics to sit in Parliament, came in 1829, just a decade before the abolition of slavery throughout the British Empire.) The American founders had grown up in such societies, and many assumed that the newly independent states would continue in the same way; but a few decades of more-or-less peaceful democratic revolutions soon brought universal white male suffrage and an end to other gradations of citizenship. As white men consolidated political equality among themselves, they intensified the legal gap that separated them from enslaved people and Native Americans, who now stood not just on a lower echelon in a system of "mutual subserviency," but radically outside legal and political life. Membership in the new United States meant an unprecedented kind of equality. Nonmembership meant exclusion with a sharpness that no other North Atlantic country matched, an exclusion more akin to those of the slave societies of Brazil and the Caribbean.

Much of the engine of this change was the land itself, at least after the balance of technology, social organization, and population shifted decisively in favor of the colonists. Edmund Morgan and other historians have shown that gradations of inequality buckled and broke because open land was available beyond the pale of the hierarchical settlements.[33] It was a continent-sized version of what William Bradford feared from Merry-Mount: servants would not stay in service when something better beckoned past the woods at the edge of town.

With the land itself a collaborator in democratic revolutions, the theory of mutual subservience in "nature's economy," so dear to generations of natural theologians, came to seem medieval and absurd. In the satirical *Modern Chivalry,* modeled very loosely on *Don Quixote* and often called the first American novel, the Jeffersonian newspaper editor and western Pennsylvania judge Hugh Henry Brackenridge mocked the idea that slavery could be justified by "the economy of nature," which everywhere illustrated "the subserviency of one thing to another."[34] That version of the unequal terrain was gone.

In the future, North American nature would instead be figured as some kind of democratic terrain. The way Americans inhabited, shaped, and imagined the land would be in line with a version of democratic society. The question was what version of environmental imagination they would develop to replace the now implausible "economy of nature."

2

GOD'S AVID GARDENERS

IN A 1788 INDEPENDENCE DAY address in Philadelphia, James Wilson, the Scottish-born lawyer and scholar who would soon help to design the U.S. Constitution, recalled the decline of Rome, and its effect on the harvest. In the prime of republican self-government, "smiling harvests bore testimony to the bountiful boons of liberty." But the Roman republic fell into imperial decadence, a rotten empire yielded to barbarian invasion, and the Mediterranean landscape changed: "Waste and barrenness appear . . . in all their hideous forms. . . . With double tyranny the land is cursed."[1] "Double tyranny" referred to political despotism and Catholicism, a pair of fetters on the people. Tyrannical government meant wasted land: deserts replaced olive groves, floods carved gullies where gentle streams had run, and serfs labored hopelessly on ground that had once belonged to upright and independent farmers.

Rome had declined; America was rising. In the republican United States, free Rome was reborn ecologically as well as politically. Wilson ended his address with what he termed an "enrapturing prospect": "Placid husbandry walks in front, attended by the venerable plough. Lowing herds adorn our vallies; bleating flocks spread over our hills; verdant meadows, enamelled pastures, yellow harvests, bending orchards, rise in rapid succession from east to west."[2] Under republican government, the new continent would flourish as a garden.

Half historical, half mythic, Rome was an essential taproot for the political imagination of the American Revolution. "Publius," the authors of *The Federalist* called themselves, making their case for the new Constitution as the voice of the people. Opponents of the Constitution answered under the pen names "Cato" and "Brutus," implying that the federal government would not vindicate the people's liberty but would instead become the dictatorial empire of the caesars. The example of Cincinnatus, the ideal of the republican leader, inspired George Washington to decline a crown or life tenure as president and, for better or worse, established an American theme of mistrust for career politicians. It takes only a look at the neoclassical architecture of Washington, D.C., to appreciate how intensely those who designed its buildings sought to identify themselves with the liberty and power of ancient Rome.

The land would be the emblem of this republican restoration. In the idiom that Wilson used in 1788, a fruitful landscape bespoke both freedom and prosperity. The land was also the resource that would make this restoration work. Thomas Jefferson argued in his first inaugural address that the plenitude of the frontier meant the United States could avoid Europe's crowded cities and political tyranny, birthing instead a thousand generations of settlers.[3] Free land was the condition for a nation of free men, because it made possible widespread and expanding proprietorship.[4]

Many of the founders, notably Washington, were large landholders of great wealth. Theirs was still a hierarchical terrain, especially in the low-country South and the Hudson Valley, where great estates and fortunes dominated public life. Hardscrabble labor was not part of these grandees' picture of republican citizenship, which they imagined as an elite affair. Many of Washington's soldiers, though, were landless immigrants and small farmers, especially the Scots-Irish, and his veterans, who had no doubt about their claims to citizenship, were rewarded with midsized frontier plots across the eastern seaboard. (I am thinking of a grandfather of mine who settled on one of those plots, having survived the winter at Valley Forge with Washington's troops as a teenager.) Federal attempts to disburse western lands in an orderly and well-supervised way all but collapsed beyond the Allegheny Mountains, where the law gave way to settlers' customs, recognizing land claims established by actual clearing and planting regardless of the state of their paperwork, and often adopting claims that enjoyed the support of neighboring pioneers, even though these communities of settlers had no formal right to disburse land. Later versions of federal land law bent increasingly toward basing claims on actual settlement, the premise of the famous Homestead Acts. This represented a triumph of the settlers' on-the-ground practice, a victory that was both practical and ideological. Where one generation of lawmakers had envisioned the supervised sale of land as the right way to advance the grid of a continental empire, a later generation imagined that expansion in more organic and populist terms, as the westward progress of a mobilized people.

So an unequal terrain of the old, English style became a landscape of revolutionary republicanism and, soon enough, a democratic terrain. North America became, in the public language of its most powerful country, the emblem of a Creation made to be developed and settled. The blooming landscape of freedom and prosperity was the reward of a democratic people unafraid to swing an ax and steer a plow. The political culture that celebrated settlement supported, too, a new ideal of personal dignity, *free labor,* in which work changed from a mark of low status to a democratic emblem of personal worth.[5] The work that brought the land to its intended, bountiful use was not degraded labor; it was a high human calling, the fulfillment of a providential covenant.

Making the continent a democratic terrain took work that was both material and ideological or imaginative. Materially, American law worked intensively to create Wilson's pastoral republic. Law deployed Americans as an army of development, not like the conscriptions of the French *corvée,* but through a scheme of opportunity and reward, in which pioneers, miners, and companies could grab and transform a portion of the frontier—making it both profitable and their own. The laws of these decades made real dozens of versions of John Locke's archetypal myth: that a person could turn wild nature into property by "mix[ing] his labor with it."[6]

Early federal statutes offered frontier acreage for sale and were modified by "pre-emption" laws that gave actual settlers first claim to the land. Later, the Homestead Acts granted ownership as the reward for clearing and planting. Speculators often used the Homestead Acts to claim vast tracts of timber, abandoning the land once it was logged; officials mostly tolerated this sleight-of-hand, despite the great waste it involved, because it resulted in more land being cleared. For genuine settlers, the standard practice was to leave one-quarter of the land covered with forest, as a source of timber and firewood; a tenant could be sued for laying "waste" to the land if he cut those trees. As settlement passed onto the Great Plains, mostly a treeless prairie, the laws shifted, and the Timber Culture Act of 1873 granted an extra 160 acres to settlers who planted trees on forty of those acres. In the same decade, the Timber and Stone Act granted unlimited logging and stone-quarrying rights on land deemed unfit for farming, a designation speculators were quick to agitate for when they spotted profitable trees. The Swampland Act of 1850 gave public wetlands to those who agreed to drain them, inspiring reclamation projects from the Florida Everglades to Illinois's Kankakee River and Michigan's Lake St. Clair, while irrigation laws exchanged ownership for canal building in dry lands. By the later nineteenth century, when it became clear that most private irrigation efforts would fail, the federal government undertook a massive reengineering of the continent's water supplies, moving the precious liquid from mountains to plains, from rivers to fields, until the tellingly named Bureau of Reclamation had left hardly a free-flowing waterway in the West. After 1909, a settler could claim as much 320 acres of the remaining dry land for ranching, and in 1916 that doubled to 640 acres.

By 1934, when Franklin Roosevelt responded to overgrazing and the Dust Bowl by withdrawing federal land from settlement, this web of laws had made private property out of two-thirds of the country's acreage, from the westward edge of the original thirteen colonies to the Pacific Coast. Today, larger and smaller pockets of federal land remain in the various states—almost 84 percent of Nevada, 45 percent of California, almost 37 percent of Colorado, and no more than 12 percent of any state farther east, where in most places the share is vanishingly small. (The national forests and parks of the East were assembled by purchase and from abandoned timberland, rather than kept in original federal ownership, as in the West.) To this day, the General Mining Law of 1872 gives any person title to valuable minerals that he or she finds on much public land. In theory, an individual can come to own the land itself by developing a mine, though there are now many bureaucratic roadblocks to this Lockean consummation. This is the last active part of the vast legal agenda of development that turned Americans into an army of clearing and settlement between 1781 and 1934.

But this material work was entwined with its imaginative dimension, the vision of progress and freedom that Wilson and other early Americans propounded. American settlers had come to see "nature's economy" in a very different way from John Evelyn and John Ray's lessons in "mutual subserviency." The nature they described and learned to see, hostile and dangerous though it could be, taught a reassuring lesson of equality and just reward. It was a commoners' terrain, provided those commoners worked it hard and well enough.

Locke and the Commoners' Terrain

This settler vision resonates with John Locke's pregnant phrase, "In the beginning, all the world was America." The sentence occurs in his account of the origin of property rights, which settlers adopted to advance their claim to North America. For Locke, saying that all the world had once been America meant that humanity had begun in a world not yet owned. No property lines marked mine from yours, and anyone could rightfully use whatever resources he or she needed for survival or convenience. Those who wandered this world were in what Locke called the "state of nature," where all were equally free to act as they wished, so long as they did not harm one another. There were no slaves and no masters, no rulers or ruled.[7]

Although it was a world not yet owned, it was not immune to ownership; in fact, it was designed by providence to invite it. Whoever used something, whether by clearing a field or gathering apples, acquired ownership over it, which others had to respect. Human labor turned nature into property. The only limit on this right to acquire property was that men had to leave enough unclaimed for others to satisfy their own needs. History thus began in a world of extensive liberty and radical equality, organized by a modest dose of natural law, a world without government but infused with order and principle. In that primordial world, the most natural activity—gathering, using, and improving things to serve one's needs—transformed nature into property. It was an orderly world that tended to generate law, to fill itself up with legal claims to ownership. This was Locke's "America."

And how could we know all this, according to Locke? There were two sources for Locke's view of natural property, both deeply involved in the human relation to nature. The first lay in revelation. The curse of Adam, the command to labor that accompanied the expulsion from Eden, was not purely a curse; rather, those who obeyed the command were a morally favored group, the "industrious and rational," and it was to them that the world *really* belonged. The second source was an interpretation of the human predicament in the natural world. People were needy, vulnerable, and poorly provided for by "un-assisted nature,"[8] but the world's stinginess and humanity's "penury" need not be permanent. Instead, when men mixed their labor with the world, it bloomed, producing a hundred times or more the wealth it yielded when "un-assisted." Property, which guaranteed to owners the fruits of their work, was the rational response to human needs in a world that met those needs abundantly when fertilized with labor, but scarcely at all when left fallow. Locke persistently referred to land that had not yet been turned to property as "waste,"[9] a word with a double sense: it connoted resources squandered or not used, an affront to the "industrious and rational," and also emptiness, a sense rooted in its origins in the Latin *vastus,* a desolate space. The natural world, to the extent that it had not come under the fruitful power of labor, was empty, incomplete.

The world taught humanity to subdue it and make it bloom. It seemed to do so on equal terms for all: the natural condition, Locke argued, was one of equality as well as freedom. Equality included the equal capacity to turn waste land into fruitful property. It also included the equal capacity for citizenship: Locke imagined government as formed by the free consent of each person who would live under it.

For these reasons, and because his ideas and even some of his phrases ripple through the Declaration of Independence, Locke has often been imagined as the Americans' philosopher, theorist of the enterprise that the United States made real. Indeed, Locke exemplified a philosophical culture of natural-rights thinking and support for development that was terrifically prominent in early U.S. political and legal culture, and he crystallized the themes of this approach systematically and accessibly. But Locke's significance for

Americans is best illuminated not by asking what he taught them to think, but the other way around: by asking what they learned to do with the ideas he epitomized.

The original purpose of Locke's imagined "America" had little to do with America. Locke wrote it to show how government might arise from natural freedom and equality. He assumed that the highly unequal landholding and political authority of contemporary England were legitimate, as long as they rested on, and adhered to, an original act of political consent by ancestral Englishmen. Locke was far from imagining North America itself in the "Lockean" terms that Americans later adopted. When in 1669 he drafted a constitution for the proprietors of the Carolina Colony, it made no provision for the settlers to mix their labor with open American land. On the contrary, Locke sketched a hereditary aristocracy in which the balance of land ownership among the noble echelons maintained an exact proportion to their share of political power. Those who actually worked the land would be hereditary serfs, bound to the soil where they had been born and subject to the jurisdiction of their manor-lords. The theorist of equality even inserted a provision for enslaved Africans, providing that their enslavement should be perpetual and their masters' power absolute.

Once the Lockean formula existed, however, it was available for other uses, including those the settlers in Britain's North American colonies gave it. It is true that the settlers did not need Locke's ideas in order to take the continent: opportunity and self-interest were enough for that. It is also true that reading Locke, even *being* Locke, was not enough to give one what today seems an obviously "Lockean" view of North America. Nonetheless, once continental settlement was under way, it made a difference that the people doing the settling had assimilated the worldview we now call Lockean, whether or not any particular frontiersman had ever heard of Locke. (The same accounts of natural law and progress were staples of political speeches, sermons, popular writing, and agricultural journals. One did not have to be a reader of jurisprudence or philosophy.)

The continent thus became, for some of its settlers, a real-life instance of a world before government, a landscape under natural law. Its settlers had a chance to replay Lockean history—to divide the continent among themselves and make, by common consent, a constitutional government. They could take freedom and equality as the premises of a practical enterprise, building an "empire of liberty" westward from the Atlantic. What had been theoretical postulates in Locke's thought now became premises of practical work. Early Americans regularly claimed that open land and rational experiments in government made them the pivotal nation in human history, the country whose success could revive Roman freedom; show the proper form of Christian government; or establish once and for all that a people could rule itself by choice and reason, not chance and inheritance. By the middle of the nineteenth century, it was a commonplace that a republic of free men, each dignified by making his living through free labor, depended on the availability of free land on the frontier. The continent belonged to those who could make it bloom, who were also the touchstone citizens of the young republic. The justification for these claims was multifarious, but never far from its heart was an idea about nature itself: that it was made to collaborate in human progress, as we were made to develop it for our needs.

That last paragraph is an account of a fantasy. More exactly, it is an account of an ideology—a pattern of belief in which the world makes convenient sense, in which its rough edges are softened and its contradictions dissolved or obscured. Of course American settlers lived under a combination of colonial rule and imported English law, not in a state of nature. Of course the continent was anything but unoccupied when they arrived, and it took centuries of negotiation, warfare, and demographic catastrophe to clear it for its new claimants. Of course the new government that the rebellious colonists eventually created was modeled on a panoply of precedent, English, biblical, and classical, and there was no neat moment of universal consent in its adoption. Nonetheless, an ideology takes hold best when it has roughly the same shape as the reality it is half-glossing, half-masking, and that was the case here. Compared with deeply settled, anciently ruled, thoroughly owned western Europe, conquered North America lay open to remaking, as Locke's imagined world had lain open at its beginning. Settlement was a mission of republican progress, and also a consummation of divine design.

Savages and Slaves: A New Unequal Terrain

The form of imagination that early Americans adopted gave them a template for remaking the continent in line with providential vision. It made nature a source of reassurance, a guarantor of the rightness of the national project. It also underwrote the exclusion of Native Americans, enslaved people, and women from the American democracy. Thus the democratic terrain of North America became a new kind of unequal terrain, defined both by an ethic of equality among its citizens and by hard lines that marked off those it excluded as natural subordinates.

James Wilson's pastoral republic, remember, was partly defined by its opposite—a wasted landscape of tyranny. A fruitful and free republic must always be vigilant against that opposite. For decades, northern polemicists described the slaveholding South in ways that echoed Wilson's imagery: as a wasted landscape, exhausted by the greed and slovenly labor that tyranny fostered. There was plenty in this condemnation that was both righteous and accurate. Plantation agriculture did exhaust the soil in much of the South, though more because of its typical crops and overcultivation than because of its labor system. Lowland southern expansion moved through a series of new plantations, ripped out of the forest with slave labor under especially brutal discipline, as enslavement was most fragile where there were few masters and little law. Labor remained degraded, not dignified, in the reality and imagination of the plantation economies. In all these ways, the South was doing something different with the continent from the Northeast and northern Midwest, and the difference undercut the egalitarian ideas of citizenship and dignifying labor that were touchstones elsewhere. Some abolitionists, notably Gerrit Smith, went beyond denouncing southern slavery and deeded plots of land in upstate New York to free black settlers, trying to carve out a place in the pastoral republic for people who were neither whites nor slaves. These efforts, though, were rare and ill-resourced, and ended up almost as fictive as the iconic forty acres that post-Emancipation Reconstruction never brought to former slaves.

The whole project of claiming the continent was, in practice, unmistakably a white one. African-American slavery was the keystone of the southern exception to the Lockean picture of the continent. The inclusive and egalitarian version of continental settlement opened up two fronts of belonging, citizenship and ownership; for critical decades of the nineteenth century, African Americans were formally excluded from the first and effectively excluded from the second. The notorious *Dred Scott* decision, which declared that the constitutional order was permanently tied to racial inequality, both denied the free descendants of enslaved blacks any possibility of becoming U.S. citizens and protected slave ownership in the frontier territories as an inviolable right of white Americans. (The decision was overturned by the Thirteenth and Fourteenth amendments to the Constitution, after the Civil War.) Opening the continent was a Lockean project for some people, then, while for others it looked more like Locke's Carolina Constitution: a scheme of permanent hierarchy and exclusion, reinforced rather than undermined by the continent's new wealth.

The even deeper irony in providential imagination, though, was its treatment of Native Americans. The land claims of these first and continuing inhabitants were erased ideologically even as the traces of those inhabitants were being wiped out on the ground. Providential imagination reworked conquest, expulsion, and genocide into a benign account of necessary and lawful progress. Fourteen years after James Wilson's Independence Day address, the young John Quincy Adams asked rhetorically: "Shall the lordly savage . . . forbid the wilderness to blossom like a rose? Shall he forbid the oaks of the forest to fall before the axe of industry, and to rise again, transformed into the habitations of ease and elegance? Shall he doom an immense region of the world to perpetual desolation . . . [and] the fields and the valleys which a beneficent God has formed to teem with the life of innumerable multitudes, be condemned to everlasting barrenness?"[10] The answer, of course, was no. The "savage," literally a creature of the *sauvage,* the forest, was the arrogant, "lordly" enemy of common men's progress—the worst thing in a young republic of property-hungry settlers. The savage represented static, unchanging nature, without the galvanizing power of labor, which cut trees so that they could "rise again," redeemed as houses and cities. The savage stood against providential design: the continent was formed for settlement by "a beneficent God," and if it remained forested, it would languish in "perpetual desolation," as good as empty, being full of nothing but disordered and useless wilderness.

The fact remained that the "savages" had been present for millennia before Europeans arrived to claim the continent. Outside the United States, there were plenty of critics of colonial land grabs, including Adam Smith and the jurist William Blackstone. Within the United States, for some of the same reasons, there was pressure to defend the European claim in richer terms than "might makes right."

So, twenty-four years after John Quincy Adams's self-assured speech on the presumptuousness of savages, the jurist James Kent claimed that a version of Lockean natural right was the foundation of European claims to North America. He offered a key to understanding why the continent had to belong to its European settlers, rather than to its original inhabitants. Chief judge of the New York Court of Chancery, lecturer in law at Columbia, and author of the influential *Commentaries on American Law,* Kent argued that when Europeans arrived, North America was legally empty. No one then had any right to the land—or at least none that a mature legal system like that of the United States or its colonial predecessors had to respect. How could this be, when Native Americans had long lived in and used territories that they treated as their own? Kent explained that people came to own property only by developing the land, turning it to cultivation. An "uncivilized, erratic, and savage race of men" could not acquire lasting ownership of their territories; their passing occupation gave them only "the loose and attenuated claim" of their usufruct, a right to "use the fruits" but not to own the land.[11] This was entirely in line with Locke and his many followers: passing over ground, or hunting and gathering there, did not change the earth enough, mix enough labor with it, to convert it to property. Indeed, if Native Americans tried to keep out settlers, in doing so they denied the settlers' natural right to acquire unowned land. Rather than rightful inhabitants, Native Americans who resisted encroachment figured as thieves in this theory.

According to Kent, Native Americans had not only failed to establish property rights; they had also failed to satisfy the human duty to make nature fruitful. This "immense continent" was "evidently fitted and intended by Providence to be subdued and cultivated, and to become the residence of civilized nations."[12] Kent embraced the theory of natural law expounded by Emmerich de Vattel, who had "observed, that the cultivation of the soil was an obligation imposed by nature upon mankind."[13] The continent might as well be unoccupied, for while not literally empty, it was devoid of its proper use: to be fruitful and support settlement.

Kent's argument, for all its fit with widespread providential ideas, was a misreading of the foundational and then-recent U.S. Supreme Court decision on the topic, *Johnson v. M'Intosh*. Decided in 1823 by Chief Justice John Marshall, the case held that Native American land claims enjoyed only limited recognition under United States law, and that the federal government (and only the federal government) could wipe out those claims and transfer the land to settlers.[14] In his opinion, Marshall explicitly sidestepped issues of "abstract justice," such as Vattel's theory that farmers enjoyed a natural right to displace nomadic hunters.[15] Instead, he reasoned from the positive law (enacted statutes, as opposed to unwritten "natural law"), as manifest in the customs of Europe's colonial powers and the early United States. Quite unlike James Kent, he hinted broadly that he had serious doubts about the justice of expropriating a populated continent, allowing that Europeans' claims to North America might be "opposed to natural right" and noting with irony that the colonizing powers had "found no difficulty in convincing themselves" of the justice of their claims.[16]

After finishing his legal reasoning, however, Marshall went on to explain that European settlers had "excuse, if not justification," for treating the continent as their own. They had arrived to find a savage people, he wrote, who made their living from the forest. Respecting Indians' use of the continent would have meant abandoning it to stasis, which would self-evidently have been unacceptable. Not far from the surface of Marshall's "excuse" was John Quincy Adams's rhetorical question: How could savages be permitted to stand in the way of the world's destiny?

Marshall declined to adopt as American law the theory that Europeans had an "abstract" right to the continent, but at the same time he embraced a view of nature and the human role in it that made the abstract claim sensible. The difference between the natural-law right to take the continent that Marshall set aside and the more pragmatic reasoning that he embraced is important as a matter of legal theory and doctrine; but if we view both in light of the worldview in which they set humanity and nature, they reveal deep affinities. The difference is between two branches of the same tree.

In *Johnson v. M'Intosh*, then, John Marshall came to a legal conclusion which drew from the same providential vision that informed the Lockean position. Unless American law favored settlers and cultivators, the continent would remain a wilderness. Nature was meant to serve human ends, which the labor of clearing and farming should secure; wilderness was the mark of failure. This is the common ecological premise of disparate strands of American thought, rhetoric, and law. All paths led to the same destination: the vision of North America flourishing under settlement. All arose, too, from the same root: a vision of nature as calling out for development through work and discipline.

Trader Imagination versus Settler Imagination

Recall Thomas Morton of Merry-Mount, icon of some early Massachusetts colonists' fears that a wild land would sustain a "lord of misrule" and help to revive paganism. Morton was not content to let William Bradford tell his story, and, after managing to return to England, made a bid for the last word. His self-exculpating and self-promoting *New English Canaan* contains a boisterously indignant, Falstaff-like account of his expulsion from Merry-Mount, belittling his tormentors as superstitious and trivial clowns, "Princes of Limbo," led by the hapless and self-righteous "Captain Shrimp" (Myles Standish). Viewed from a distance of almost four hundred years, this polemical broadside inadvertently highlights just how much Morton shared with his enemies. Different though they were, neither saw the new world as a permanent home, for themselves or for their people. Both were sojourners, though Bradford's expedition was more spiritual and Morton's fleshly and commercial. The colonies they sketched were, therefore, not mainly colonies of settlement, and that made a great difference.

The heart of Morton's book was a paean to the commercial promise of the continent. He wrote with vivid, sensual interest in the place and its life. His report is also studded with lists of the uses and market prices of North American goods. His persona is Falstaff but also Prospero, a colonial master and a voluptuary who takes the time to gaze with wonder at the "hunning bird," though not to the neglect of his accounts. He opens *New English Canaan* with a verse description of North America as "a faire virgin, longing to be sped / And meet her lover in a Nuptiall bed," then moves smartly to announce a ledger of commodities, "The worth of which, in each particuler, Who list to know, this abstract will declare."[17]

Morton's "abstract" allows diversion but also returns promptly to profit. He describes "Squirils of three sorts, very different in shap and condition": the gray, the red, and "a little flying Squirrill, with batlike winges, which hee spreads when hee jumps from tree to tree, and does no harme." Bears are innocent creatures, frightening only to "some effeminate person who conceaved of more danger in them [than] there is cause," although "the Beare is a tyrant at a Lobster." The wolf, which sometimes hunts "puppy dogg[s]" to feed its whelps, is a "discommodity" in North America as in other "Countries of Christendome"; the "Salvages" (a spelling that reminds the reader that "savage" means people of the forest) treasure its hide and will trade forty beaver skins for the pelt of a black wolf, which makes it "worthy [of] the title of a commodity."[18]

"Commodity," meaning both what is useful and what can be sold, is the key to Morton's discussion. Though he promises a description of the "bewty of the Country" and does give a cursory, admiring account of "her naturall indowements," the emphasis is on profit. His account of trees ends by observing that American musk roses produce a better rosewater than their English cousins, and that sassafras "doe[s] perfume the airs" in spring; but his focus is on the uses, and markets, for oak, ash, beech, walnut, chestnut, maple, birch, and evergreens. (The last were essential for seafaring, a source of materials ranging from masts to sealing pitch.) The "curious bird to see, called a hunning bird, no bigger than a great Beetle," wins Morton's admiration for its "glosse like silke . . . of a chaingable colour," but is the last bird mentioned after the many edible species whose abundance he trumpets. The "beasts," too, he addresses in order of usefulness, beginning with deer and moose, reliable sources of meat, and the latter showing promise as a harnessed draft-animal (striking thought!) for the new world.[19]

All these edible things are commodities in the sense that they are useful; they will keep colonists alive, like the North American salad greens whose "maskuline vertue" Morton praises. The heart of his analysis of "commodity," though, is market value, which has a double-headed currency: English money on the one hand and beaver skins on the other. The latter are "the best marchantable commodity," fetching ten shillings a pound, and Morton provides the value of many other skins in terms of beaver pelts: between two and four to a deer hide, and, as mentioned, forty for the skin of a black wolf. But because the otter's market was in England, and not in the Indian trade, he prices an otter skin in cash, at "3 or 4 Angels of gold."[20]

Morton's "abstract" is a bestiary for a trading colony, not a blueprint for a settler colony. There is no discussion of the fertility of the soil; and the plants that interest Morton, besides trees, are the wild "Potthearbes and other herbes for Sallets," not greens for gardens or grains for fields. Usefulness, *commodity,* refers to those things that traders can live on during their sojourns in America or sell on the home market. Accordingly, Morton's interest in Native Americans is strikingly unburdened by any need to demonstrate a superior claim to the continent. They are trading partners in his eyes, not competitors for productive land, so there is no pressure to demonstrate the inferiority of their practices, or hold them to a European, agricultural standard of land use. Instead, Morton offers a portrait of New England's Native Americans that includes an insightful account of the ecological effects of their practice of burning undergrowth, and generally stresses their goodwill and capacity for civilization. Even his wilder claims, that indigenous languages descend from Latin and Greek, tend to put them on the same plane as their European counterparts.

The move to settlement produced a new set of ideological pressures. The question was now how to establish a superior claim to the continent. This meant reinterpreting North America so that Europeans could become, at least to their satisfaction, more American than the indigenous people who greeted their first arrival. They interpreted America, in short, as the place that had been waiting for them, which meant interpreting all the natural world as a place meant to foster and reward the life they would make, or imagine themselves making, in America. Under this pressure, the providential view of American nature took shape and became a prominent, even dominant, element of American civic identity. Settlement, and the need to make sense of settlement in a place already inhabited, incited the creation of providential imagination, and powered both its inclusive spirit and its brutal exclusions.

A Road Not Taken

The American politics of nature might have grown in a different way if the early decades of independence had made more room for the legacy of Thomas Paine—and, ironically, for that of his great opponent, Edmund Burke. Paine is best remembered as the radical pamphleteer of the American Revolution, whose *Common*

Sense sold a half-million copies and stirred the colonies' appetite for independence more than the works of any other author. His famous declaration that "we have it in our power to begin the world again" captures the utopian spirit of a writer-politician whose creed was human equality and peaceful coexistence. History, for Paine, was a series of usurpations of the natural human conditions of social cooperation and mental independence. Kings and aristocrats had replaced equality and cooperation with hierarchy and exploitation. Priests had usurped the mind, trapping thought in fear and superstition. "It is from the Bible that we have learned cruelty, rapine, and murder," Paine wrote, "for the belief of a cruel God makes a cruel man."[21]

Paine was exorcised from mainstream American political culture in the 1790s and the start of the 1800s, as part of a general reaction against the radical egalitarianism that had been one critical strain in revolutionary culture. The French Revolution alarmed conservatives and moderates, especially in New England and the South, and ministers and politicians inveighed against "infidel" philosophy and the politics of "leveling," or radical equality. Figures such as Lyman Beecher of New Haven (father of Harriet Beecher Stowe) called for a revival of the Christian element in American political culture, which they took as a limit on social, political, and philosophical radicalism, and a firm basis for orderly liberty. Paine made a perfect target: so committed to the French Revolution that he joined the National Assembly as a representative of Pas-de-Calais and became an ally of the Girondin faction. Denouncing received religious doctrine in favor of deism and reason, he was easily painted as a hubristic, atheistic foe of settled order.

He had the double misfortune of being too moderate, or too reasonable, for the leaders of the Jacobin Terror. Jailed and nearly executed by Robespierre, he returned to North America embittered by the Washington administration's lack of revolutionary solidarity with the French, as well as its refusal to seek his release from his

Paris cell. He vented his frustration in a fierce denunciation of Washington's character, which he called opportunistic and hypocritical, and from then on was a public target for Federalist contempt. Some combination of alcoholism and mental illness ruined his last years, and when he died in Greenwich Village in 1809, only six people attended his funeral. (Two of them were free blacks who were likely aware of his radical defenses of liberty.)

Paine's writing enlists the natural world as an ally of democracy. One might say the same of the theorists of providential settlement, but Paine's idea of democracy was more open-ended and radical than theirs. For him, nature was a refutation of all divisions and hierarchies within humanity. He abhorred slavery, calling even before the American Revolution for total abolition; unlike many later abolitionists, he also urged integrating freedmen into the economy and society of a post-emancipation North America. He was a lifelong supporter of universal male suffrage. Human solidarity seemed to him a natural fact: denouncing an opponent's description of France as "the natural enemy of England," he called the very idea of natural enemies "an unmeaning barbarism."[22] Nature meant that the community of mankind knew neither limits nor hierarchy.

Nature stood, too, for the power Paine ascribed to revolution, the power to begin the world again. A return to the rudiments of things meant a chance to throw off the accretions of history and build a new order, fairer and more equal. History was full of surprises, he wrote, and when unforeseen circumstances arose, "none but the man of nature can understand them," for they required fresh eyes and a simple, almost unfiltered clarity.[23] Writing to Lord Howe to defend the American colonists in 1776, he sneered at the king's defender: "Your master has commanded, and you have not enough of nature left to refuse."[24] Nature was the capacity to respond to "purely original" events in an equally original spirit: it was the power to begin the world again in everyday political events, to look beyond habit and, especially, habituation to hierarchy and division, which were always artificial and generally pernicious in Paine's eyes.

As for the natural world itself, Paine saw it in two lights. On the one hand, it grounded a principle of economic equality. "Natural property" was the inborn right of every person to an equal share of the unimproved world, which was the common inheritance of humanity, now artificially divided into private property. Paine's "Letter on Agrarian Justice" argued for a tax on wealth that would amount to "ground-rent" paid to society by those who owned the world, to compensate the dispossessed. The money should go to universal benefits: a payment to each person at birth, as a kind of social inheritance to start them in life, plus pensions for the aged. Paine argued that this scheme would make the artificial institution of private property beneficial to all, whereas without his reforms it preserved both wealth and great poverty. Paine also insisted that property could be justified only if it did benefit everyone—since it was, after all, extracted from humanity's common birthright. There was a baseline human relationship to nature, then, based on equal claims to the natural world. Any departure from that equality needed justification, and the justification, in turn, must be to a political community of equals.

Paine's second theme was that, beyond the baseline of equal common inheritance, dealings with the natural world presented a *political* question. When he confronted opponents who were inclined to resolve difficult questions by turning politics instead into a "natural" relationship, he rejected that easy answer and insisted on the responsibility to come to political terms with political problems. He denied the claim made by the loyalist pamphleteer "Cato"—that the clearing and development of the eastern seaboard, done under British government, tied the colonists to British jurisdiction as if they were children tied forever to their parents by their early dependence.[25] In a lengthy dispute during the Revolutionary

War on the question of American access to the fisheries off Newfoundland, Paine mocked his opponent's claim that "natural rights" to fish could resolve the issue, and insisted that although "Americanus" might be intimately acquainted with the customs of fishermen (as his opponent claimed to be), "as a great political question, involving with it the means and channels of commerce, and the probability of empire, he is wholly unequal to the subject."[26] Paine insisted on negotiating explicit guarantees of American access, and set out the advantages to the young country of developing a fishing fleet that would serve as a "nursery of seamen" and so as a kind of incubator for naval power. Whether sparring against traditional conservatives who saw the American colonies as saplings grown from and bound to the English oak, or against natural-law theorists who proposed to resolve political questions by Lockean principles, Paine insisted on the competence and responsibility of the present political community to reach its own judgment, limited by its own foundational—he would have said *natural*—principles of equality and inclusiveness.

Paine represents the strongest tendency in early American culture toward the democratic politicization of nature that was already latent in Thomas Hobbes's thought a century earlier. Hobbes had few admirers among the Americans: they received him as a monarchist and absolutist, and he would have mocked their commitment to natural rights as superstitious. But Paine, for all the differences between his views and Hobbes's philosophical skepticism, spoke for and helped to shape an American strain of politics with the same basic tendencies: a foundational commitment to political equality, a rejection of the idea that nature or revelation could answer political questions, and an insistence on giving to the political community the task of supplying the interpretations and judgments that nature itself could not. If Paine's strand of thought had not been so thoroughly shut down in the early decades of American independence, the providential strain of interpretation might have obscured fewer contradictions and provided less chauvinistic self-certainty to the project of continental settlement. Americans might have approached nature somewhat more as a democratic problem, and less as a religious or quasi-religious endorsement of their settler democracy, with its intense blend of inclusive and exclusionary elements.

Paine did not find a way to take the political equality of Native Americans seriously while also establishing an agricultural empire of democracy on the continent. Probably there was no remotely satisfactory solution to this most basic paradox of settler democracy. Indeed, one of Paine's less attractive proposals for emancipated African Americans was to settle them on the frontier, where, he predicted, they might combat Native American incursions.[27] Despite his blind spots, however, his thought represents a real alternative, a path not taken that would have deepened the democratic engagement with nature in the independent United States. He was not a voice in the wilderness but, for a time, the very opposite: a writer who formed American sentiment, at once catching the spirit of the moment and helping to shape it with words that others read, traded from hand to hand, pirated into unauthorized editions, and argued over in the streets and taverns.

Paine's greatest limitation was the corollary of his decisive radicalism: he placed his faith in spontaneous human cooperation. Like other eighteenth-century theorists of "sociability," he insisted that interdependence and natural affections were all people needed to bind them together for peaceful and beneficial cooperation. Government, he famously wrote, came in only as a secondary measure, a remedy for residual "wickedness," and it was always susceptible to opportunism and tyranny. Violence and disorder, on Paine's account, came from outside the true human community, introduced by kings and priests, and a healthy revolution would throw these off and reestablish cooperative harmony—unless wickedness snuck back in through politics. He was hardly able to see perennial violence and injustice as products of human nature, rather than as incursions by some corrupting principle.

Maybe this ideological blindness accounts for Paine's ability to hate fiercely individuals (such as George Washington) who disappointed him, while retaining, in principle, his faith in all humanity. It certainly made him a less sophisticated political thinker than Hobbes, who saw that the need for government was rooted in the tragic character of human nature: that stable cooperation does not arise naturally, but must be secured by artificial rules, grounded in the "artificial man" of sovereignty. The same blindness accounts for Paine's almost total lack of regard for custom, culture, habit, tradition, and the loyalties and sympathies that these instill in people. For Paine, these were only the happenstance form of natural human sociability, usually with an admixture of corruption from political power and religion. By contrast, a more pessimistic view of human nature, one that saw violence and abuse as rooted in widespread, everyday passions, would have given him more reason to respect those forms of culture that hold back the worst impulses and channel human life into peaceful cooperation.

Such moderate pessimism was the lifelong theme of Paine's greatest polemical target, Edmund Burke, the Irish-English parliamentarian and man of letters. Burke's complex career defies easy characterization, especially because the world of politics in which he acted all his life was deeply different from what we know. He was, in any event, a champion of India against the abuses of the East India Company, and of the American colonists against the British government. He hated slavery and seems to have been genuinely nonracist, once answering a critic of his defense of India, "I do not care what the white people think." He combined ordinary parliamentary duties with extraordinary acts of political imagination, delivering multi-day speeches in which he worked to bring his listeners into the lived experience—as he portrayed it—of Indians, American colonists, and others who were far away yet subject to British rule. At the end of his life, Burke's hatred of violence and fanaticism, his reverence for tradition, and his almost overpowering imaginative gifts brought him to an unforgettable denunciation of the French Revolution. His *Reflections on the Revolution in France* remains the work that defines his memory, making him, somewhat anachronistically, an anti-totalitarian prophet to the right, while inspiring an anti-Burkean tradition of the left that runs forward unbroken from Paine's answer to the *Reflections, The Rights of Man.*

Paine's great objection to Burke was that he insulted human nature by treating political order as a kind of mystery, a blend of habit, deference, self-conception, and implicit constraint that checked power and kept it humane. For Paine, there was no mystery, and Burke's apologies for tradition amounted to a defense of priestcraft and privilege. There was much to support Paine's complaints, particularly in Burke's writings on France. But had Paine been better able to listen to Burke, he might have heard something else: a recognition that part of the reason appeals to nature are often disingenuous and dangerous is that, as Burke once put it, "art is man's nature." That is, as social creatures, living in the mediums of culture and language, we are what we have learned to be, and we live as we have taught one another how to live. Burke's argument against the French revolutionaries was that, drunk on abstract concepts, they were stripping away the habits that upheld political order, leaving nothing but the unbounded appetite for power, domination, and spectacle that he evoked in passages that later readers have taken as a forecast of the Terror. But his arguments were not always so dire. Fifteen years earlier, describing the rebellious Americans' ability to organize themselves with no outside power, he had admitted that it was simply a mystery, one rooted in the peculiar set of political ideas and customs that the colonists had brought from Europe and cultivated in their settlements. The unifying point, for him, was that the key to peaceful order lay in how people imagined themselves and saw one another. It could not be enough to say that people were naturally peaceful—first, because they were not; and, second, because they were not *naturally* much of anything, art and culture being the heart of human nature.

Listening to Burke, for early Americans, would have meant understanding two interlocked points. First, politics could never be simply "natural," in the way that Paine took human equality, inclusiveness, and "natural property" to be. Behind every human thing that people call natural, there is artifice: storytelling, imagination, ways of seeing that become a kind of second nature. A democratic, inclusive, egalitarian nature is a nature people have learned to see, in the natural world and in one another. Listening to Burke might have modified Paine's conclusions to this effect: the natural world can never be simply a political problem. That is, we do not make bare, instrumental choices about how to dispose of forests, rivers, and wildlife, any more than we make bare, abstract judgments about whether political power in general is legitimate, or whether another person is a compatriot or an enemy. These judgments about the natural world reflect how we have learned to see it, the place it has come to occupy in our identities—for instance, as the reassuring ground of a settler colony, or as the inspiring, quasi-divine outdoor cathedral of a Romantic pilgrim.

In the end, the American politics of nature did develop—as Burke would have said it must—through successive, interwoven waves of environmental imagination, ways of encountering and envisioning the natural world that were deeply linked to visions of the nation and of the American self. It has also developed, as Paine would have urged, in a direction that was increasingly democratic—more and more committed to explicit, shared decisions about the meaning of the world and the human place in it. The historical narrative that extends from the providential beginnings of a settler colony has been a long one, though, and even its most recent chapters still cling to the politics of nature.

3

NATURE AS TEACHER

AT ABOUT THREE IN THE AFTERNOON in the high summer, at the end of July 1831, Alexis de Tocqueville and his traveling companion, Gustave de Beaumont, reached Detroit via Lake Erie on a steamboat called the *Ohio*. Detroit, Tocqueville reported, was "a little town of two or three thousand souls," founded by French Jesuits and still full of French families.[1] Earlier in the day, the French-built Catholic church in British Fort Malden (now in Windsor, Ontario) had reminded him of a village near Caen or Evreux, with a rooster-shaped weathervane atop its bell tower. A Parisian whose aristocratic family was rooted in Normandy, where the village of Tocqueville sits just out of sight of the English Channel, the young traveler sought restlessly for such points of contact between the Old World and the New; they were essential aids in his effort to make sense of the Americans for his European audience.

Such comparisons failed him in Detroit. In what Norman village would the bell-tower cock look down on a British soldier of the Highland regiments, fully uniformed in kilt, red tunic, and ostrich-feather cap, on guard at the border of the empire; then pivot in an east wind to behold "two stark naked Indians, their bodies streaked with dyes, rings in their noses . . . in a little bark canoe"?[2]

The frontier of European settlement was also the border country of empires, where civilizations crossed. Unsettlement, the mutual jostling of people displaced by choice or force, was what Tocqueville found in the Northwest Territories. The emblems of European nations that he met on the frontier were fragmented images on the vast canvas of the continent.

Strangest and most fascinating to Tocqueville were the American pioneers, the forest-clearing, town-building leading edge of settlement. In them, the French visitor found a people entirely without *terroir*. They had, he reported, none of the flavor of a place and its soil, no regional idiosyncrasy or rough peasant culture. The man one met in New York on disembarking from a transatlantic voyage was the same man one met at the doorway of a log cabin on the very edge of settlement. Unlike the laborers and aristocrats of France—at least as Tocqueville imagined his compatriots—these Americans did not spring from the land and carry its mark in rooted cultures. They were indifferent to the detail and variation of the continent they were mastering, except where these promised wealth. Tourists from a culture soaked in Romanticism, the two Frenchmen wanted to see trackless wilderness for its own sake. This made no sense to their American hosts. As Tocqueville reported—playing up the scene for effect—he and Beaumont had to pose as speculators, then "maneuver" into a faux-casual question about where the least desirable land lay, in order to get directions to the wilderness they sought.

These directions led them to a woods northwest of Pontiac, in what is now Michigan. The scene was one of devastation. The first sign of settlement was burnt-over ground, scorched limbs, and trees dead but standing, having been strangled by girdling, the labor-saving trick of stripping off a ring of bark to stop sap from circulating: "all the trees seem to have been struck by sudden death," and "in full summer their withered branches seem the image of winter."[3] In this deathly forest, a proliferation of weeds and wheat, corn and oak shoots, grew on ground newly opened to the sun. At the center of this crude clearing, dead trees gave way to stumps not yet grubbed up, and amid the stumps stood a log cabin.

In this crude building, with a window hacked out of the log walls and furniture assembled from untrimmed tree limbs still sprouting leaves, a few details pointed to the meaning behind the rough labor of frontier survival. A muslin curtain and cracked teapot indicated hope for a gracious domestic life in decades ahead. A Bible, a prayer book, and "sometimes, a poem of Milton or a tragedy of Shakespeare" formed the cabin's ties to the past, while a few newspapers maintained a desultory link to present events.[4] Other than a deerskin or eagle feathers, Tocqueville mentioned only one pure decoration, one piece of visual display: a map of the United States, hanging to the right of the fireplace, rippling in the breezes that passed through cracks in the cabin wall.

The map was an apt symbol. If the American pioneers lacked *terroir* and took no pleasure in the details of unsettled land, if the terrain they shaped was haphazardly ugly, they were nonetheless in the grip of a continental vision. Tocqueville, who adored paradox, saw in the Americans a heroic spirit deployed for workaday ends, the vitality of savage warfare joined with the cool calculation of self-interest. He called the settlers "a race to whom the future of the New World belongs, a restless, calculating, adventurous race which sets coldly about deeds that can only be explained by the fire of passion . . . that submits to living the life of a savage without ever letting itself be carried away by its charms, that only cherishes those parts of civilization and enlightenment which are useful for well-being." The American nation, he judged, "like all great peoples, has but one thought, and presses forward to the acquisition of riches, the single end of its labors, with a perseverance and a scorn of life which one could call heroic, if that word were properly used of anything but the strivings of virtue." Here was something new in the world: heroic effort for everyday purposes, self-sacrificing devotion without self-immolating passion. These were the qualities of a people who could both achieve the focused violence of conquest and sustain the orderly power of rule. Thus, Tocqueville called the Americans "a nation of conquerors . . . whom rivers and lakes cannot hold back, before whom forests fall and prairies are covered in shade; and who, when they have reached the Pacific Ocean, will come back on its tracks to trouble and destroy the societies which it will have formed behind it."[5]

What such a nation meant for the continent was palpable: clearing, settlement, cultivation and also a kind of devastation. What did it mean for the people? How did it feel, to be such a person, one of these new Americans? It seemed to Tocqueville that these calculating conquerors grew emotionally flat, almost two-dimensional, and lost the savor of living. He described the pioneers as cold-blooded, austere, and so emotionally isolated that they hardly took pleasure in ordinary sociability. Consumed by their nation-building vision, they could hardly acknowledge the reality of fellow human beings: "Even [the pioneer's] feelings for his family have become merged in a vast egotism, and one cannot be sure whether he regards his wife and children as anything more than a detached part of himself." This was, for him, part of the paradox of a "great" people, a nation that would turn the wheel of history, that spent its energy in chilly, deliberate fashion, turning a continent to production and profit, from wilderness to property. The image of the pioneer as what we might today call a narcissist—self-aggrandizing, emotionally truncated, isolated from others to the point of seeing them as projected aspects of one's self—would later form a central and enduring image of the second volume of Tocqueville's *Democracy in America*. There he portrayed not just frontier settlers, but Americans in general and, by extension, the democratic personality of the future, as emotionally insensate, set among others yet unable to *feel* them, with each man shut up alone in himself. In this report from frontier Michigan, the same idea seems to originate in Tocqueville's observation of Americans' relation to land and the natural world.

Although Tocqueville saw no *terroir* in Americans, he did see the settlers as shaped by a relation to the land. That relation was abstract and general: nature was a field of economic value for extraction and exploitation. Its consequences came in the casual destruction that had turned a midwestern summer to sun-stricken winter and left trees to decay and collapse, as weeds and new crops grew up together under their dead limbs. Tocqueville's intuition was that Americans' isolation from one another, their evasion of their own warm and passionate energies, and their relentless, muscular, but cold-blooded struggle with nature were parts of a coherent outlook, which would foster both wealth and devastation.

I find Tocqueville's passage fascinating—I must have read it a dozen times since discovering it—and haunting. It has a prophetic quality that suggests the author has seen the future prefigured in a fragment of the past. Reading it, I think of images of the Dust Bowl, of Wallace Stegner's memoirs of his family's exhausting, ultimately failed pioneering on the dry Great Plains. In Tocqueville's forecast that the pioneers will finally reach the Pacific, then turn to harry those they left behind, I think of Los Angeles, last destination of the westward migration, then, soon after, the crucible of the Reagan revolution, which (to my mind) propagated frontier fantasies in a post-frontier country. In the end, though, Tocqueville's prophecy does not convince me, despite its literary art and its chilling picture of the sapping labor of the frontier, which turns summer to winter, not just in the forest but in the faces and hearts of the pioneers.

Throughout his work, Tocqueville presented the young United States as a forecast of democratic modernity. In the passages we are considering here, his thought seems to have been that democratic peoples would take a purely utilitarian view of the natural world.

They would cut themselves off from it and define themselves by conquering it, and these acts would make them both powerful and inhumane, infusing them with a terrible kind of greatness. What Tocqueville missed, like many later critics of utilitarian, capitalist, and democratic approaches to nature, was how intensely Americans continued to regard nature as a teacher, a shaping source for learning how to live. American nature's lessons ratified the program of continental development that Tocqueville witnessed in Michigan, infusing it with the providential significance that flickered through James Wilson's Independence Day speech, Thomas Jefferson's first inaugural address, and John Marshall's opinion in *Johnson v. M'Intosh*, as well as in many popular speeches, editorials, and sermons. It lent a specifically democratic cast to nature, and a reciprocal naturalness to democracy, at least of the settler kind that white Americans were developing. Tocqueville's pioneer may have been exhausted by his work, and his clearing and burning must have given a nightmarish impression to a visitor accustomed to a settled and orderly landscape; but he was involved in an intense vision of nature's purpose that contributed meaning to the lives of those who carried it out and to the democratic communities they were working to form. There were many problems with those communities, and many qualifications are necessary in calling them "democratic"; we have been considering some of those. But the problem was not the bleak fanaticism, veering toward isolate nihilism, that Tocqueville evoked.

In fact, the first fifty years of American independence show an intense and continuing interest in nature as the teacher, the source of refinement and also reassurance, that a democratic people required. The continent was a storehouse of material wealth, but was also full of aesthetic riches. From the late eighteenth century, Americans regularly used an aesthetic distinction that would figure centrally in the development of the modern environmental imagination: the distinction between *beauty* and *sublimity*. Beautiful scenes were defined by gentle contours, regularity, symmetry, and a quality of welcoming the human observer. A pastoral landscape with mildly sloping fields, repeating lines of furrows or hedges, and an air of fertility and hospitality exemplified the beautiful in nature. Sublime scenes, by contrast, were reminders that nature is not designed for human purposes: they were vast, intimidating, inhospitable; often impossible to compass in one person's gaze, they overwhelmed the eye. Niagara Falls, with its thundering wall of water and bone-crushing force, was an early American paradigm of sublimity. High mountains, sheer cliffs, and the sea were also sublime. These two aesthetic qualities named different aspects of the American landscape, but they also named different qualities in the human response to the natural world: a sense of being at home and cared for, in beautiful places, and a feeling of shock, alienation, but also inspiration, in the face of the sublime.

Thomas Jefferson wrote in his *Notes on the State of Virginia* that the state's arched-stone "natural bridge" was "the most sublime of nature's works," where "the rapture of the spectator is really indescribable!"[6] Jefferson purchased the bridge and a 153-acre surrounding tract, and reflected on building an idyllic rural retreat there, a "little hermitage" where he could spend part of the year. Jefferson's emissaries to the American West, Meriwether Lewis and William Clark, also brought a keen aesthetic appreciation of the continent to the report of their Corps of Discovery Expedition (now better remembered as the Lewis and Clark Expedition). They confronted regular threats to their lives, ranging from unknown rapids to recurring bear attacks, at one point finding themselves so beleaguered that they marched in military formation into the portion of a river island where they believed a bear population to be holed up. Nonetheless, they regularly found energy for admiring the landscapes they crossed, and dedicated some of their report to an account of the balance between beauty and sublimity in the West.

In one passage, Lewis follows thunderous sound and hints of mist to the Great Falls of the Missouri, where he "enjoyed the sublime spectacle of this stupendous object, which since the creation had been lavishing its magnificence upon the desert, unknown to civilization."[7] A moment later, he contrasts the sublimity of the "stupendous," dangerous cascades with the beauty of a small, regularly formed waterfall slightly above them, a gentle geological anomaly that welcomed the eye, whereas the cascades overwhelmed it. Both the curiosity about nonutilitarian features of the landscape and the precise use of aesthetic classifications are typical of the expedition. Its report evinces interest not just in the ways the United States could make use of the West, but also in what Americans would see there, and how they might be moved by it.

Such sentiments were not peculiar to the Europhilic and fashion-conscious Jefferson and his scientific representatives. Timothy Dwight—conservative minister, president of Yale University, and arch-opponent of what he styled French-Revolutionary atheism and anarchy—was far from Jefferson in his vision of the young country; but when he wrote his *Travels in New England and New York,* he explained that he dedicated some pages to scenery because it was what readers wanted: "Not a small number of readers are delighted with landscapes, and their taste is as reasonably consulted . . . by a writer, as that of graver minds. When I hear so many individuals converse on the scenes of nature of with so much pleasure, I . . . believe that, wherever justice is done to such scenes in a book, it will be read by them with some degree of the same pleasure." Making good on his promise, he wrote later of New England's variety of "immense ranges, bold spurs, and solitary eminences . . . delightful succession of sublimity and grandeur." The beauty of more modest and hospitable landscape forms and gracious, useful waterways was interspersed with the grand and sublime, so that "the variety, which Milton informs us Earth has derived from Heaven 'Of pleasure situate in hill and dale' is nowhere more extensively found." The land was endless inspiration for those aesthetes who sought it: "Neither the poet nor the painter can here be ever at a loss for scenery to employ the pen or the pencil." Much the same notes, then, sounded from both the Republican and the Federalist poles of American public life.[8]

Nature contained both the wild terrain that called out to be cleared and settled and the beautiful and sublime landscapes that offered symbolic, aesthetic, and moral lessons. Three moments in those lessons are worth close consideration: the poetry of the revolutionary soldier and Jeffersonian newspaper editor Philip Freneau; the theory of moral improvement put forward for the Whig Party by then-former president John Quincy Adams; and the aesthetic agenda of the Hudson River School of painters, with its civic ambitions for American landscape.

A Pause for Flowers: Philip Freneau

Philip Freneau, known as the "poet of the American Revolution," served as a privateer—a licensed pirate—before assuming the editorship of the *National Gazette*, a Philadelphia-based newspaper that existed to attack George Washington's administration and promote Washington's secretary of state, Thomas Jefferson. Freneau never tired of shouting down old Europe's aristocracies and tyrannies, or of comparing his domestic opponents to them. He was also the first American Romantic poet, with a keen aesthetic interest in the natural world.

Freneau's poetry voices the fierce republicanism of a writer who supported Tom Paine and the French Revolution. Kings, for him, were "source of discord, patrons of all wrong [who] / On blood and murder have been fed too long . . . / The curse, the scourge, the ruin of our race . . . / Who made this globe the residence of slaves." He urged his fellow republicans to "haste the period that shall crush them all."[9] One of the pleasures of reading Freneau—and the pleasures are not mainly literary—is that his work evokes the un-abashed radicalism of the American Revolution. He mocked mon-archists as idolators and slaves to their own superstition and fear, and voiced every confidence that Reason sided with the Amer-ican cause. Independent America, he promised in the midst of the Revolution, would enjoy "a second golden reign," an era of peace and freedom, restoring the highest achievements of the ancient world.[10]

Nature, in Freneau's view, was the unfailing ally of republican freedom, and kings were usurpers against her. She was a Deist Cre-ation, uniform in her laws, with no miracles or "special provi-dence": "All, nature made, in reason's sight, is order all, and *all is right*."[11] Nature taught "the path of right, fair virtue's way": liberty, equality, and peace.[12] Society should arise from the natural soli-darity of free and equal individuals.

Freneau foresaw a spiritual consummation as well as a political one. When republicans finally drive superstition from the human mind, "Then persecution will retreat / And man's religion be complete."[13] His hints at the meaning of "man's religion" were a far-rago of Deism, classical paganism, and humanism. His "Creatress Nature" is the only nonhuman figure in a poem on "Religion." (God makes no appearance.) In other poems, he asserted that the soul was mortal, a view he shared with Epicurus, and which seems to have meant, for him, that this world is humanity's only home and the place where the "golden age" must come about, if it does at all.[14]

Freneau regarded North America as humanity's last chance to reclaim Roman and British freedom—and on the grandest scale yet, one that might inspire the rest of the globe and become uni-versal. This millennial promise would arise when the continent was enriched by labor and science. Settlers would "tame the soil, and plant the arts" to harness the vast, useless energy of the living land-scape, the "savage stream" of the Ohio and the "princely flood" of the Mississippi, which surged through a country where for mil-lennia "forests bloomed but to decay." Now at last, that power would be turned to usefulness and wealth: the soil would feed new nations, and as for the rivers, long the lifeblood of "a darksome wood . . . unnoticed," now "commerce plans new freights for thee."[15] This portrait of North America as the material basis for a new chapter in human freedom is the poetic answer to Jefferson's promise that the frontier offered "room enough for our descendants to the thousandth and thousandth generation"—at last, time and world enough for an "empire of liberty" to enter history.

For all his commitment to reason and progress, Freneau was also attached to wild places. Repeated notes in his poems suggest that there is something incomplete in the plan of rational freedom and something charismatic, even essential, in the primitive. As he put it, reflecting on the charm of an Indian burying ground, in the presence of myth "reason's self shall bow the knee / To shadows and delusions here."[16] It is telling that Freneau uses the image of political or religious submission, which he scorns when it is rendered to kings or priests: the same impulse, to kneel to power and mystery, wins a kind of respect from him when it responds instead to enchanted nature—or, more exactly, to an image of another, more primitive people's idea of enchanted nature. Here, sentimental and aestheticized submission is a safe way to acknowledge the irrational in ourselves.

He returned often to a well-rehearsed theme from Virgil's *Eclogues:* the peace of the rural retreat, in contrast to the corruptions of urbanity and power. This sometimes led him to the implausible conceit that American villages and forests were populated by pipe-playing shepherds. Lacking real peasants (who were amply accessible to, say, Wordsworth) and without much capacity or inclination to convey the texture of labor or its effect on the human body, the republican Freneau in these poems inadvertently resembles Marie Antoinette playing shepherdess. His pastoral settings were unreal, even bizarrely so, in a society mobilized to open the frontier. The main thrust of his treatment of nature was utilitarian: prosperity and improvement would be the basis of a free and self-governing society. One might pause to admire a fast-dying flower for its own sake—but not for long, and not during working hours. Americans should keep such useless, fanciful decorations around, but not at the sacrifice of nature's real purpose, which was to make men productive and rich.

Learning from the Land: John Quincy Adams

Three years before his death in 1848, the aged ex-president John Quincy Adams returned to the theme of continental development. Forty-three years earlier, he had given an oration against "the lordly savage," insisting that North America must belong to the settlers who made it bloom. This time, as a grand old man in the Whig Party, he set out to explain how mastery over nature built moral and intellectual progress. The argument appeared in the *American Review,* a Whig journal of the later 1840s devoted to national unity, continent-binding infrastructure, a strong federal government, and the development of an Atlanticist literary culture.

Adams treated the changing ways humans had wrested a living from the earth as a moral education designed and administered by providence. Humans' social nature, he explained, was rooted in sexual attraction, so each kind of relation to the earth had also been a sexual economy, a form of the bond between women and men. Each way of life also produced a specific religious or philosophical mood, a way of seeing and reflecting upon the natural world. A way of living on the earth shaped the social bonds and the intellectual and religious life of humanity.

Adams thought little of the primitive life of hunters, whom he described as inconstant in every way: the urgency of the chase was followed by long periods of lassitude; hunters' sexual passion, too, was inconstant, opportunistic, lacking social and moral shape. "The life of the hunter," he wrote, "is a life of action, intent upon the pursuit of his game—or of idleness, in which the mind feels no call for the exercise of its powers. His passions are all violent and fierce. There is nothing in the aspect of nature with which he is conversant, tending to melt his soul into tenderness, or to allure it into contemplation. His very domestic affections are languid and cheerless. He is the tyrant rather than the friend and protector of his wife."[17] Here is an elaboration of Adams's much earlier dismissal of the "lordly savage's" claim to North America: an unworthy human type with a primitive relation to the earth should not delay the providential development of the continent.

In the historical path that Adams supposed all developing societies took, hunting gave way to the herding (pastoral) and farming stages of history, and these new eras deepened human consciousness. With herding, Adams claimed, the erratic character of the hunter passed into depths of devotion and contemplation. Since his survival now depended on his care for particular animals, the herdsman became accustomed to a steadier, more affectionate form of life than the savage hunter. This new scope of affection, in turn, influenced the domestic sphere, where herders learned a deepened love of particular women.

Adams also portrayed pastoral humanity learning for the first time to contemplate nature. He pictured a shepherd watching his flocks by night and considering the stars' movement across the sky. From this sort of steady, relaxed attention, which was the basic attitude of a man protecting his herd, came religious contemplation and a sense of wonder.

Still, there was something basically boundless in the life of the herdsman; an open horizon was implied in the way he followed his flocks across open country, with no tie to particular places. In their starry skies, Adams reported, shepherds imagined many gods, and they likewise expressed their sexual desire in polygamy, wishing to attach both love and appetite to as many women as they could have. The pastoral life deepened human nature to produce the raw material of the modern soul and society, but its culture remained as sprawling and ill-defined as the territory of herders (at least as Adams imagined them).

A new form of consciousness came with the farming life, anchored in a new relation to landscape. Adams described what happens when a people labors in a settled place:

> The foot of man becomes thus fastened to the earth. He constructs his dwelling place to outlast his own existence. It passes as a heritage to his children. . . . The ties of mutual dependence between man and his neighbor gain strength. The kindly affections first awakened in the bosom of the shepherd, for the cattle of his flock . . . extend their influence even to the inanimate nature that surrounds him. The roof that sheltered his infancy, the fireside at which he has listened in comfort and security to the howling of the winter's blast; the lawn at the cottage door, the streamlet that courses through the neighboring vale; the trees planted by his hand, which, as they rise and flourish, and yield their delicious fruits, or spread forth their refreshing shades, seem like children grateful to parental care; the mountain that borders the horizon, immoveable and unchanging in the lapse of years, and insensibly leading the mind from the transient objects of time to the boundless ages of eternity, all silent witnesses of the first emotions of infancy and the dearest joys of youth, grappled to the soul by ever multiplying recollections, chain the heart of man to his home, and become the primary elements in that strong, beneficent and virtuous impulse, the love of his country.[18]

Adams asserted that, in such a setting, a farmer would naturally realize the value of monogamy and find one woman to be "the partner and companion of his life," a collaborator and an intimate.

The age of farming, then, brought "the foundations of civil society and of rational religious worship," and also the anchor of the modern family, tied together by love in a shared home and labor.[19]

The settlement of North America took the continent from indigenous peoples' hunting lives directly into the farming stage, and from there to the consummation of human development, which Adams called civilization. This fourth and final stage was marked by widespread trade and the rise of commercial cities, but it did not leave the earlier stages behind altogether. Civilization rested on the bedrock of virtuous husbandmen, who formed the cultural and moral anchor of commercial society. Adams recognized the "mechanic arts, and the division of labor," which "multiply to an indefinite degree the occupations of men," but he did not seriously consider that an industrial economy, or a class of property-less laborers, could much complicate his picture of civilization's "two great classes, husbandmen and merchants."[20]

Settlement followed a providential course, but there were urgent tasks for government. Like other Whigs, Adams believed that these included building the infrastructure of settlement—railroads, canals, and highways—that would tie the country together. He also forecast "the great problem of legislation": to harmonize self-interest with the interest of society, care for self and family with care for the country and all humanity.[21] This was a matter of legislation, but also of enlightenment: moral growth and good law must go together in a harmonious society.

Nature encouraged this harmony through its influence on consciousness and culture. A properly settled landscape was a kind of moral and civic education. These levels of harmony were mutually reinforcing.

James Wilson had argued similarly more than fifty years earlier. Wilson maintained that all levels of experience and reality followed the same pattern, from the cosmic order to the "moral sense" of right and wrong: "Order, proportion, and fitness pervade the universe. Around us, we see, within us, we feel, above us, we admire, a rule from which a deviation can not, or should not, or will not be made."[22] Aesthetic response was an exercise of the moral sense, a spontaneous admiration for virtue and good work. So, for Wilson, development and morality inspired "in every beholder possessed of sensibility and taste, an effect far more pleasing, and far more lasting, than can be produced by the prettiest piece of unreformed nature."[23] The rebirth of political freedom in North America was beautiful; perceiving that beauty was the eye's tribute to the continent's development, which was a project of both material and moral perfection.

Even as John Quincy Adams was reviving Wilson's optimistic view of the harmonies of development, his allies around the *American Review* were coming to doubt it. An unsigned article titled "California" treated the nation's move to the center of world history as providential, but left open the question as to whether it would end in a triumph of civic and moral culture or a collapse into a new barbarism. Of the westernmost state, the article warned: "The foundations . . . of a new social order, are being laid there. What a hell upon earth, if the boundless lust of gold be unrestrained, unsanctified by better influences! Pandemonium [Hell's capital city, according to John Milton] was built of molten gold." The problem was that "the spirit of the age is a spirit of hard worldliness and self-willed pride."[24] The problem lay in habits of the heart, in the way a culture focused on wealth and the way competition shaped the character of its members. The solution, the author of "California" argued, must be to intensify the Christian influence in American life, the inherited orientation to higher things.

Training the Eye: The Hudson River School

There was, however, another approach to cultivating moral order in a continent-spanning commercial republic. This was to draw on the morally educative power of nature, the harmonies among land-scape, character, and society that both Wilson and Adams em-phasized. Yet whereas these harmonies had expressed themselves almost automatically through providential history, they would now have to arise intentionally, as a part of cultural self-creation. Ad-ams's passage on how a settled landscape trains both the eye and the heart to virtue could have been a manifesto for the landscape artists who, from the 1830s forward, aimed to improve Americans' character through images of American landscape. The pioneering Thomas Cole and, some two decades later, Frederic Church and Asher Durand, depicted the landscapes of New England and the Hudson Valley in canvases that integrated images of settled culti-vation; icons of development such as railroads; distant cities where commerce drew the products of the subsisting yet dynamic countryside; and, often framing the whole image, sublime and unchanging mountains, reminders of the moral and religious principles that should undergird the whole composition.[25] In part, these artists aimed to present the New World landscape as the basis for America's membership among the great cultures of the world, substituting the grandeur of the continent for European legacies of literature, architecture, and the fine arts. Another aim was to form a civic identity, drawing the eye and the mind to the same morally instructive landforms that Adams had sketched in his portrait of a farmer's relation to his locale.

How could art assist this work? As Angela Miller has argued, the landscape artists of this era kept up a tenuous but productive harmony between two ideas of how aesthetic response shaped the mind. On the one hand, Church and Durand held to a visual and painterly version of moral-sense theory, the eighteenth-century Scottish-born view that perceptions of right and wrong came nat-urally from the exercise of innate faculties, just as perceptions of color arise from the ordinary power of sight. Thus, people should respond to landscapes in convergent ways, as (on the moral-sense theory) they would to kindness or cruelty. On the other hand, the aesthetic and psychological culture of the time owed much to associationist theories of the mind, which held that images and ideas grew attached to one another by repeated exposure. Both theories are evident in Adams's passage: on the one hand, he writes that viewing mountains all one's life *just will* inspire reflections on eternity and a healthy tendency to monotheism; on the other hand, he refers to the intellectual and emotional meanings of the landscape as "grappled to the soul by ever multiplying recollections"— the same process that associationist ideas of the mind envisaged. Repeated exposure to art that showed an ideal American landscape could train viewers in the right ways of observing actual terrain, teach them to identify that terrain with the civic and religious sentiments that the art expressed, setting up a circle of virtuous perception. Seeing in the right way would be the proof of good training and, itself, the source of more training.

Both Cole and Durand made the case in polemical theories of American landscape, Cole in 1835, the younger man twenty years later. Both insisted that aesthetics cultivated qualities of character and mind that were essential to high civilization. Too much of American life, they complained, was no more than wealth-getting and "money-pride."[26] As Cole put it, the danger was that a "meager utilitarianism" would leave "the bright and tender flowers of the imagination . . . crushed beneath its iron tramp."[27] American minds would be reduced to selfishness, unspiritual and uncivic: "It is bitter to those who love their race, to see men shut up into themselves year after year, pursuing that which can belong to themselves alone."[28] By contrast, exposure to beauty always cultivated an appreciation of goodness, while sublimity raised the mind to higher things, above and apart from selfish desire. Attention to the "stern sublimity of the wild" and the gentler harmonies of homeplace and cultivated lands could make Americans both reverent toward ultimate things and brotherly toward one another.[29] In an increasingly democratic culture, even the rougher sort might be trained for social life by beauty: Durand described "a group of boys rollicking through the street" in lower Manhattan who, coming upon a heap of discarded marigolds, gathered the flowers and proceeded in a different spirit: "locked arm in arm . . . voices . . . softened, and their bearing harmonized."[30] Durand's roughs were a set piece for an emerging American nation, which would have to refine its businessmen and raise up its urchins into a spirit of citizenship.

Painters could assist this work by rendering on canvas the edifying power that was immanent but unrealized in the landscape. The landscape itself was spiritualized, both Cole and Durand insisted, so didactic art did not falsify but captured the truth. Yet simple imitation would not convey landscape's lessons: the artist's work was to go beyond mimesis to a portrayal that put truthfulness over mere accuracy. The key was to learn to see, because seeing was not mere surface perception—it was insight. The most successful painting would be true to vision, and would train the gaze of others. Cole observed already in 1835 that the painterly aesthetic culture he hoped to cultivate was not only a matter of canvases in studios: it took strength from the land itself, which narrow-minded development jeopardized. Cole insisted, comparing Americans to biblical prophets, "The wilderness is YET a fitting place to speak of God," and he lamented that "the ravages of the axe" were "destroy[ing] Nature's beauty without substituting that of Art."[31] Although he praised the development of the continent as nearly "magical" progress, Cole also insisted that something was being lost, which Americans might hope to preserve in landscapes, but which, even more imperatively, they must achieve anew in the second nature of art.

The American landscape had always been a collective project as much as a natural (or even material) fact. By participating correctly in nature's providential design, settlers might contribute to a free and prosperous republic that completed divine intent. This providential idea coexisted with another that was more artificial and self-conscious: that Americans should form a national landscape that could sustain a complex integration of wealth and virtue at the endpoint of an ordained procession through developmental stages—hunting, herding, farming, and commercial civilization. Working on, and imagining, the American landscape became aspects of collective self-creation. The painters' ambitions were ratified, if imperfectly, when ordinary New Yorkers lined up around city blocks to pay a nickel apiece for views of their heroic landscapes, and when cheap copies of these paintings appeared everywhere, in settings ranging from living rooms to Sunday-school primers, producing a vernacular of wonder. These changes set the stage for new registers of civic and aesthetic ambition, which yoked ideas of nature to nationalist and imperial projects and to new aesthetic and spiritual claims.

4

NATURAL UTOPIAS

IN DECEMBER 1874, John Muir climbed to the top of a hundred-foot Douglas spruce on the forested lower slopes of California's Mount Shasta to experience a windstorm from the standpoint of a tree. Lashed to the trunk for safety, he closed his eyes and listened to the hissing needles, the bass boom of the larger branches, the click of a hard leaf driven against another, and, every two to three minutes, the crash of some felled giant. Eyes still closed, he savored the resin-scented air, caught a hint of Pacific salt beneath the evergreen, and imagined just a touch of the coastal redwoods and the wildflowers of the Central Valley in the gusts that reached his nose. Looking again, he found the currents of air as visible as a river in the dancing trees and eddying debris of the storm.

Storms, Muir reckoned, were not violent at all—just spectacles of sublimity, like a waterfall or sunrise over the peaks of Yosemite: dramatic, yes, but part of a larger harmony, there for the delight of all. This was no senseless destruction, no Darwinian struggle for existence, but a joyous shouting-out of the world's vitality. When the wind had stopped, he untied himself and climbed down with a consummate sense of peace.[1]

That, anyway, is how Muir recalled it in 1894, when he published *The Mountains of California,* one of a series of books that made him an icon. That was two years after he cofounded the Sierra Club and became its president, an office he held until his death in 1914. Muir presented himself as a literary and spiritual descendant of Ralph Waldo Emerson and Henry David Thoreau. In his carefully crafted account of meeting the aging Emerson in Yosemite Valley, he claimed that the mantle of Transcendentalism had passed from New England to California.

Muir's tree-climbing adventure was not the sort of thing either Concord writer would have undertaken: Thoreau was more likely to stand stock-still by a stream until he could tickle a complacent fish than to go in search of violent excitement, and his one journey into sublime terrain, on Maine's Mount Katahdin, left him shaken and anxious to return to gentler ground. Muir had learned a way of seeing from the Transcendentalists, though: to sort a natural scene into its elements, carefully naming each, then join them into a single pattern by a grand act of intuitive perception—that was Thoreau's style, which Muir adopted in his popular and influential high-country travelogues.

Muir's choice of inheritance fit the solitary, ecstatic persona he created in his writing. He portrayed himself as a kind of paladin in restless search of sublimity. His touchstone writings gave no hint that he was a husband, farmer, and, for some years, one of those industrious truck farmers that Thoreau portrayed as slaves to conformity and busyness in the early pages of *Walden*. Muir's inconvenient entanglement with other people and lowland life mostly stayed well off the page.

Muir learned a way of writing about nature from Thoreau and Emerson. In turn, he trained his contemporaries in actively seeing nature. His Sierra Club, the much smaller seed of today's environmental organization, was an outing group devoted to mountain sunrises, ascents to snowy peaks, hard-earned picnics atop mountain waterfalls, and, at every summit, a feeling of having touched the source of things. Muir's writing mapped the routes, literal and imaginative. Sierrans drew on this writing as they taught one another to think of hiking as pilgrimage. Much of the teaching took place on shared expeditions to the high country, where club members camped together by the scores or hundreds for weeks in July and August. Some came through shared writing, images, and speech, which imparted living force to their language of epiphany and the sublime.

The club's ideal was the personal encounter with nature that Muir conjured up, even as its activity was intensely social, even communal, to the point where one member described its encampments (with only the lightest irony) as short-lived socialist utopias. Club members relied on one another for comfort, survival, and companionship in the high country. Even more, they relied on one another to confirm and amplify their quasi-mystical experience by hearing it and saying it back to them. The movement was one part action, one part language, and neither of those could go far in isolation (language even less than action). But because the touchstone of the movement was personal epiphany, its social dimension tended to waver in and out of sight, even recede to invisibility. As the club rapidly became a force in public-lands politics, it was, ironically, a political movement dedicated to the aesthetic and spiritual experience of the solitary wanderer. Club members mobilized together to move the lever of the state, all to preserve some acreage where a person could be alone in the wild.

A Choice of Inheritances

In choosing the ancestors they did, Muir and the Sierra Club almost unwittingly took a philosophical position in a long debate over how nature could contribute to radical change in human experience. In making Thoreau their touchstone, they put spirit over structure, and the individual over the common, in ways that both energized and limited the politics they created.

Fifty years before Muir helped to found the Sierra Club, Thoreau reviewed a book that proposed a technological utopia. The work, by J. A. Etzler, was *The Paradise within the Reach of All Men, without Labor, by Means of Nature and Machinery*, published in 1842. Etzler, a follower of the French social visionary Charles Fourier, argued that men could build a paradise on earth (and, he promised, within a decade) by harnessing what the twenty-first century calls renewable energy. Wind, tides, and the sun would replace human labor. These new powers would "level mountains, sink valleys, create lakes, drain lakes and swamps, and intersect the land everywhere with beautiful canals, and roads for . . . traveling one thousand miles in twenty-four hours."[2]

Thoreau agreed with Etzler that unused energy was plentiful: air surged and plunged over the earth; New England's few windmills were a farcical tribute to its power. The waves and tides were even stronger, and the sun's vast energy promised limitless power, if only people could capture it. There was no scientific reason to deny Etzler's forecast that future man would "lead a life of continual happiness, of enjoyments yet unknown" and "free himself from almost all the evils that afflict mankind, except death."[3]

But Thoreau thought Etzler had left out the most important change, the one that had to happen before any other would really matter. Etzler proposed giving people what they wanted, in such abundance that scarcity would no longer define social life. Thoreau replied that people could be happy only when they shaped what they wanted. He insisted that what he called "reform of the world," which aimed to change attitudes and appetites, must come before Etzler's "reform of the globe," mastering nature to fulfill the appetites that existed.

Thoreau maintained that reform of the world—his kind of change—had to begin with the individual. He replied to Etzler's call for new kinds of social cooperation, "Nothing can be effected but by one man. . . . We must first succeed alone, that we may enjoy our success together." In contrast to Etzler's forecasts of plenty, Thoreau argued for simplifying needs and avoiding new wants. Instead of chasing ease and luxury, train yourself to find pleasure in everyday beauty, and make thought and imagination your luxuries. Thoreau wrote, in a typical sentence, "When the sunshine falls on the path of the poet, he enjoys all those pure benefits and pleasures which the arts slowly and partially realize from age to age." In Thoreau's view, while the material reformer worked to make wind and tides more productive, the spiritual reformer made sunshine brighter and winds sweeter. These were the dividends of having eyes to see, ears to hear. Riffing on Etzler's calculations of the untapped horsepower of wind and tide, Thoreau reflected, "Suppose we could say . . . how many horse-power the force of love, blowing on every square foot of a man's soul, would equal." As New England's windmills insulted the world's winds by their paltriness, so her hospitals, poorhouses, and Bible societies insulted the power of love, showing "how little it is actually applied to social ends."[4]

Although Muir and Thoreau were not entirely aware of it, they were replaying a much older quarrel between versions of utopia, a debate in which North America had never been allowed to be neutral. From the time Europeans first made landfall, the Americas became canvases of moral and political imagination. Even though tens of millions of indigenous people lived there already, the continents sparked in European minds the idea of a land not owned, ungoverned by any dynasty or inherited law—a *new* world. To some, this promised the chance to start again, this time on a better plan. At the least, it opened space in imagination to consider how a better society might begin.

Two sixteenth-century classics put this question in high relief. Both were social theory in the form of fictional travelers' tales from the far Atlantic. Thomas More's *Utopia,* the ironically titled traveler's report from "nowhere," described an island whose inhabitants lived peacefully and with mutual respect because, by abolishing most private wealth, they had eliminated inequality, jealousy, and ambition. The Utopians trained children to regard gold and silver as unclean, and gems and finery as fools' toys. Raised in conditions of strict equality, Utopian children had no wish to dominate others, and no fear of being dominated. Utopians lived a quietly sociable life of six-hour workdays, edifying public lectures, and orderly self-government. By remaking their social world and training their desires, they had remade the human condition.

Francis Bacon's *New Atlantis* portrayed a very different earthly paradise beyond the western sea. More's Utopians transformed human desire: they eased and drained the passions that made people competitors and enemies. Thoreau would have called their strategy the reform of the world. The Atlantans, Etzler's intellectual ancestors, mastered nature to fulfill desire. As they explained to Bacon's fictional emissary, their power rested on "the knowledge of causes, and secret motions of things; and enlarging of the bounds of human empire, to the effecting of all things possible."[5] The Atlantans commanded submarines, telephony, sources of heat akin to the sun, wondrous medicines, and the means of producing meat from inert matter, as well as audio gear that today's remixers would recognize: "We make diverse tremblings and warblings of sounds, which in their original are entire" and "diverse strange and artificial echoes, reflecting the voice many times and as it were tossing it: and some that give back the voice louder than it came, some shriller, and some deeper." The Atlantans had remade the human condition, not by disciplining appetite but by expanding the power to satisfy it, the power of "empire" over raw nature.

When the Romantic strand of American environmental imagination made Thoreau a prophet, it carried a version of consciousness-changing "reform of the world" into public life and lawmaking. It has made Thoreau its own because it, too, prizes nature for the power to change consciousness and enrich experience. It agrees with Thoreau that human freedom involves refining our desires and distinguishing between what we want and what we need.

The other major forms of environmental imagination in the first 150 years of American history made North America a staging ground for Francis Bacon's utopia, a world remade by technology and wealth. Only the Romantic strain has aimed mainly at consciousness, the prize in More's Utopia. Romantics have insisted that self-knowledge depends on connection to the natural world, and may even require being able to escape everyday social life to a rural retreat or into the wilderness. Because of this strand of environmental imagination, it made sense for Idaho senator Frank Church to say in 1961 that if Congress failed to preserve wilderness, the country "would become a cage."[6] For wilderness to be the thing that keeps us free, nature must be a storehouse of special insight, open to whoever walks into the mountains for a night or a week.

Romantic environmentalism has followed Thoreau in treating changed consciousness as an individual goal, a matter of improving the personal relationship with nature. It has tended to treat politics and social order as a web of distractions, woven from trivial and corrupting fixations that fall away from a clarified mind. Consciousness changing thus works from the inside out, and is quite different from what it was for More's Utopians, who changed their institutions so that they could change their minds.

This Romantic style of individualism and skepticism toward politics has contributed to both success and failure for environmental politics. Romantic environmentalism proved an easy fit with established American attitudes, especially in its early constituency of the wealthy and traditional elites. Its ideal encounter with nature proved easy to package as a consumer experience. The failure is the other side of the same coin. Because consciousness takes shape in relation to the institutions of social life, an ideal of radically different consciousness that takes social life pretty much as it is will have trouble being very radical at all. This is part of the reason that Romantic environmentalism, for all its high gestures and rhetoric, has tended to become vacation and consumption.

Romantic reverence for wild nature paradoxically disserved the natural world, idealizing nature to the point of obscuring much of its reality. When Romantic environmentalism did not own up to the ways that law and technology produce both the nature we encounter and the ways we encounter it, its ideal of pristine, wild nature grew narrower. This narrowing encouraged the Romantic habit of disregarding, even disdaining, places that do not meet high standards of sublimity and inspiration, segregating the natural world into a few cathedrals and vast tracts of profane land, with most of human life relegated to the profane regions.

Arguing over Concord: Transcendentalism and Its Uses

Along with his friend, mentor, and sometime landlord Ralph Waldo Emerson, Thoreau belonged to the first, small generation to argue in secular terms that American freedom was a spiritual challenge. They argued that it was not enough to conquer the continent materially and create political liberty. Instead, freedom entailed a new goal, what today we might call *authenticity*: acting from one's own conscience and mind, rather than from habit or tradition. To act freely was to overcome rote and ritual and fully inhabit each moment of one's action. Such action would become a kind of worship, a celebration of the self that could act freely and of the world in which it acted.

Emerson was a major figure in his long life. Thoreau, in his brief life cut short by tuberculosis, was a substantial literary figure but not, by his ambitious lights, entirely a success. At the younger man's funeral, Emerson lamented Thoreau's unfinished work, sketched in his often beautiful journals. Thoreau looms so large in American environmental imagination because later figures canonized him as they made his twin themes of nature and spiritual freedom central to a much broader public argument than he stirred in his life. Thanks to the Sierra Club's founders and their allies and successors, by the middle of the twentieth century Thoreau sat at the center of a pantheon of American environmentalist pioneers.

In adopting Thoreau as a source, the creators of American environmentalism were also remaking him, turning him into a figure they could prize. The Thoreau that emerged from his environmental canonization was a different figure from the one who took his daily walks through the Concord woods: the new Thoreau was committed to wilderness, prized untouched nature, and saw human incursions on natural beauty as a kind of sin. In the late 1950s and early 1960s, Howard Zahniser, longtime secretary of the Wilderness Society, drew on this Thoreau in his stump speech on the importance of wilderness, which Senate supporters entered into the Congressional Record. Calling wilderness the key to conservation as a whole, and warning that without its lessons humans would face "annihilation," Zahniser devoted about a quarter of his address to long quotes from Thoreau, crediting him with teaching Americans the value of preserving a nature beyond human control, where they could "witness our own limits transgressed, and some life pasturing freely where we never wander."[7] He drew a line from Thoreau through Muir and Verplanck Colvin, the leading advocate of Adirondacks preservation, to the icons of the Wilderness Society: Stephen Mather, Robert (Bob) Marshall, and Aldo Leopold. The acolytes of this Wilderness Thoreau completed a transformation in their hero that John Muir had begun: Muir had conceded that Thoreau was not really a wilderness man, but insisted that most people, lacking his subtlety, could get at Thoreau's ideal only through literal wilderness. Muir devoted his own advocacy to making that claim true, turning the Transcendentalist legacy into a doctrine for the Sierra Nevada, the northern Rockies, and the Cascades.

Reading Thoreau in a different light shows that there is just as much in him to support an Anthropocene reading of his work as to confirm the commitment to wilderness that his Romantic admirers found there. The point is not that Thoreau was "truly" an Anthropocene figure, or that Thoreau's words must matter to people thinking about nature today. What an Anthropocene reading of Thoreau shows, though, is just how long and actively Americans have been dealing with, interpreting, and learning from a transformed world, and how much wilderness advocates simplified and obscured when they focused the Romantic legacy on pristine nature. It also highlights that much in the old canon remains useful, even illuminating and exciting, in an Anthropocene time, if only we claim it.

This, however, is getting ahead of the story.

The Transcendentalist obsession with nature began with the very opposite of a pristine wilderness. In his first major published work, "Nature," Emerson reflected on a world transformed by human powers. Technology was amplifying the harmony between human needs and the natural world's order, Emerson argued. Once, people had looked to the cycles of rainfall, seasons, and fertility as signs that the world was made for dwelling in; now the man-made landscape of cities, canals, and bridges, traversed by railroads and ships, served human needs at every point, and economic life built a system of mutual service that elaborated the original interdependence of all creatures. And the transformation had only begun. Emerson concluded, "At present, man applies to nature but half his force"—meaning his contemporaries had learned to change the world only through material power; next they should learn to *see* differently, which would transform the world yet again, this time from within the mind.[8]

Emerson also treated the natural world as an answer to the problem of individuality: How can a person, molded by habit and pressed by convention, know who he or she *really* is? His answer was to trust spontaneous intuition—a kind of inward light flashing through the dust of custom. Emerson proposed that the highest view of nature revealed it as a kind of mirror of the mind. We should feel and trust that the natural world, despite all its manifest diversity, arose from a single underlying principle, and that our minds had the same source. The mind had to display the same spontaneity and harmony that nature did. The world thus served as a kind of master analogy for one's self, and to contemplate it was to turn an epistemic somersault and observe one's own self, if not directly, then at the nearest possible remove.

This vastly egotistical view (the phrase is merely accurate, rather than pejorative) did not treat nature as a source of specific, didactic lessons, as Puritan and evangelical New Englanders had done. For Emerson, it was nature as a whole that had meaning, and this meaning was not a series of instructions expressible in words. Nature's meaning was intuitive: knowing it meant grasping a living, ordered, spontaneous unity that was at once all of reality and, mysteriously, coextensive with one's self. One considered the whole universe to illuminate the self.

Emerson, who was a sympathetic and supportive reader of Thoreau, claimed that his friend's ideas were all Emerson's own, only "very originally dressed."[9] Whether that was fair or a stray instance of Emerson's principle of self-knowledge through egotism, an important part of Thoreau's task in *Walden* was to refine Emerson's all-consuming exhortation—know the world to know yourself—to a practical form. When Thoreau went into the woods, he did something new in the young United States. To be sure, the idea of retreating to a virtuous rural redoubt to draw a bead on the decadent capitals of culture and power was a classical notion with plenty of American instances, from Philip Freneau's pastorals to George Washington's emulation of farmer-ruler Cincinnatus. Thoreau's project was different. It was that of the ascetic hermit-errant, whose careful attention to his "life in the woods" would help him to see life at large. The backdrop of Emersonian faith helped Thoreau to declare that "the highest reality" came in contemplation, both of the self and of the world's natural wonders, and that in this fleeting state, "all nature is your congratulation, and you have cause momentarily to bless yourself."[10]

Thoreau and Emerson shared a posture: always on the move, bent in anticipation toward new light about to rise, with new harmonies, however fleeting, set to emerge. Thoreau concluded *Walden* with the prophecy that "the life in us . . . like the water in the river . . . may rise this year higher than man has ever known it, and flood the parched uplands,"[11] a sentiment of nearly religious expectation quite consistent with this formula from his review of Etzler: "The Divine is about to be, and such is its nature."[12] Thoreau's aim was to describe the flow of experience through an intensely receptive consciousness, not to generate a specific formula for living.

Although *Walden* is sometimes imagined as a story of settlement, it is just as much about transience. It ends with Thoreau's explanation that "I left the woods for as good a reason as I went there. Perhaps it seemed to me that I had several more lives to live, and could not spare any more time for that one."[13] This transient spirit was so strong that Thoreau expressed horror at "how easily and insensibly we . . . make a beaten track for ourselves," as he had between his cabin door and the pond, and worried wryly that "others may have fallen into" his tracks at Walden since his departure. In this way, *Walden* resembles the essay "Walking," in which Thoreau exhorts his fellow Americans to realize their destiny by pressing always westward, not so much by the compass as into the unrealized wilds of their own experience: they should follow the paths of pilgrims toward a Holy Land that is always receding from reach but also visible to truly open eyes. These themes made Thoreau a ready source for the early Sierra Club, which gave practical life to a new way of encountering the natural world: secular pilgrimage, a seasonal passage into landscape whose sacral quality lay in its power to bring on the epiphanies Thoreau urged. Thoreau had made Emerson's theory of nature as a key to self-knowledge practical in one life; the Sierra Club's founders made Thoreau's use of nature as a pilgrimage site the basis for a new movement and a new form of sociability.

Thoreau's remark—that he left Walden because he had several more lives to live—turned out to be true of his posthumous literary career. In his own time, Thoreau was mainly received as a picturesque-nature writer. Reviewers often acknowledged that he had philosophical ambition, or at least conceit, but they seemed not to find this aspect of his work worth engaging with care. When he came into the literary canon of the late nineteenth century, inducted by the publishing decisions of Brahmins clustered around Harvard and the *Atlantic*—which had also been important institutions for him in life—Thoreau continued to figure as a literary student of American nature. His most-anthologized writing was more or less pure nature description. *Walden,* which in the twentieth century came to be regarded as his masterpiece, in his own day was viewed as being on a par with much less philosophical, book-length accounts of expeditions on Cape Cod and on the Concord and Merrimack rivers. An early edition of his works relegated "Civil Disobedience" to a tenth volume of "Miscellany," along with his slashing, near-despairing attacks on the Fugitive Slave Law and his defense of abolitionist John Brown's attempt to spark a slave revolt at Harper's Ferry, Virginia (later West Virginia). He was being ushered into the pantheon of hortatory, pastoral men of American letters, alongside other New Englanders such as James Russell Lowell, Henry Wadsworth Longfellow, and Oliver Wendell Holmes Sr., the Renaissance-man father of the Supreme Court justice.

A twentieth-century storm swept away this pantheon but lifted Thoreau higher. From the 1920s forward, critics reoriented the

American canon around an "oppositional" tradition that attacked the country's mainstream as complacent and materialist.[14] The opaque, sometimes phantasmagorical world of Herman Melville's *Moby-Dick,* which was all but ignored by earlier generations, consumed the sunny ground recently occupied by Longfellow's "Song of Hiawatha." Thoreau, whose old supporters had carefully defended him as a patriot and a Christian despite his moods of cranky disrespect for both church and state, now reemerged as a dissenter with marked pagan impulses, a strange man who found himself a stranger in society and pointed others' eyes to a strange nature, both outside the villages and within the self.

Making the Sierra Club's Nature

Muir's Thoreau stood somewhere between the pastoral canon and the oppositional one, in time and spirit. So did Muir himself, in the persona he created through his writing and in the version of American nature that he helped to compose.

Muir's writing centered on description of landscapes, particularly those of the Sierra Nevada. At reliable intervals, the prose broke into soaring evocations of nature's beauty, which for Muir was morally instructive and a form of revelation. These passages portrayed everyday life as spilled out in drab settings and spiritless work, which left the eyes dull and the mind blunt. Muir offered his writing, and through it his sacred terrain, to the "tired, nerve-shaken, over-civilized" people who suffered from "the stupefying effects of the vice of over-industry."[15] Among mountain peaks, endless vistas, and sheer rock faces, something entirely different broke through in the mind: wonder, awe, even ecstasy. Muir wrote of coming into the Sierra, "Never before had I seen so glorious a landscape, so boundless an affluence of sublime mountain beauty. . . . I shouted and gesticulated in a wild burst of ecstasy."[16] When opened to this place, "the whole body seems to feel beauty when exposed to it as it feels the campfire or sunshine, entering not by the eyes alone, but equally through all one's flesh like radiant heat, making a passionate ecstatic pleasurable glow not explainable."[17] This is the language of religious conversion, akin to accounts of the experiences of saints and, probably more pertinent, to William James's study of conversion in *The Varieties of Religious Experience,* which appeared in the years when Muir was writing and captures the tone of the time's popular religion and spiritualism. The bodily sensation of epiphany, like sunshine from within, accompanying the breakthrough of a concealed insight into the nature of things, was James's paradigm of spiritual transformation. He found it alike in evangelical accounts of coming to Christ and spiritualists' tales of more esoteric conversions.[18] At the same time, Muir and his allies were putting it to work in a new religion of nature.

The world communed with and taught the spirit: this idea was the thread that Thoreau tugged from Emerson's writings, and Muir from Thoreau's. But the uses they gave it were quite different. Emerson had promised this harmony abstractly; Thoreau had experimented with it; Muir gave it an instruction manual. He placed his epiphanies along specific trails and before named vistas where others could follow. Walden Pond had been a metaphor and set piece, but Yosemite Valley was a destination, where Muir invited his readers to repeat and deepen his track. His widely read books and essays offered a field guide to epiphany, working Romantic aesthetics and Transcendentalist spiritual ambition into training for experience. Muir's writing laid out a journey on foot over spectacular landscapes; a precise, appreciative, even reverent way of seeing the terrain; and overwhelming yet exquisite emotional response, with a benign interpretation latent in it. To read Muir was to begin learning to make that experience one's own. His writing was aesthetic and a practical how-to for a social movement of heartfelt tourism.

This experience taught that the world was good and beautiful, and so was the human mind that could be moved by it. Mind and world vibrated together to harmonies that Muir compared to mystical intuitions of divinity. Muir wrote of Yosemite Valley's most distinctive massif, "South Dome . . . seems full of thought, clothed with living light, no sense of dead stone about it, all spiritualized, neither heavy looking nor light, steadfast in serene strength like a god." Seen in the proper light, as Thoreau might have put it, droplets of water passed from "form to form, beauty to beauty, ever changing, never resting, all are speeding on with love's enthusiasm, singing with the stars the eternal song of creation." Indeed, "the whole landscape glows like a human face in a glory of enthusiasm."[19]

Club members described Muir as one of the "prophets and interpreters of nature," who trained others to see through his eyes.[20] The *New York Times* observed in 1917 that Muir had produced a new mode of popular seeing: "Many who have sought a vision of truth beneath the surface of nature have found it through the eyes of John Muir."[21] His Sierra Club comrade William Frederic Bade eulogized Muir in the same spirit, predicting that "thousands and thousands, hereafter, who go to the mountains, streams, and can[y] ons of California will choose to see them through the eyes of John Muir, and they will see more deeply because they see with his eyes."[22]

Club members thus ratified Muir's own ambition: to stand in a line that ran through Emerson and Thoreau and tied Concord to California. Bade tellingly entitled his eulogy "To Higher Sierras." Muir had used that phrase in describing how Emerson, then an old man, had visited Muir in Yosemite accompanied by a small entourage. As Muir told it, Emerson was tired and confined by his keepers, and although the younger man would have liked to talk all night around the fire, or dance amid the shadows of the trees (Muir was full of such displays of enthusiasm), and thought he glimpsed an answering spark, the weary Emerson was soon escorted to his bed. When they parted, Emerson gave a wave, which Muir interpreted as a call onward "to higher Sierras."[23] The Transcendentalist spirit had exhausted itself in the cautious and aging precincts of the East, and its new home would have to be the vast and dramatic West, its prophets the men and women of that terrain, Muir first among them. Bade assured an emerging public that Muir's claim to prophetic succession was valid.

Contributors to the *Sierra Club Bulletin*, which was a beautifully produced movement organ from the early years of the club, adopted Muir's voice, describing glimpses of the sacred in their high-country expeditions. One correspondent reported "hours pass[ing] like moments" in "this sacred spot";[24] according to another, "We . . . learned to interpret and love the 'various languages' in which nature speaks to the children of men. . . . We were acolytes in the grand temple of the eternal."[25] Marion Randall, a longtime club member, wrote that, on an outing, "for a little while, you have dwelt close to the heart of things . . . and in the whispering silences of the forest you have thought to hear the voice of Him who 'flies upon the wings of the wind.'"[26] These passages are typical in mixing biblical phrases with a sense that all nature is sacred.

According to the *Bulletin,* high-country pilgrims saw one another face to face (as they might have put it themselves, following their penchant for biblical paraphrase), without the masks that their lowland lives imposed. Describing how a plutocrat congressman and a socialist radical rediscovered their common humanity around a campfire, one correspondent explained, "The varnish of civilization rubbed off, and the true strata of individual organism developed."[27] As genuine qualities shone through, "natural aristocracy" prevailed and bonds formed around affinity and admiration, not wealth, status, or refinement.[28] These themes crystallize several of the Sierra Club's paradoxes: a collective, even communal pursuit of pure individuality; radical dissent that disowned any political or social program beyond the voluntary affinities among pilgrims; and a principle of human equality that was, in practice, quite at home with the hierarchies and divisions of labor that marked its time. (Marion Randall's enthusiastic descriptions of weeks in a Sierra Club camp pass in perfect equanimity over "Charlie Tuck," the Chinese cook and laundryman. She does mention that some of the women on the outing, though seemingly none of the men, did their own laundry in the river as a lark.)

These paradoxes in the club's ideas and practices were also present in its geography. Sacred nature was intensely concentrated in the high Sierra, not in the fallen and disappointing lowlands. Epiphany waited in a special place visited a few months of the year. Club members saved their radicalism for personal relations in the exceptional space of the high country: a utopian vacation.

During that vacation they sought perfect respite from an imperfect world. For those who believed that most lives were, as Muir once wrote, neither sane nor free, high-country outings meant a measure of personal restoration, in which the projects and distinctions of ordinary life fell away for a few weeks. The everyday world would reassert its claims when the summer's expeditions were over. The goal of club members was not to change their lives, as Thoreau urged, nor to change the world, as radicals in the same time tried to do. For most, it was enough to share for a few weeks in the beauty of the world.

A Romantic Cultural Politics

The Sierra Club and its allies created a public language in line with this vision of nature. Their program came to be called *preservation* because they argued, for the first time in American politics, that large areas of land should be publicly owned, open to hikers and campers, and permanently protected from the settlement and extraction that had defined more than a century of land policy. The purpose of preserving this land was to cultivate a kind of experience—rapt appreciation of the living world, spontaneous joy, free activity, and unaffected sociability—that club members saw as endangered by a social world that turned every thing, moment, and human being to profit. Theirs was a Romantic social movement: they spoke for values of feeling and spontaneity that their version of nature confirmed, and which they believed American society had pressed to the margins of human personality.

For them, settlement and development had become disenchanting forces. Frontier culture had cast nature as a mere storehouse of productive resources, ignoring it as a source of inspiration, enlightenment, and spiritual restoration. It had pressed people, too, into endless activity that left them sheltered and fed, yet also anxious and unaccountably disheartened, at once materially richer and spiritually poorer—if not poorer than their ancestors had been, then poorer, surely, than they needed to be.

Touching wild nature was a way of denying that the world had to be drab and wearying—though the preservationists held that too much of it was exactly that. Muir lamented that in "these hot, dim, strenuous times . . . [when people are] choked with care like clocks full of dust, laboriously doing so much good . . . they are no longer good for themselves."[29] Anxiety, a wearying restlessness, was the major emotion of the lowland life as these critics portrayed it. Thoreau had made this anxiety a theme, memorably in the famous description of most lives as consumed by "quiet desperation." The Sierra provided balm. There one found "no pain . . . no dull empty hours, no fear of the past, no fear of the future."[30] There was rest in the high country, and also inspiration. When "one's heart [went] home" to wild country, as Muir promised, it met a "divinity" that was immanent in nature and could be reached through it.

If one motive was to deny that life must be gray and flat, another was to reject an image of "Nature, red in tooth and claw" (as Tennyson put it), scene of a relentless struggle for survival. This Darwinian picture seemed to make traditional moral views obsolete:

naïve, pious words mumbled over selfish conflict. Against this un-settling conclusion, Muir insisted on nature's moral harmony. The most dramatic landscapes brought a feeling of fraternity among all living things. When Muir climbed down from his Douglas spruce, he reflected, "We hear much nowadays concerning the universal struggle for existence, but no struggle in the common meaning of the word was manifest here . . . but rather an invincible gladness as remote from exultation as from fear." This led him to meditate on the flow of natural forces through the mountains, from the waterways to the winds that had just leveled the woods: "After tracing the Sierra streams . . . learning their language and forms in detail, we may at length hear them chanting all together in one grand anthem, and comprehend them all in clear inner vision. . . . The setting sun filled [the storm-wrecked trees] with amber light, and seemed to say, while they listened, 'My peace I give unto you.' "[31] Violence might be one of nature's basic facts, but its meaning resided in a larger harmony that an attuned observer could feel and share.

Some argued that their experience of nature need not contra-dict Darwinism: it could perfect it instead. Sierra Club cofounder and longtime officer Joseph LeConte, a professor of geology at the University of California, Berkeley, devoted much of his career to arguing that evolution was compatible with theism because na-ture's patterns bespoke the orderly mind of God. He recast evolu-tion, and the whole natural world, as an elaboration of the mind of God. In this divine thought, rendered as earth and flesh, humans played an essential role. When people admired the earth, they, as self-conscious elements of nature who also reached toward the di-vine, brought nature to awareness of its own beauty and harmony.[32] LeConte wrote, "In plants and animals, spirit is deeply submerged, and, as it were, drowned in Nature, and in perfect darkness. In man alone, spirit appears above the surface and emerges into the light. It looks downward upon Nature; it looks around upon other entities like itself; it looks upward to the heavens above. It rises out of Nature, above Nature, and becomes the interpreter of Nature."[33] LeConte answered an atheistic interpretation of evolution as driving God out of nature by proposing "a God *immanent,* a God resident *in* Nature," so that "the phenomena of Nature are ... objectified modes of divine thought."[34] Understanding this truth, he contended, would bring believers "*home* to our inner higher life." It was by understanding themselves as the highest expressions of "Nature, gestative mother of spirit,"[35] that people could turn to their role as "interpreter[s] of Nature."[36] LeConte's supreme human activity, grasping and admiring nature, was just what the Sierra Club most prized. LeConte's theology underwrote Muir's promise that life was no arena of meaningless struggle, but, approached in the right spirit, a higher home.

Club members insisted that ordinary social life stood in the way of humanity's higher calling. Previously, such criticism of everyday life had been mainly religious. Revivalists had long claimed that the country was distracted from its true aims, lost in worldly pursuits that—to borrow a phrase of Thoreau's from *Walden*—murdered eternity by killing time. The several Great Awakenings of American Christianity are only the best remembered of these episodes, which form a perennial theme in American history. But in the Sierra Club's hands, the revivalist goal was recast as in a pantheistic form: people had fallen away from nature, and, with it, from God.

Ironically, the club's Romantic consciousness did not run all that hard against the culture that produced it—a fact that frequently holds of the most successful waves of dissent. As we have seen, the beauty and sublimity of the West transfixed members of the Lewis and Clark Expedition at the beginning of the nineteenth century, even as they scrambled to survive an inhospitable terrain. An interest in picturesque landscapes, both pastoral and wild, was well established in the early nineteenth century, although more among those with the leisure of the parlor than in districts where pioneers attacked the actual wild to build their farms. The paintings of the Hudson River School, along with countless cheap imitations, spread the idea that mountain vistas, sunlight softened by mist, and crashing waterfalls opened the mind to powerful natural harmonies that might also foster civic virtues. It was a commonplace that these landscapes were America's answers to Europe's ancient cities and cathedrals, that natural sublimity elevated the country to a higher principle than moneymaking. For much of the nineteenth century, Americans had enchanted themselves with images of wilderness even as they opened the continent to development.

Sierra Club members made few true innovations in this culture, but they made Romantic commitments concrete as a political program. Romantic themes had been sentimental supplements to the real work of clearing and economic development. Club members *did something* with these commitments—at the scale of a vacation, to be sure, but the Sierra outings were still expenditures of time and energy and, just as important, bases for political community and mobilization.

The Sierra Club and Public-Lands Politics

The Sierra Club came onto the scene at a pivotal moment. After more than a century of distributing land to settlers and developers, whether by sale or in exchange for settling, planting, draining, or irrigating, the federal government had begun reserving lands for permanent public management. Congress created Yellowstone National Park in 1872, in response to a range of interests, including railroads angling to carry tourists to the geysers. In 1891, Congress authorized the president to reserve forests for public benefit; supporters feared that unregulated logging was wiping out the country's timber reserves and depriving big game of habitat. (The second concern was especially keen among the elite sportsmen who gathered around the young Theodore Roosevelt at New York's Boone and Crockett Club.) Loud controversy ensued when presidents used the new power. Opponents called it "tyranny" to forbid pioneers to clear wild forests, but an 1897 statute confirmed the president's power to create national forests and established a framework for managing them. These debates came in the last decades in which land of much economic value still lay unclaimed. They focused attention on whether any large tracts at all would remain public and, if so, what purposes that land should serve.

Debating how to manage Yellowstone in 1883, supporters had to defend the very existence of such parks: "The best thing that the Government could do with Yellowstone National Park is to survey it and sell it as other public lands are sold," one opponent insisted.[37] Ironically, defending public lands could mean arguing that Yosemite was "for all public purposes, worthless,"[38] and that Yellowstone beyond its tourist-enchanting geysers was "simply useless . . . mere leather and prunella."[39] These, it may be worth repeating, were the arguments of the parks' *supporters*. These debates still assumed that the "public purposes" and "worth" of land meant economic productivity. The wild high country of the parks was eligible for preservation partly because it offered little to conventional development.

George Perkins Marsh, the pioneering American conservationist, showed the shape of these constraints in his influential 1864 book *Man and Nature*, which contains some of the first serious arguments for preserving wild lands. Like other educated Americans, he could use a Christian-Romantic literary idiom to praise natural beauty; but he knew that was not the way to influence the politics of public lands and resource management. Marsh wrote admiringly of the man "whose sympathies with nature have taught him to feel that there is a fellowship between all of God's creatures . . . he who has enjoyed that special training of the heart and intellect which can be acquired only in the unviolated sanctuaries of nature, 'where man is distant, but God is near.'" Such a person, Marsh wrote in tones that resemble Thoreau's, "will not rashly assert his right to extirpate a tribe of harmless vegetables, barely because their products neither tickle his palate nor fill his pocket." These, however, were asides, tokens of Marsh's refined sensibility, not weight-bearing parts of his argument for conservation. When he argued for preserving "some large and easily accessible region of American soil . . . in its primitive condition" as a scientific and recreational resource and a refuge for indigenous plants and animals, he was careful to emphasize that his reasons were not "poetical" but "economical," squarely centered on conserving soil and water resources.[40]

At the turn of the twentieth century, public environmental language opened much more widely to poetic appeals. From its founding in 1892, the Sierra Club worked to preserve the wild lands where its expeditions and epiphanies took place. As early as 1895, club meetings were devoted to support for national forests, and, in the decade before World War I, the *Bulletin* gave ever more space to disputes over forest management and parks policy.[41] In 1911, it ran a series of technical reports on the prospect of a unified system for administering the national parks, a system that Congress would create in 1916.[42] Editorials staked out the club's positions on expanding Sequoia National Park (the members were in favor of it), increasing funding for Yosemite National Park (in favor of it), and damming Hetch Hetchy Valley for San Francisco's municipal water supply (emphatically against it).[43] A movement founded on aesthetic and spiritual experiences of nature had fully entered federal land-use politics.

Although the club was one in a network of pro-conservation groups, including forestry associations, sportsmen, and progressive reformers, its Romantic commitments gave it a new and distinctive rationale for preserving open lands, one that would become increasingly central to public language on the environment. In a letter to state governors attending a 1908 presidential conference on natural-resource conservation, Sierra Club representatives set out their "strong sense of the paramount value of scenic beauty among our natural resources. The moral and physical welfare of a nation is not dependent alone upon bread and water. The deeper need for recreation and that which satisfies also the esthetic sense [is] an ever present human desire. Our . . . wealth of natural beauty . . . is an untaxed heritage . . . whose influence upon the life of the nation, physically, morally, mentally, is inestimable, and whose preservation is the greatest service that one generation can render to another."[44] This passage contains plenty of respectful gestures toward the utilitarian reasoning that was standard among progressives: using the paradigm of "natural resources" management, treating public "welfare" as a touchstone, and honoring trusteeship for the interests of Americans not yet born. At the same time, the club's letter introduced a Romantic perspective, embracing a "deeper need" for recreation, "esthetic" satisfaction, and "moral" influence, the values the club located in the High Sierra.

The club's language was soon at the center of the public case for national parks, which progressive conservationists like Theodore Roosevelt had previously defended on more utilitarian and civic grounds. While serving as director of public education for the recently formed National Parks Service, Robert Sterling Yard argued in 1919: "The national parks are far more than recreational areas. . . . They are the gallery of masterpieces. Here the visitor enters in a holier spirit. Here is inspiration. . . . It is the hour of the spirit. One returns to daily living with a springier step, a keener vision, and a broader horizon for having worshipped at the shrine of the Infinite."[45]

This is the language of John Muir and Joseph LeConte on the value of nature's most spectacular places as sources of self-knowledge and spontaneity. Reworked from its Transcendentalist roots by the social movement of the Sierra Club, this idea became the central public justification for a new public-lands policy, which already governed tens of millions of acres in 1919.

How Nature's Utopia Became Less Radical

As the Sierra Club and its allies drew on the canon of Thoreau, Emerson, and Wordsworth (whose grave Muir visited at Grasmere), they also transformed it. The approach to nature that these activists put at the center of twentieth-century public language departed markedly from its nineteenth-century roots. The alterations were rhetorical, but also philosophical: they changed the conception of human freedom that nature promoted, and so also changed the challenge that nature presented to everyday life.

The most basic departure was a move away from the philosophical engagement with character, desire, and need that lay at the heart of Thoreau's project. He quarreled with those who thought renewable energy would make a paradise on earth, because he believed that no sum of satisfied appetites could bring lasting satisfaction, or heal pervasive anxiety, before people became clear on what they valued and why. These questions required reflection on who people were and how they fit into the world—the goal of his expedition to Walden.

The Sierra Club's spokespersons, notably Muir and LeConte, also set themselves against rote activity and materialism. Club members, too, saw their excursions as balm for the bruises that everyday life left on the spirit. At the same time, Muir's prescription was essentially to take a vacation, some stimulating and restorative time off from numbing workaday tasks. This was not Thoreau's goal, which had been to develop a relentless practice of exploring and transforming one's own purposes. The effect of Muir's vacations might be subversive, but not so subversive as to spoil a high-country pilgrim for ordinary life and work. The "springier step" that Robert Sterling Yard promised parks visitors was not the sauntering stride that carried Thoreau across Concord's woods while his neighbors were working, nor was it the civil disobedient's willing step across the threshold of a jail.

Most sojourners in the high country could not afford to remake themselves too radically. Muir and his comrades needed to appeal to acolytes who had duties at home and ambitions at work. They also needed to persuade federal officials that their view of nature was a properly American one. They succeeded—within systems built on the very ideas of humanity and nature that they said they wished to overcome: the market economy, with its demand for productive effort from all; and the nascent administrative state of the early twentieth century. Both of these systems treated the natural world as a storehouse of goods to serve human appetites. This was very different from Thoreau's idea that close observation of nature could teach and train desire.

The Sierra Club thus got involved in very practical contradictions between high and esoteric goals and popular and administrative means. Muir organized his 1901 advocacy work, *Our National Parks,* around the preservation of spectacular places, on the one hand, and, on the other, ready access for visitors with limited time. The book promised readers a "profound solitude . . . full of God's thoughts," and also assured them that thanks to highways and railroads, "in a few minutes you will find yourself in the midst of . . . the best care-killing scenery on the continent."[46] It did not take much subtlety to appreciate that these promises could not stand together—that the solitude would be shared with everyone else who had come on the same train.

Muir and his allies simplified the Transcendentalist inheritance in other ways. There had been an ambiguity in Thoreau and Emerson's work, an inconsistency about the relation between nature and self-knowledge. On the one hand, Emerson often wrote as if behind all confusion there resided a perfect and abiding True Self, whose manifestations might be flawed or oscillating but whose essence was unchanging. On the other hand, he described identity as a river of experience, at once one thing and forever changing, to which one owed the highest degree of attention from moment to moment. He stresses the simpler view in his early and hortatory writing, such as "Self-Reliance," and gives greater weight to the subtler approach in his late writing, especially "Experience," which shares its title and some of its spirit with the last of Montaigne's *Essays*. There are, however, flashes of the simpler conception of nature and self throughout Emerson. Thoreau had less of the simple idea: he followed his thoughts through vagrant tacking, and when it came to the ability to describe moments and things, which in Emerson often evanesced upon touching his rarefying mind, Thoreau could give readers a sense of participating in his own movements. For Thoreau, the natural world was an interlocutor, goad, whetstone, and provocatively imperfect mirror of thought. Answers composed from reflection on nature tended to dissolve soon enough and become new questions.

Treating nature as a partner for his wandering and often burdened mind, Thoreau wrote in his essay "Slavery in Massachusetts": "I walk toward one of our ponds; but what signifies the beauty of nature when men are base? We walk to lakes to see our serenity reflected in them; when we are not serene, we go not to them. Who can be serene in a country where both the rulers and ruled are without principle? The remembrance of my country spoils my walk." This is quite different from the "care-killing" role of nature that Muir offered and the Sierra Club's early members flocked to accept. The Romantic nature that club members celebrated was a reliable tonic, a healing force regardless of the state of mind one brought to it.

In Sierra Club culture, the mind was less engaged in its own transformation than simply present for the event, which the Sierra Nevada landscape accomplished. Whether nature disclosed a true self or just provided a reliable stimulant and comfort, its meaning was simpler for the Sierra Club than it had been for the

Transcendentalists. Accordingly, club members portrayed nature as literally filled with the meaning that, for Emerson and Thoreau, emerged in the mysterious circuit of mind and world. This meaning was concentrated in the most spectacular places, those most remote from everyday concerns: mountain peaks, valleys rimmed by sheer cliffs and plunging waterfalls, and vistas of white snow, blue water, and silvery stone. Muir captured his difference from Thoreau in a telling passage written from Glacier Bay, Alaska: "In God's wildness lies the hope of the world—the great fresh unblighted, unredeemed wilderness."[47] Muir was following Thoreau's iconic formulation, "In wildness is the preservation of the world."[48] In "Walking," the essay in which that sentence appears, Thoreau presents "the wild" variously: as childlike playfulness, a principle of virtue ("all good things are wild and free"), a literary principle associated with Homer, Shakespeare, and the pathos of mythology, and an epistemic source connected with knowing one's true nature by intuition and symbol rather than by abstract propositions. In Muir's semi-plagiarizing equivocation, these values of a mind at play with itself, its culture, and the natural world collapse into literal wilderness, open and undeveloped land—a change that left the idea of wilderness considerably less complicated and actual wilderness acreage a good deal more charged with importance. The Sierra Club contributed much to producing, in hindsight, a Thoreau who would have embraced such uncomplicated thoughts about wilderness: a simplified but useful Thoreau, who could be cast straightforwardly as a patron saint and founder of the Romantic environmentalism that the club brought into public language.

Natural Utopias

"Utopianism" has two broad meanings as a political practice. On the one hand, it can mean radical reform by blueprint: a top-down program to bring the actual world into line with an ideal vision.

This is the sense in which the term has served mainly as an insult in the twentieth century. It gets saddled with the visionary lunacy of Mao's Great Leap Forward and Cultural Revolution, and the Soviets' killing of entire classes of the czarist Old Regime. When these violent impositions on social reality are the paradigms of utopianism, the very idea can seem one short step from tyranny.

The other version of utopian practice is more experimental and eccentric. It begins not with a plan, but with a foray into unfamiliar ways of doing things. Insofar as these experiments succeed, those who undertake them bring back essential information about how people might live differently. In this sense, Thoreau's time at Walden was a utopian experiment in personality, as the Sierra Club's expeditions were utopian experiments in sociability.

Writing in the second decade of the twenty-first century, it is easy, nearly reflexive, to embrace the second as the good side of utopianism, the kind that chimes with all the decentered innovations of the present, from crowdsourcing to micro-finance. Mistrust of law and government ripples through the canon of environmental imagination, from Thoreau's near-anarchism; through Muir's indifference to the political struggles of his time, such as the contest between labor and capital and the rise of the trusts; to founding literary ecologist Aldo Leopold's impatience with the role of bureaucrats, experts, and laws in environmental policy. All these figures opposed government with their conviction that reform of individual conscience must come first.

Yet in practice, both these emblematic writers and the movements that adopted them have recognized that conscience does not spring fully formed from the head of the enlightened. In Thoreau's asides in favor of preserving open land, in the Sierra Club's program for public-lands preservation, and in Leopold's administrative and polemical efforts to establish wilderness as a legitimate public goal, each worked to shape the physical and aesthetic landscape in which the conscience would arise. They believed that if their prized landscapes disappeared, the form of conscience they treasured would be endangered, too. In other words, they recognized that conscience and aesthetic openness—the qualities they worked so hard to cultivate—arise from experience and interaction. These human qualities are ecological products, and also social products. How we experience nature is a product of law, of organized power that shapes and makes intentional the massive human impact on the earth.

In practice, then, the pioneers of environmental imagination have seen that the conscience they prize needs public power. Nonetheless, they have also fostered an impulse to disown collective power and evade politics. In the Romantic environmental imagination, nature's freedom has meant the freedom of the individual conscience from social habits. Admitting that conscience is itself a social thing—not simply, not reductively, but really—runs against the idea that the free conscience could be a thing apart from society, anchored in nature.

Charismatic as it is, the idea of a pure conscience rooted in nature has to give way in a reckoning with the Anthropocene. We shape the nature that we encounter, and it shapes us in turn—shapes the eyes that take it in and the conscience that draws on it. This means that the two kinds of utopianism, the small experiments and the collective shaping of the world, are tied together inescapably. Experiments need the landscapes that collective power produces, and collective power draws ideas, motivation, and lessons from those experiments—as the national parks show.

Thoreau was right to say that our desires have to change if we are to change our relation to the world. He was wrong, though, to say that we must do this alone, that change begins only in the individual. The work belongs to conscience, of course, but also in very important ways to shared and mobilized conscience.

A Walden for the Anthropocene

The Romantic strand of environmental imagination has been at once the most radical, because it has asked what changes in human identity might arise from a different relation to nature, and the least radical, because its utopianism has been of the personal, conscientious, and unsystematic kind. The fact that founders of environmental movements have chosen Muir and Thoreau as touchstones shows much about the style of conscience, and the attitude to politics, that the activists prized and cultivated.

This suggests an experiment. Muir and his Sierra Club allies looked back to, and helped to create, a Thoreau who presaged their own ideas about humanity and nature, a prophet of wilderness and solitude. What if we instead read *Walden* as a work engaged with Anthropocene themes? How might Thoreau look as part of a different chosen inheritance, one oriented to a different environmental imagination? The point of this is not to rescue a true Thoreau from Romantic kidnappers; nor, on the other hand, is it to kidnap him anachronistically for a twenty-first-century agenda. It is, rather, to approach a familiar past through new, Anthropocene eyes. There is much in Thoreau to support an Anthropocene reading, and it comes into focus when we read him with these themes in mind.

Such a reading of *Walden* might start with an observation about how the book arrives at its most classically Transcendentalist moments, the epiphanies where mind and world appear as elements in a continuous harmony. A reader looking for the Romantic Thoreau might expect to find these moments in wilderness, or at least the nearest thing to wilderness landscapes that Concord provided in the mid-nineteenth century, after two hundred years of clearing, planting, and regrowth. Even Muir, who acknowledged that Thoreau himself could see the divine in small things, nonetheless imagined the prophet gazing on a perfect green shoot alongside a path outside his house. Either way, Thoreau's aesthetic touchstone and spiritual source would be a bit of unspoiled nature, lovely and whole.

Consider, though, a defining epiphany in the chapter titled "Spring," culmination of *Walden*'s season-by-season progression through a year in the woods. Reflecting on the patterns formed by the loose, thawing soil of a slope, Thoreau declares, "This one hillside illustrated the principle of all the operations of Nature." In its swirling, flowing forms, joining and parting from moment to moment, Thoreau found proof that "the very globe continually transcends and translates itself," moving from one form to another in ever-shifting expressions of one all-pervading impulse to self-organization, to *take form*. This impulse, it seemed to him, infused all nature's patterns and flows: leaves bursting from buds, grubs becoming butterflies, and eerily similar branching patterns of blood vessels, lightning, and the human hand. All of this was an invitation to imagine one's own body in the same terms: "What is man but a mass of thawing clay?" he asked, and went on to imagine hands as leaves, and the human face—signal expression of the unique and self-subsistent individual—as a slipping slope of clay and earth. The whole scene is a kind of ecological mysticism. It dissolves the nineteenth-century man, the bearer of legal and natural rights, the citizen-participant in the social contract, and merges him into a whole whose essence is change, self-dissolution that opens the way to other forms.[49]

This passage from "Spring" has a reconciling, even healing power in the motion of the book. A few chapters earlier, in "Higher Laws," Thoreau exudes self-disgust, denouncing the "reptile and sensual" in humans, the "slimy, beastly life" of eating and drinking, and seems to endorse the ethical regulation of every bodily function, a program he identifies with "the Hindoo lawgiver." He announces, rather startlingly, "Nature is hard to be overcome, but she must be overcome." On his springtime slope, though, Thoreau forsakes the impulse to segregate and regulate unclean bodily life, and instead identifies all the lovely and inspiring forms with muck and all that it connotes. He writes of that life: "True, it is somewhat excrementitious in its character, and there is no end to the heaps of livers, lights, and bowels, as if the globe were turned the wrong side outward; but this suggests at least that nature has some bowels, and there again is the mother of humanity." It is a defining quality of disgust to imagine the slimy parts of bodily life in the wrong places, outside its natural tubes and sacs, exposed in ways that cast doubt on the solidity of the body itself: mucus on the face, excrement on the hands, bowels violently made visible. In his portrait of harmonious nature, Thoreau does not shy away from this, but assimilates all of life to it. He celebrates the fact that we are all in the shit. In the ecological mysticism of these passages, there is no essential difference between the earth's bowels and its "living poetry like the leaves of a tree." This vital, filthy, gorgeous unity persuades him that that the earth is alive at every point, and only beginning its passage into future forms. This, in turn, suggests to him that the same is true of human lives and institutions—"plastic like clay in the hands of the potter."[50]

Now consider where, in Thoreau's telling, all this takes place: on the cut of a railroad bank, a quarter-mile gash in the earth. Earlier in the book, the railroad is "devilish" and has "profaned" Walden, and Thoreau does not withdraw that thought.[51] But the earth's wholeness is disclosed in a place that has been ruptured and profaned. The bowels that show the harmony and aliveness of all matter have been spilled out, cut as if with the bodily violence that reveals literal bowels. The choice of setting brings to mind, however anachronistically, W. B. Yeats's declaration: "Nothing can be sole or whole / That has not been rent."[52]

When one has taken this as a clue, others fall into place. Another of *Walden*'s key passages of mystical harmony comes in the chapter entitled "The Bean-Field," where Thoreau identifies a series of symmetrical principles uniting the various realms of matter: "The hawk is aerial brother to the wave which he sails over and surveys, his perfect air-inflated wings answering to the elemental un-fledged pinions of the sea."[53] Carried away by his reflections, Thoreau judged that the moment's political passions, the Mexican War and the patriotic drilling of militias on the Concord common, seemed incidental and dispensable, like the "plastic" institutions revealed by his meditation on the railroad cut.

Again, consider the setting. In this chapter, Thoreau has become a farmer for a season. This is easy to misread, today, as part of the pastoral conceit of *Walden*. But for Thoreau, farming is not an admirable form of self-reliance; it serves, alongside buying and selling, as the model of a conventional life, in which energies and years get frittered away for no worthy purpose. Farmers were the serfs of their fields, self-enslaved to their own labors. It is almost as if Thoreau had set up to sell knick-knacks on the Concord green.

He also emphasizes the scar he is putting on the world, the violence of farming. His work is a form of warfare, a martial campaign against weeds, a colonizing project for his beans. All of this is ironic and metaphorical, as Thoreau so often was. Some of his target is the military clearing of the Southwest for Anglo settlement. But it is nonetheless by breaking land that he achieves insight into the unity of things. The field of heightened perception is, once again, a place ruptured by technology and work, and for purposes Thoreau elsewhere disdains or denounces. As with farming, so with the railroad.

Thoreau reported a myth that Walden Pond itself, the namesake and center of the book, was another ruptured place. According to that story, Walden was formed when Native Americans, holding a pow-wow on a high hill, "used so much profanity" that, in punishment, the earth broke and the hill became a vast hole, as deep as it had been high. Although Thoreau expresses doubt about this story, protesting that Native Americans did not use profanity, he has nonetheless suggested that Walden is no part of a timeless and perfect nature, but another profaned tear in the world. In the same chapter, he emphasizes that, quite apart from the status of the myth, the pond is entirely profaned: "the wood-cutters, and the railroad, and I myself have profaned Walden."[54] Thoreau's inclusion of himself in this list is especially telling: by the very act of making the pond the object of his meditation, Thoreau has profaned it—though he is only one in a long line of people to do so.

In *Walden,* insight into nature seems to arise from, even require, rupture and profanation. These may be the necessary conditions of an appreciative relation to the world. To take another anachronistic phrase from a poet, this time Wallace Stevens, "The imperfect is our only paradise."[55]

Once one reads key passages in this light, other features of the book come into view. *Walden* takes place, quite self-consciously, in a landscape transformed by long and intensive habitation. Thoreau tells us that the woods around the pond have been cleared, that boats have sunk to its bottom, that it is regularly harvested for ice. His Concord is full of the artifacts of old and new settlement, down to the soil itself, seeded with stone tools and potsherds that tinkle against the hoe as he works his bean-field. There is nothing pristine in this place, no basis for a fantasy of original and permanent nature. There is only a choice among relationships with and attitudes toward ever-changed places. These do not just accommodate the damage and ruptures of the landscape: they begin from and depend on them. It may be that even to think of nature, let alone act on it, is to make it a joint product of human and natural activity, so that to come to the pond is already to profane it. But profanation is simply the condition of the world, which is redeemed, if at all, by our deeper apprehension of that condition.

Is this the right, the true Thoreau? The question may be needless and artificial. If we who live in the Anthropocene do not simply discard the once-canonized past, then we are going to regard it

A CONSERVATIONIST EMPIRE

ALBERT BEVERIDGE, A TWO-TERM REPUBLICAN SENATOR from Indiana, was a devotee of President Theodore Roosevelt and gave the keynote address at the 1912 Progressive Party convention that nominated Roosevelt as the "Bull Moose" candidate for president. He backed Roosevelt's push for forest conservation, labor regulation, antitrust law, and the U.S. occupation of Cuba and the Philippines. Beveridge shared and in many ways embodied Roosevelt's ideal of the engaged American man: he was a politician, a biographer of Abraham Lincoln and Chief Justice John Marshall, and above all a moralist, convinced of the consummate meaning and urgency of national life, and on fire to persuade others of it. For Beveridge, as for Roosevelt, the early twentieth century marked the height of the era of Manifest Destiny. The American mission was no longer to conquer the continent but to remake the world, especially its fallow lands and benighted peoples.

Beveridge and his reformist allies greatly expanded the role of government and, at the same time, worked to limit the reach of democracy. They developed a technocratic ideal of governance as the neutral, scientific pursuit of an objective public interest—a government, as they often put it, of administration.

Their social vision relied strongly on a picture of the natural world. They cast it as a servant of human needs, as it had been for the theorists of the frontier; but for Beveridge, Roosevelt, and their generation of reformers, nature was too complex for a laissez-faire scheme of private property. Clearing and farming by individual pioneers could erode land and exhaust resources. The continent needed administration by trained and public-spirited officials. In this way, nature resembled social and economic life: all three demanded expert management. This meant intensified governance, but it did not imply greater democracy. In fact, keeping democracy in check while expanding government was the task that the Progressives enlisted nature to help them accomplish.

Conquest and settlement of North America were merely "modes of preparation" for the real hinge of American history, when the national mission must turn to "administration and world improvement."[1] As Beveridge told it, the doctrine of Americans' political ancestors, stretching back to George Washington, had been "perpetual growth" in a land ruled by law and animated by free enterprise.[2] The conquest and development of North America expressed a principle—progress—and also a national fate: "From irresistible impulse, from instinct, from unwritten racial laws . . . our pioneers reclaimed Kentucky and the Mississippi wilderness . . . crossed the Rockies and seized Oregon . . . explored new regions and claimed new empires, and left behind them the crimson trail of their own blood. . . . They did this because they could not help it."[3] Americans' national destiny, which was also their racial destiny as Teutonic stock, was to be "steward under God of the civilization of the world."[4] This meant extending American power around the globe, for "with the twentieth century the real task and true life of the Republic begins."[5] This would be a new kind of empire, an "empire of liberty and law, of commerce and communication, of social order and the Gospel of our Lord."[6]

The language Beveridge called on to conjure up the American mission abroad echoed earlier calls for the settlement of the West: "wilderness" and "waste" had to be "redeemed" by labor and freedom. "It is destiny," he explained, "that the world shall be rescued from its natural wilderness and from savage men."[7] Through an evolutionary principle, "superior nations" displaced or remade "inferior races": "It is thus that America itself was discovered; thus that this Republic was builded; thus that South Africa was reclaimed; thus that Australia was recovered from the Bushman and made the home of civilization; thus that Ceylon was taken from wild men and tangled jungles and brought beneath the rule of religion, law, and industry. It is thus that Egypt is being redeemed, her deserts fertilized. . . . It is thus that the regeneration of India has progressed."[8] To fall away from this mission would give "the whole world back to barbarism and night"[9] and let "history say that we renounced the holy trust, left the savage to his base condition, the wilderness to the reign of waste."[10]

In these phrases, Beveridge carried the language of providential settlement beyond America's borders. The progress that Americans must bring to new lands was now rooted in an evolutionary principle, a progressive logic of nature with underlying providential design. Although it was closely related to the "general providence" that underwrote settler claims to the continent, the new vocabulary of national destiny also chimed with the Darwinian thought of the later nineteenth century: it would have been alien to James Kent or John Quincy Adams to say that settlers "did this because they could not help it," a phrase that suggests the biological compulsion of racialized evolutionary theory.

In Beveridge's imperial vision, "inferior races" would not always be displaced, as Native Americans had been; instead, imperial powers should often manage subject peoples to bring them into the circle of civilization. So Beveridge pivoted from American settler colonialism, which had insisted that North America *belonged to* its European colonists, to the model of British empire in India, Egypt, and other administered colonies. Subject peoples were not to be eliminated, only "improved": managed for their most productive use, which was also their highest end. In this respect, Beveridge portrayed colonized peoples much as early Americans had imagined the land itself: as a resource whose productive use was an imperative of civilization. Beveridge's move from settlement to administration meant that the American "empire of liberty" would need complex, long-distance governance, of a kind that the domestic frontier had seldom seen.

Beveridge believed that the American frontier project had to evolve from settlement to administration at home as well as abroad. The conquest of the frontier brought wealth and liberty, and these, in turn, produced a complex industrial economy unlike anything the first settlers knew. "From the labor-saving machine to the modern office building, from labor union to steel combine, the whole tendency of modern times is toward organization of industry. All the politicians in the world could not prevent it; the people themselves could not destroy it; because at the bottom and in the final analysis this tendency is based on human progress itself."[11] The world the settlers had made was too complex to govern with laissez-faire laws: it required intelligent, extensive, and powerful government, competent for national regulation of industry, labor relations, and natural resources. Beveridge read this preoccupation back into his racialized history of American settlement, declaring, "Our race is the most self-governing but also the most administrative of any race of history. Our race is, distinctly, the exploring, the colonizing, the administrating force of the world."[12] An empire of liberty, at home or abroad, was not just a landscape properly settled, but one correctly administered.

Although some reformers, notably Roosevelt, labored to reconcile progressive management with the frontier legacy, their program was inescapably a rejection of the old providential republicanism. Progressives argued that yeoman ownership, far from sustaining liberty and prosperity, had brought crises of waste and depletion. Progressive reforms withdrew much of the country's natural wealth from the rivers of privatization that had run so richly since the eighteenth century. Naturally enough, this change inspired resistance. In the old republican schema, where private property was the key to both liberty and development, the federal government's enlarged role in the West looked like resurgent tyranny.

Resistance to Progressive reforms emerged as early as 1878, when Interior Secretary Carl Schurz moved against unlicensed commercial timbering on federal lands, fining and seeking to prosecute "timber pirates."[13] For nearly a century, federal officials had tolerated massive and often wasteful tree cutting on public land. Now senators reacted furiously to Schurz's new strictness and trumpeted settlers' right to harvest the public domain. They argued that Schurz's policy turned pioneers in the territories into second-class citizens, denied them development, and established tyranny in the West. They called clearing and using land an inviolable human right, comparing the policymakers of Washington, D.C., to the colonists' despotic King George.[14] (After all, the right to settle the West—then the region beyond the Alleghenies—had been one of the bases of the Declaration of Independence.) Recalling the wasted landscapes that providential rhetoric associated with political tyranny, critics accused Schurz of locking settler families into poor and primitive conditions.[15] Senators warned that the Interior Department's "spoliation" and "robbery of the poor" would drive settlers into "barbarism" and end by "depopulating the Western lands."[16]

Albert Beveridge took a very different view. For him, Roosevelt's national forests, which expanded federal management far beyond Schurz's first restrictions on timbering, was a model of the country's need to overcome the frontier experience and learn to manage a more complex reality. The conquest of the frontier, he lamented, had been a "period of destruction," marked by "ruinous exploitation which was called 'development' but was the reverse." Too many acres had been cut too quickly, with too much waste and too little attention to regrowth. The laissez-faire rush across the continent had turned land to "desert" and neglected the subtle interplay that tied the health of forests to that of streams, rivers, and irrigation systems. After this heedless destruction, Roosevelt's program of reserving federal lands for permanent forest management was "a great work—and how characteristically American it is—the work of reclaiming, saving, developing." The U.S. Forest Service would restore American woods to "great natural wood factories" and the "great reservoir of nature."[17]

In both domestic government and empire abroad, the work of reclaiming unregenerate nature now belonged to the administrative state. Nature's meaning changed with the new emphasis on administration. In the early republic, undeveloped nature, "waste" or "wilderness," called out for settlement and development; because nature was also infused with providential design, it answered the ax and plough by blooming. Beveridge kept the old tone of offense at anything wild and undeveloped. In the Philippines, he announced, "a hundred wildernesses are to be subued. Unpenetrated regions must be explored. Unviolated valleys must be tilled. Unmastered forests must be felled. Unriven mountains must be torn asunder."[18] In Beveridge's picture, though, what wild nature called out for was not settlement—that might only make it a desert, as frontier clearing had done in American forests—but administration. Unregenerate nature would answer sound governance with bountiful and sustained production. Federal management would make forests the factories they should be and give the country "streams now dry, running bank full for the welfare of the people."[19] This was the benefit a country could win by complying with the principle of evolution that produced—and demanded—ever-greater complexity in all systems, human ones above all.

Beveridge and Roosevelt insisted that global empire would strengthen American character. The closing of the frontier meant a crisis of identity and threat to national vigor. For Beveridge, "the whole object of civilization is character" and so "the purpose of this republic is to produce manhood and womanhood."[20] If Americans idly enjoyed their prosperity, they would "rot in our selfishness, as men and nations must, who take cowardice for their companion and self for their deity—as China has, as India has, as Egypt has"— phrases Roosevelt also used in his pro-imperial praise of the "strenuous life."[21] Imperial responsibility would inoculate Americans against ennui at the final station stop of progressive history. Beveridge concluded a long meditation on whether the Americans still had great deeds to perform: "You need not despair of the possibility of winning one of the highest of honors . . . of fighting for your country and of dying for your flag."[22] Besides literal war, young people could seek glory in its political and moral equivalents: the meeting of East and West in China and Japan, the need for law and policy to address an industrial economy's problems, and the ever-advancing frontier of science and technology. Taken together, science, administration, and imperialism issued a reassurance, "*You can be a man* and do a man's work," and also an injunction: "*Be a man.*"[23]

The heroic, dignifying work of the time, then, was different from that of the republican pioneer. Important work now meant grappling with collective problems—national challenges and the administrative needs of a complex society. For those who had the chance to shape national policy, the literal frontier was replaced by an administrative and technical frontier of ever-greater complexity in all areas of life. Those with more modest gifts or prospects would have to satisfy themselves with a clear understanding of their inkdot's place in history's long arc.

Beveridge's web of themes was typical of conservationist reformers. His thinking about nature and the nation, the frontier and the future, was broadly that of Roosevelt, who shared his preoccupations: national greatness or decline, individual virtue or decadence, and the need to redirect the energy of continental settlement toward administration. Reformers turned away from the frontier but not from nature, and made a new concept, "conservation," the keystone of programs for social renewal and progress.

At the beginning of the twentieth century, nature defined a purpose for American government and, at the same time, marked the limits of democracy. In the providential republican vision, the frontier had fostered a community of political equals, proprietors and free laborers, in contrast to the class societies of crowded Europe. A nature that rewarded clearing and settlement by yeoman landowners was a great support for this ideal of political community.

As discussed in earlier chapters, the settler republic was marked by a sharp line between those it included and those it shut out. The regnant theory of nature did much to justify that line. Apologists for expelling Native Americans insisted that the continent called out for ownership and development while indigenous peoples remained idle and vagrant, thus forfeiting any claim to the land. Ideas about nature also supported the political exclusion of African Americans, as defenders of slavery invoked theories of natural racial hierarchy. Similarly, those who defended women's exclusion from political, social, and economic life appealed to biological differences between the sexes and the innate need for women to devote themselves to creating the next generation. Although racial and sexual hierarchies were not rooted in a theory of the human relation to the nonhuman world in quite the way that treatment of Native Americans was, a pseudo-scientific picture of nature also underwrote these types of exclusion.

The old vision of a nature designed to become private property had helped to naturalize the market economy: "free enterprise" arose organically from ownership and exploitation of the natural world. Progressives, however, denied that the economy naturally regulated itself to serve the common good. To curtail concentrated ownership of industries, they devised antitrust laws that made the shape of the economy explicitly a matter for political decision. To protect the health of workers and balance unequal economic power, they set minimum wages, maximum hours, and mandatory working conditions. To promote the health of the next generation, they imposed sanitation laws, required vaccinations, and expanded free, mandatory public education. In sum, they took both the economy and, in some measure, childrearing—and so the family—out of the realm of supposedly natural phenomena and subjected them to political judgments.

Regulating the economy, land use, and others areas of social life in the common interest raised the question of just what the common interest was, and who should decide. One answer would have been democratic: that the question was for the whole political community. Instead, a central line of Progressive reform held that the content of the common interest was, like the management of forests and waterways, a technical question, suited not for democratic majorities but for expert administrators. A technically administered natural world and a technically administered social world came into being together.

In this new vision, the line that nature inscribed in the political community was between the experts and everyone else. Administrators might earnestly weigh the interests of, say, women, children, and nonwhites; Progressives expressed a new concern for the health and life-prospects of vulnerable workers and city-dwellers, and did not always uphold the old boundaries of racial prejudice (though plenty of them did). But the Progressive program did not ask citizens to decide what the common interest was. As Progressive reform expanded the scope of the community's concern, and so of its social and moral membership, it contracted the scope of political judgment, the scope of questions open to majority decision.

Progressives defended their expansion of government by calling on an idea of nature: the world, natural and social, was complex, fragile, and easily thrown out of equilibrium. The private, self-interested decisions of pioneers, farmers, businessmen, and workers often did harm: they produced erosion, burnt-over forests, choleric slums, and dangerous workplaces. From landscapes to factories, these systems needed looking after: they required management. By treating such management as a technical rather than a democratic problem, the same reformers who pressed government into new areas of life quashed the democratic potential of this change, both at home and abroad.

Progressive Management and the Idea of Conservation

A single concept, *conservation,* organized both a new kind of law for the natural world and the Progressives' approach to government and social life. It began as a theory of natural-resource management and returned again and again to that touchstone, but also became a general theory of reform and an all-purpose rhetoric for reformers. Past a certain point, it meant different things depending on who was using it and what they aimed to achieve; but it was unified by its core conception of the problems a government confronted and how it could solve them.

Two statutes, the 1897 "organic act" of the U.S. Forest Service (creating the service and setting out its structure) and the 1916 counterpart for the National Parks Service, expressed conservation ideas very concretely. Both laws reserved land for federal management, land that would otherwise have been on track to become private property. The statutes set up administrative frameworks for this permanently public land, directing administrators to manage the federal acreage for maximum benefit to the American public.[24] National forests were to provide "a continuous supply of timber" and control downstream erosion and drought.[25] The parks' "fundamental purpose" was to "conserve the scenery and the natural and historic objects and wild life therein . . . for . . . enjoyment . . . such . . . as will leave them unimpaired for the enjoyment of future generations."[26] Both statutes embraced scientific expertise and administration as the techniques for managing the new public lands.

On their face, the two statutes serve quite different purposes—economic production on the one hand, aesthetics and recreation on the other. Historians of this period often cast these values as antagonists, their conflict crystallized in the famous dispute between the Sierra Club and the Department of the Interior over damming Hetch Hetchy Valley in Yosemite National Park.[27] Despite such conflicts in emphasis, though, the statutes were unified by the organizing concept of conservation. The word expressed a core commitment to economically rational resource management, but it also had richer significance. "Conservation" meant imagining both natural and social life as complex systems that required educated management. It embraced a moral vision of the national community, centered on a government with the power and competence to maintain the health of all the country's systems, economic, environmental, and cultural.[28] Gifford Pinchot, Theodore Roosevelt's chief forester and the country's most visible theorist and advocate of conservation, put it this way: "There is . . . no interest of the people to which the principles of conservation do not apply . . . in the education of our people as well as in forestry . . . to the body politic as well as to the earth and its minerals. . . . It applies as much to the subject of good roads as to waterways, and the training of our people in citizenship is as germane to it as the productiveness of the earth."[29]

"Conservation" was partly defined by its antithesis, "waste," an old word that conservationists endowed with a new sense.[30] "Waste" had been used interchangeably with "wilderness" to mean undeveloped terrain; as mentioned in Chapter 2, this sense was present in its Latin root, *vastus,* meaning "empty" or "desolate." The more familiar meaning today, a fruitless expenditure of energy or wealth, was already in use (as we've seen, it went back to Locke), but in Progressives' hands this sense of "waste" became an obsessive indictment of any system or process that failed to get the most value from its materials, whether those were minerals, trees, or human bodies and energy.[31] As Progressive reformers told it, waste occurred when a country disregarded the insights of conservation. Waste arose from ignoring the complexity of natural and social systems; putting personal interests over the public good; and failing to implement rational public policy. For Progressives, these waste-making attitudes seemed typical of people stuck in the mentality of the frontier. "Wasting" a resource, for progressive reformers, meant using land, forests, or labor in ways that diminished their health and productivity. Conservation was the principle and technique of eliminating waste.

Pinchot, the spokesman for conservation ideas and the architect of conservation policy, was part of a network of foresters, engineers, and sportsmen who warned that, without a change of course, the country's forests would soon be cleared, its mines exhausted, and its rivers clogged with sediment from erosion. These arguments came before Congress as early as 1890, in a memorial from the American Forestry Association, a central node in the conservation network.[32] Already in 1891, the Interior Department's annual report to Congress had warned that, without timbering limits, "there will be little timber left to protect," and urged the president to use his new power to reserve timberlands from settlement or harvest.[33]

Human beings were among the resources that conservationists set out to manage. Theodore Roosevelt declared, "The health and vitality of our people are at least as well worth conserving as their forests, waters, lands, and minerals,"[34] and Charles van Hise, a leading Progressive scholar of regulation, concluded his landmark study, *The Conservation of Natural Resources in the United States* (1910), with a section entitled "The Conservation of Man Himself," which focused on public health.[35] The 1909 National Conservation Commission report to Congress and the president, which set out a sweeping conservation agenda, included *A Report on National Vitality: Its Wastes and Conservation,* opening with this assertion: "The problem of conserving our natural resources is part of another and greater problem—that of national efficiency [which] depends not only on the physical environment, but on the social environment, and most of all on human vitality."[36] Progressives warred against spoliation of human bodies and energies as much as they did against waste of timber and coal.

This interest in human health made natural beauty and outdoor recreation essential elements of the conservationist program. Sanitation laws saved Americans from epidemics in crowded cities; parks restored them after the mental abrasions of loud, fast-paced neighborhoods and workplaces. Laborers and city-dwellers should be able to contemplate gorgeous landscapes in their leisure hours. As early as 1865, Frederick Law Olmsted urged the California legislature to preserve Yosemite Valley for public recreation. By dedicating its most spectacular land to parks, Olmsted argued, the United States could grant citizens the vigor of outdoor life and the healing of aesthetic contemplation, balms that Old World nations reserved for aristocrats in private parks.[37]

Management of nature and management of people wove together in the imagery of Woodrow Wilson's first inaugural address. Elaborating on a conservationist theme, Wilson described the nineteenth century's legacy as both "riches" and "inexcusable waste," the latter evident in the failure "to conserve the . . . bounty of nature" and in "the human cost . . . of lives snuffed out, of energies overtaxed and broken."[38] Throughout the speech, images of neglected forests and waters and "waste places unreclaimed" come alongside evocations of sick, exhausted, and vulnerable bodies. The Progressive responses to such social waste—resource conservation, public-health regulation, and labor laws—figured in Wilson's language as a single remedy: "to purify and humanize every process of our common life" by replacing shortsighted self-interest with a commitment that law shall "keep sound the society it serves."[39]

The Roots of Conservation

Building stronger states and shaping governance through science were great themes of the later nineteenth century on both sides of the Atlantic. American reformers owed much to European administrators who pioneered the welfare state, to political economists who described society as an organic whole rather than a constellation formed of self-reliant individuals, and to the foresters who developed silviculture as their countries' woodlands dwindled. (France's central government had been wrestling with its regional authorities over forest management since the seventeenth century; the young Gifford Pinchot absorbed some of the lessons of this experience in a year he spent studying at the National School of Forestry in Nancy.) These were decades of intense transatlantic influence around new problems that were pressing on all the industrialized countries.

The American version of conservation was indebted, especially, to the work of George Perkins Marsh, whom we met in Chapter 4. His 1864 book *Man and Nature* is often described as a precursor of ecological science and environmental policy—but in truth, it is stranger and more distinctive than that. Marsh brought together two literatures and combined them with his own New England moralism to enlist the natural world in a campaign of managerial reform. Marsh drew on the natural histories of the Comte de Buffon and Alexander von Humboldt, who had blended empirical inquiry with philosophical speculation about how nature's order arose and changed. He also continued a literature of jeremiads against resource exhaustion that went back to England's Civil War–era forester, the Royalist John Evelyn, and his contemporary Jean-Baptiste Colbert in France. Marsh imbibed these European influences as a polylingual traveler who, among other excursions, logged a period as U.S. ambassador to Italy. The distinctly American element in his work was a Protestant and republican moralism in which nature's health, and the survival of the human species, formed a judgment on the country's intelligence, discipline, and public spirit.

In a diagnosis that was both environmental and moral, Marsh denounced "the ravages committed by man [that] subvert the relations and destroy the balance which nature had established," leaving "well-wooded and humid hills . . . turned to ridges of dry rock." He warned that "human crime and human improvidence" might bring the planet to "such a condition of impoverished productiveness, of shattered surface, of climatic excess, as to threaten the depravation, barbarism, and perhaps even extinction of the species."[40] On one level, this passage expresses Marsh's protoecological theory, which was that nature tends toward stability and that disruptive human action sets off a spiral of breakdown. On another level, the energy of the passage is moral and polemical. Marsh describes ecological change as driven by criminal and profligate behavior. If humanity went extinct from resource exhaustion, we would deserve it.

Marsh's footnotes gave running commentary on the political morality of his ecological argument. He footnoted the passage just quoted with bits of a sermon by the Protestant divine James Martineau: "By relaxing . . . [the world] tend[s] downwards, through inverted steps, to wildness and the waste again. Let a people give up their contest with moral evil; disregard the injustice, the ignorance, the greediness, that may prevail among them, and part more and more with the Christian element of their civilization; and . . . the portion they had reclaimed from the young earth's ruggedness is lost; and failing to stand fast against man, they finally get embroiled with nature, and are thrust down before her ever-living hand."[41] In Marsh's picture, civilization and virtue are always under threat from misdirected human powers and the natural forces they unleash. Instead of American founder James Wilson's fruitful dance of human effort and natural wealth, Marsh describes a grappling match between the natural world, which is both fragile and dangerous, and people, who are heedless of their power to set ecological destruction in motion. Mutual degradation, slow violence, results.

"Of all organic beings," Marsh wrote, "man alone is to be regarded as essentially a destructive power." Unlike other predators, "man pursues his victims with reckless destructiveness" well beyond his need or appetite, and "has ruthlessly warred on all the tribes of all animated nature whose spoil he could convert to his own uses." He "gradually eradicates or transforms every spontaneous product of the soil he occupies." Marsh thought the ecological violence of human action bespoke our origin in "a higher order of existence than those born of [earth's] womb and submissive to her dictates."[42]

Humans were destructive, but the earth also needed them to keep it vital. Without human disturbance, Marsh insisted, most landscapes would become forest: he was so convinced of this point that he believed the Great Plains must have been cleared by a lost race with more powerful technology than Native Americans. Mature forests, in Marsh's eyes, were biological deserts, where old trees and the occasional bird sleepily bided the seasons. Without humans, the earth would settle into early senescence.[43] The world's productivity, then, came mostly from deliberate disturbance, such as clearing forests and marshaling four-legged armies of labor.

The problem: humans had gone too far and had thrown off the balance between their disruptive vitality and the somnolent steadiness of the rest of creation. Beginning with "the destruction of the woods . . . man's first physical conquest, his first violation of the harmonies of nature,"[44] human power was wrecking the earth. Forests held water, slowing its release into streams and rivers, each rainfall restoring a natural reservoir. When the forests were gone, the rains rushed across bare soil, washing it into flooded waterways and leaving the headwaters and slopes naked and soon dry and barren. Healthy soil and steady-flowing streams gave way to intermittent floods, silt-choked channels, and eroded hills and fields. Other human activity was also destructive—killing birds could unleash swarms of insects suddenly freed of predators—but recklessly clearing forests and overusing soil were the deadly sins.

Any solution required the knowledge to understand the problem, the cultural maturity for self-restraint, and government to enforce limits on exploitation. Marsh set out ecological destruction as a tale of civic and moral decline. He opened *Man and Nature* in the landscape of the classical Mediterranean: spared the corrupting luxuries of gold and jewels, blessed with a climate that gave nothing for free but rewarded work, enjoying a quiet beauty that inspired "sympathy . . . with the inanimate world," the Greeks and Romans built great civilizations. Now much of the same land was sparsely populated semi-desert. Political tyranny brought the ecological fall: Marsh wrote of "the brutal and exhausting despotism which Rome herself exercised [and] the host of temporal and spiritual tyrannies which she left as her dying curse to all her wide dominion." Medieval exploitation of peasants and serfs, abandonment of lands, and the ignorance and abjection that Catholic doctrine fostered reduced people to "naked, sunburnt, wild animals, male and female, scattered over the country and attached to the soil" by feudal bonds.[45]

Marsh summarized his judgment: "Man cannot struggle at once against crushing oppression and the destructive forces of inorganic nature. When both are combined against him . . . the fields he has won from the primeval woods relapse into their original state of wild and luxuriant, but unprofitable forest growth, or fall into that of a dry and barren wilderness."[46] Throughout the history of Europe, political brutality fed into ecological destruction, as kings devastated forests to root out robbers and rebels. Then peasants, after the French Revolution, cut and burnt trees in sylvan riots that showed their contempt for the aristocrats who had held the forests. This is as much fantasy as history, and ignores the centralized forest management that was well over a hundred years old in France when Marsh wrote. The republican Marsh, though, saw a country's management or mismanagement of its lands as a symptom of civic virtue or vice, which the earth answered in the destructive forces of ecological misrule.

In the young United States, the challenge was to overcome the ignorance and greed of too-rapid clearing and development, which had stripped forests and eroded slopes from the Green Mountains to the Mississippi Valley. The same forces were moving into the Pacific region, leaving only Oregon, in Marsh's judgment, with a healthy share of land in forest. Although he lamented the privatization of so many acres of public forest as "a great misfortune to the American Union," he did not expect either government or private owners to manage their holdings well as long as Americans lacked "the diffusion of general intelligence on this subject" and the salutary effects of "enlightened self-interest." Marsh called the moral and cultural climate in which he wrote "the semi-barbarism of modern times." Too much of the country's energy served organized greed. Corporations pursued profits above all and seized control of state governments for private ends. Marsh hoped that moral reform, together with practical forestry, would convert Americans from cutting wild timber to managing their acres for the highest sustainable yield. He thought an enlightened United States would emulate Europe, with its large stock of state forests.[47]

Carl Schurz's Interior Department deputies knew Marsh's *Man and Nature*: in 1878, under its influence, they set out to stop the uncontrolled timber cutting that they saw as robbery and waste of public forests.[48] Well before the 1891 statute that first authorized the president to create national forests, Marsh's heirs were asserting a new role for government: disciplining frontier excess and sometimes replacing private property with public management. Marsh recast westward development as an episode of national immaturity, destructive excess that arose from ignorance, greed, and the lack of a strong and competent state. The test of the country would not be conquering the continent, but finding the self-restraint to grow within the harmonies of nature. Otherwise, the United States would end up as desolate as the Near Eastern and North African deserts of the former Roman Empire. Marsh's nature was a severe judge, and it demanded the knowledge of scientists and the steady hand of administrators.

Social and Moral Reform

Later reformers followed Marsh in tying conservation policy to moral decline and revival. Some conservationists tried to reclaim frontier virtues in the industrial era, others to root out the frontier's legacy of selfish individualism. Some focused on the country's civic culture, others on the quality of private life. They agreed, though, that the country had to change, and they found a fulcrum for reform in Americans' relation to the natural world.

These questions carried an old American fixation on moral revival into a new era of social regulation. Conservation policy, now expanded to include social and economic governance, shaped the experience of workers at their jobs, children in the family and school, citizens in parks and public squares, and consumers in the marketplace. There was no avoiding the question: What kind of lives did reformers hope to foster in their fellow citizens, and what gave them the authority to mold others to the shape they thought best—assuming they could succeed?

The most straightforward answer came from Gifford Pinchot, who aimed at guiding Americans toward an ideal of shared prosperity, in the present and for future generations. Pinchot denounced "short-sighted" measures and called on Americans to "make ourselves . . . responsible for [the country's] future." Conservation's basic goal was well-being: it aimed to make "the difference between prosperity and poverty, health and sickness, ignorance and education, well-being and misery." Conservation's success would be "patriotism in action": it made the interests of all Americans the standard of government.[49] This was a moral as well as a political ideal: conservation should teach each citizen devotion to the good of all.

Pinchot's conservationist patriotism implied two distinct civic perspectives, which together formed its whole. One was that of the citizen devoted to the common good. This could only be an abstract loyalty, because finding concrete ways to serve the public interest required expertise that most people lacked, and usually took place on a scale that only large institutions could manage. The commonweal required expert engineering of systems, whether forests, schools, or markets. Thus, Pinchot's account also implied a second moral standpoint, that of the public-spirited manager who interpreted the public interest and put it into practice. Conservation took its democratic authority from the public that embraced it, but drew its epistemic authority, its claim to know how to govern, from elite expertise. Frequently, conservationists treated the authority of expertise as more basic, the real justification for their use of public power. Their program thus established a vexed bond between a democratic public and the expert managers who claimed authority to identify and pursue that good.

The Conservation of Civic Virtue

Pinchot's fellow conservationists Theodore Roosevelt and Albert Beveridge shared his wish for citizens to be committed to the long-term interest of the whole country; but they also doubted whether that civic spirit could survive in modern times. An anxiety rippled through their cohort of elite reformers: that a prosperous, peaceful, and sanitary democracy would undermine itself. Comfortable citizens might grow indifferent to anything more demanding than their own pleasures.[50] Small-spirited Americans might hurry to consume the country's natural resources, leaving their descendants impoverished and vulnerable;[51] they might fall into selfish class conflict;[52] or they might simply give up all great initiative, political or industrial, and "rot by inches, like China."[53] What united these concerns was not so much a theory as a mood and a pattern of fears. As these reformers imagined it, the United States had been built in a spirit of individualism that, although it contained a healthy dose of self-interest, was daring and oriented to high ideals. The decline of that spirit would mean the end of national greatness and might even make national unity impossible.

Some, Roosevelt among them, saw answers in war and imperial projects. In his famous speech on "the strenuous life," the future president defended U.S. imperialism in the Philippines as strong medicine for an ailing national character: "If we do our duty aright in the Philippines, we will add to that national renown which is the highest and finest part of national life. . . . If we . . . seek merely swollen, slothful ease and ignoble peace . . . then the bolder and stronger peoples will pass us by, and will win for themselves the domination of the world. . . . It is only through strife, through hard and dangerous endeavor, that we shall ultimately win the goal of true national greatness."[54]

Militarism was not the whole story, though. Reformers searched for civilian modes of character-building adventure, the famous moral equivalents of war.[55] Roosevelt's call for a "strenuous life" of adventure was soon worked into a celebration of outdoor adventure. According to the 1928 *Report of the National Conference on Outdoor Recreation*, with the closing of the frontier and the rise of industry, "the individualism of the pioneer has been submerged in collective enterprise."[56] In such circumstances, recreation was "a needful social force," a source of "physical vigor, moral strength, and clean simplicity of mind."[57] Nature, then, could be the ligament that joined American life across its eras, giving access to old virtues in new times. If the American landscape were to play this role, however, public-lands management would have to shape it for the role. Daring and adventurousness were to be, just a bit paradoxically, products of planning and administration. These individualistic qualities were recast as "needful social forces" to be husbanded like timber and coal.

Roosevelt also saw forests and parks as civic commons where Americans could overcome the class segregation of urban, industrial life.[58] In these commons, Americans could mingle across economic divisions, developing the quality that Roosevelt called "fellow-feeling," the germ of the utilitarian public spirit that he and Pinchot both praised as patriotism for their time.[59] This was the civic value of the "free camping grounds for the ever-increasing numbers of men and women who have learned to find rest, health, and recreation in the splendid forests and flower-clad meadows of our mountains."[60]

Despite his interest in civic virtue, Roosevelt saw social and economic regulation as fundamentally technical, not political. The technocratic attitude saw its highest development in the role that "national efficiency" played in his program. Roosevelt called for an economy that would reward individuals in line with their effort, talent, initiative, and contribution to the public good. He insisted that this version of economic fairness had enforced itself automatically among pioneers, but would require deliberate regulation in a complex, industrial economy.

Trying to reclaim the presidency as a third-party candidate in 1912 after despairing at the conservatism of his successor and fellow Republican, William Howard Taft, Roosevelt called national efficiency simply "the principle of conservation widely applied."[61] He similarly explained in his presidential introduction to the massive 1909 report of the National Conservation Commission, "The policy of conservation is perhaps the most typical example of the general policies which this government has made peculiarly its own."[62] Roosevelt's examples of conservation-modeled regulatory policy included antitrust, limits on corporate involvement in politics, and, above all, laws denying corporations "unregulated control of the means of production and the necessaries of life."[63] The aim of "national efficiency" was to deploy all productive forces, especially human beings, without waste. As he put it, "every man will have a fair chance to make of himself all that in him lies; to reach the highest point to which his capacities, unassisted by special privilege of his own and unhampered by the special privileges of others, can carry him, and to get for himself and his family substantially what he has earned."[64]

Part of the reason that national efficiency was urgent for Roosevelt was that it seemed to promise a solution to labor strife and social division. Roosevelt was personally horrified by class conflict and saw in it an elemental threat to order. In "The New Nationalism" and other conservation addresses, he portrayed a landscape of brutally clashing interests, especially labor and capital, which only national efficiency could reconcile. His 1901 annual message to Congress declared, "The most vital problem with which this country . . . has to deal is the problem which has for one side the betterment of social conditions, moral and physical, in large cities, and for another side the effort to deal with that tangle of far-reaching questions which we group together when we speak of labor."[65] He insisted that national efficiency, the principles of conservation rightly applied, could redress all the inequity and social waste of industrial capitalism and provide a just basis for resolving the harshest conflicts.[66]

Conservation of natural resources was the model for Roosevelt's larger ideal of a just and legitimate economy. Renewable resources such as forests exemplified the gains to be won from expert public management; by contrast, hurried clear-cutting presented a picture of selfish exploitation and a vivid antithesis to public-spirited man-agement. Compared to the notorious difficulties of economic reg-ulation, such as reconciling formally free choice with substantive opportunity and distinguishing distributive fairness from selfish grabs at special privileges, rational management of natural re-sources was straightforward. It was a natural rhetorical redoubt for the reformer eager to persuade his audience that conservationist principles could reconcile competing interests and produce an ef-ficient and just version of industrial capitalism.[67]

The thought that there should be scientific answers to political questions appealed to elites who were confident in their judgment and wary of the democratic public. It is often observed of progres-sive reformers, Roosevelt in particular, that while the public interest was their touchstone, fractious partisan politics left them impatient or disgusted. H. L. Mencken, not a pleasant or a fair observer, but an acute one, famously quipped of Roosevelt, "He didn't believe in democracy; he believed simply in government."[68] Roosevelt and his allies confronted a politics riven by clashes of economic interest and social vision, which threatened the New Nationalist ideal of an all-reconciling public interest. In resource conservation, by con-trast, expert managers could preside over mute landscapes, seem-ingly achieving governance without politics. They governed in the name of a public interest that they had considerable liberty to de-fine without ever conceding that they were making political choices.

The Humanism of Socialized Consumption

Progressive conservation took a third and distinct direction in Walter Weyl's argument for "the socialization of consumption." Weyl, co-editor of the *New Republic* with Walter Lippmann and Herbert Croly, helped to redefine American ideas of freedom during the early twentieth century. As Eric Foner notes, "During the Progressive era . . . a consumer definition of freedom—access to the cornucopia of goods made available by modern capitalism—began to supplant an older version centered on economic and political sovereignty."[69] Although Weyl's defining work was titled *The New Democracy* and made the case for strengthening democratic elections, his program was based less on self-government by the whole public than on expert government in the public interest.

In contrast to Roosevelt, Weyl was sharply critical of individualism and the frontier ethos, which he portrayed as national curses. Contradicting Frederick Jackson Turner's influential claim that the frontier had fostered grassroots democracy, Weyl argued, "It made America atomic. It led automatically to a loose political coherence and to a structureless economic system."[70] Thus, the symptoms of exploitation and inequality, "the trust, the hundred-millionaire, and the slum were latent in the land which the American people in their first century of freedom were to subjugate."[71] In Weyl's eyes, the Progressive embrace of social regulation, "an energetic campaign of human conservation,"[72] was a necessary advance beyond the destructive chaos of the frontier.[73]

Weyl called for the "socialization" of economic life; this did not mean public ownership, or even public control. Socialization for him was "a point of view" defined by utilitarianism: "It is such a coordination of business as will permanently give the greatest happiness and the highest development to the largest number of individuals, and to society as a whole."[74] The other side of this program was "the socialization of consumption," which meant providing the consumer goods and experiences that people most needed. What they needed might be different from what they wanted; it was a moral, and moralizing, standard. Parks mattered to Weyl for the satisfaction they gave to individuals, not for their capacity to support civic virtues; but Weyl cared that park-going, unlike drinking and gambling, represented a refined form of pleasure.[75] Americans would have to learn to use leisure well. Recreation thus presented a cultural challenge, one Weyl believed the aesthetic and recreational qualities of parks and other outdoor preserves could help to serve by refining popular taste.

Improving taste was part of what Weyl called "an energetic campaign of human conservation"[76] that included public health, labor laws, food regulation, and extensive education alongside public-lands management. This campaign aimed to make economic, cultural, and physical environments, from parks to cities, from the grocery to the workplace, less dangerous, more equitable, and richer in opportunities for personal development. More than either Pinchot or Roosevelt, Weyl accepted that political regulation of social life raised questions that no model based in nature could solve, questions that had to be addressed democratically. Weyl's aim was to enrich people's experience and character, and, unlike many of his contemporaries, he fully grasped that this goal had no neat parallel in forest management.

But Weyl went further. In putting human values and judgments first, he mostly set aside the idea that people might learn from encounters with the natural world, that a landscape could be part of a culture. Other than his support for public parks, which was less central to his thinking than to than Roosevelt's, Weyl saw nature as a reserve of materials for human projects, nothing more. It is not just that he rejected any mystical view of nature as a quasi-divine source of wisdom and goodness, such as John Muir held; Weyl had little interest in the cultural meaning of the landscapes that people shaped.

These three reformers shared a managerial approach to the natural world. Roosevelt and Pinchot also shared the idea that the social world could be regulated on the same terms as, almost as a subset of, the natural world. In earlier eras, the idea that the social world was continuous with a meaningful natural world had justified versions of social order and hierarchy, as in monarchical Europe or the U.S. clearing of Native Americans. For utilitarian reformers at the beginning of the twentieth century, nature was almost wholly disenchanted, and its only rational use was to serve human projects. Notionally, at least, the question of how to approach nature was just an extension of the approach to social order, which the reformers insisted had to be a matter of explicit political design, rather than the willy-nilly of laissez-faire.

By a kind of ideological jujitsu, though, their utilitarian idea of nature turned back on their approach to society: instead of an open democratic question of how to live together, politics became an increasingly technical question of how to manage life. This technocratic attitude was an ironic return to an older habit of relying on nature for social judgments, but with a twist. Earlier, a meaningful nature imposed certain kinds of meaning on human order— shapely, in a way, but unequal and constrained to specific kinds of morality, such as the frontier ethic of clearing and production. Now, it was nature's status as a fungible resource that carried over to social regulation, presenting most of economic and social life as just the total array of consumer satisfactions, which a technocratic manager should maximize.

Conservation was an empire-building doctrine. Abroad, it helped Albert Beveridge, Theodore Roosevelt, and others to expand Manifest Destiny into a global program. At home, it was a central rationale for creating a strong national government with authority to reach into every area of life. Under the flag of conservation, the federal government reserved the public acreage that, today, keeps nearly a third of the nation's land under the administration of the Forest Service, the National Parks Service, and the Bureau of Land Management. It also began to build an administrative empire for a new governing ideology: a technocratic approach to social and economic life that turned political questions into scientific ones, restricting the scope of democratic choice and participation even as progressive reform opened up governance in areas of life that had long been imagined as natural and self-regulating.

Progressivism marked a revolution in the governance of nature and society, but one in which the same attitude toward a complex, fragile natural world both helped to open new frontiers of governance and also handed off that governance to technocrats. That, at least, was the interpretation that the technocrats offered and managed to enforce.

Conservation, Eugenics, and Racism

Any thorough accounting of the rise of conservation must give a place to Madison Grant, another of Theodore Roosevelt's prominent friends and allies. Madison was the prime organizer of the Save-the-Redwoods League, an organization of wealthy and influential men (John D. Rockefeller donated one million dollars in 1924) that created many of the coastal preserves where California's redwood trees now survive. Grant and Roosevelt came together in the Boone and Crockett Club. Roosevelt founded the group of socially elite, conservation-minded, and adamantly blood-seeking sportsmen in winter of 1887–1888, restricting it to one hundred members at any time and setting entrance requirements that included having killed specimens of at least three of the large species of North American game animals (bear, bison, caribou, cougar, deer, elk, moose, mountain sheep, musk ox, pronghorn antelope, white goat, and wolf). Grant joined in 1893 and became one of the club's most active members, throwing its members' considerable influence behind state bans on commercial hunting, helping to create the network of preserves that saved the American bison from extinction, and pressing to establish Glacier National Park in 1910. He was instrumental in establishing the Bronx Zoo, whose naturalist and conservationist overseers largely overlapped with those of the Roosevelt-centered American Museum of Natural History and, unsurprisingly, the members of the Boone and Crockett Club. Grant reckoned, like John Muir and Aldo Leopold, that "nature itself has some rights," and that the United States could respect those rights by leaving some areas of the continent in "their pristine condition of wilderness."[77]

Here is Roosevelt on one of Grant's books: "This book is a capital book; in purpose, in vision, in grasp of the facts our people most need to realize. . . . It shows a habit of singular serious thought on the subjects of most commanding importance. It shows a fine fearlessness in assailing the popular and mischievous sentimentalities and attractive and corroding falsehoods which few men dare assail. It is the work of an American scholar and gentleman; and all Americans should be sincerely grateful to you for writing it."[78] The book was not a work of conservation advocacy or nature appreciation. It was *The Passing of the Great Race,* a torrid work of racial alarmism and pseudo-science that Adolf Hitler called "my bible" in an admiring letter to Grant.[79]

Here is Grant on "the result of unlimited immigration" into the United States just before the country's entry into World War I: "The man of the old stock (Anglo-Saxon) is being crowded out of many country districts by these foreigners ['the Slovak, the Italian, the Syrian and the Jew'] just as he is to-day being literally driven off the streets of New York City by the swarms of Polish Jews. These immigrants adopt the language of the native American, they wear his clothes, they steal his name and they are beginning to take his women."[80] Grant was a committed eugenicist, and here he was arguing that Americans should stem the low-quality tide of short, stocky, round-headed Alpines ("always and everywhere a race of peasants")[81] and dark, slight Mediterraneans (who thrived in "the cramped factory and crowded city" because of their racial aptitude to "work a spindle, set type, sell ribbons or push a clerk's pen").[82] The same was true of the Negro, who had neither "self-control" nor "capacity for cooperation," and displayed "low vital capacity" in comparison to Europeans.[83] Grant argued that allowing open immigration was a "suicidal ethics" that would wipe out the group that had created the country—"the Nordics," a people of courage, initiative, and leadership, whose noble spirit and unsuspicious nature made them vulnerable to peoples better adapted to factories and ghettoes.[84]

Grant's conservationism was closely intertwined with his elitist, nostalgic, anti-democratic racism. His *New York Times* obituary captured the unity of his governing sentiments: "The preservation of the redwoods, of the bison, of the Alaskan caribou, of the bald eagle . . . of the spirit of the early American colonist . . . and of the purity of the 'Nordic' type of humanity in the country, were all his personal concerns, all products of the same urge in him to save precious things." Grant's biographer, Jonathan Spiro, remarks, "There can be little doubt that Grant identified the redwood trees with the Nordic race"—noble survivors of a heroic age, now being laid low by commerce and home building for the democratic swarm.[85] This is speculation, but it does express themes that always united Grant's projects: elegy, a sense of threat, and a heroic call to save a vanishing world. The tone was established as early as his 1894 article "The Vanishing Moose," in *The Century,* a clearinghouse of progressive thought and letters. Grant began:

> So much has been written . . . of the great achievements and rapid development of the United States that sometimes we lose sight of the fact that we are still in a period of transition. The old order of things has largely passed away, but we are yet within sight of the primeval state of a savage and beautiful wilderness, and can obtain some idea of what this country once was by the untouched or only partly mutilated corners that remain. The end, however, is near. . . . Of the great forests . . . scarcely anything is left. That little will be destroyed by fire and ax within two decades, and with the trees will vanish the last of the game.[86]

The themes are all there: "development" has been a kind of muti-
lation, and only fragments remain to remind us of past greatness.
Those fragments, however, should command our attention and
affection.

The Boone and Crockett Club was an Olympus of conservationists. It included the former Interior Secretary Carl Schurz, who
first restricted timbering on federal land, outraging western populists; Albert Bierstadt, the celebrated painter of sublime western
landscapes, including Lake Tahoe and Mount Rainier; Theodore
Strong van Dyke, the popular outdoors writer; Clarence King,
former director of the U.S. Geological Survey, Sierra explorer, and
theorist of art who was heavily influenced by John Ruskin; Owen
Wister, the literary proponent of the frontier nostalgia that shaped
Roosevelt's early experience and public persona; and, a little later,
Aldo Leopold. There was no uniform view of race in the club, but
Madison Grant was not an anomaly. His fellow members included
his very close friend and collaborator Henry Fairfield Osborn, the
director of the American Museum of Natural History, who contributed the introductions to Grant's two major works of explicit
racism, *The Passing of the Great Race* and *The Conquest of a Continent,* both times (nearly twenty years apart) praising the author
for providing a thoroughly racial account of the causes and
meaning of human history. Gifford Pinchot, a Boone and Crockett
member, was a delegate to the first and second international eugenics congresses in 1912 and 1921 and a member of the Advisory
Council of the American Eugenics Society from 1925 to 1935.[87]

Madison Grant and his central place in the conservationist
milieu provide several discomfiting reminders. Conservationists
regarded the living world, human and nonhuman, through the
eyes of utilitarian managers. For many, such as Pinchot's fellows
in the American Eugenics Society, human beings were so much
raw material for manipulation and improvement. Their belief in

administration rather than democracy extended to public lands such as national forests, conquered territories such as the Philippines, and the bodies of citizens.

Conservation sprang up, too, in an atmosphere of nostalgia, militarism, and racial nationalism. Grant's redwoods, trophy mammals, and Nordic heroes, and his fear of losing all three, form a familiar nostalgic constellation. He, Roosevelt, and their fellow Boone and Crockett Club members were obsessed with the decline of heroism. Owen Wister's frontier novels, most famously *The Virginian,* spoke to the same sentiment. So did Roosevelt's lifelong search for adventure and physical trial—on Dakota ranches, African safaris, and military excursions such as his Rough Riders' bit part in the Spanish-American War. Familiar institutions such as the Boy Scouts have their origins here, in Ernest Thompson Seton's efforts to preserve frontier experiences and put some rawhide in American boys' character, and in Daniel Carter Beard's aim to do the same with stereotyped American Indian woodcraft. (Both movements merged into the khaki-clad, paramilitary-toned British import known as the Scouts' Association, founded by the Roosevelt-like imperial enthusiast Lord Robert Baden-Powell.)

Nothing in these impulses guarantees racism; but sentimentalism, nostalgia, and a sense of demographic threat to one's own status all have affinities that way. Talk of Anglo-Saxon virtues born in the misty forests of northern Europe ran far back in American rhetoric. Emerson had indulged in it without misgivings. Thoreau described the westward movement of the American "star of empire" as the national ingestion and absorption of the ancient, raw vitality of the American landscape, harbored in its forests and swamps, which would sustain Americans and fuel their creation of a new body of myth, as great as what had sprung from the Nile, the Ganges, and the Rhine before those once-wild places were exhausted. Conquest, expansion, and fantasies about a people's identity becoming inseparable from the fertile and dark depths of its land ran together throughout the nineteenth century. These tropes established a certain kind white man, often elite, adventure-seeking, and tough yet sentimental, as the "natural" inhabitant and interpreter of the continent. They tended to erase or simplify the Native American presence: in Thoreau's image of a continent full of untapped vitality, the past is, at best, prehistory, preparatory to the self-realization of the American nation. John Muir erased Native American history in a more pedestrian way when he took pains to assure his readers that Indians had been broken to docility on U.S. public lands, so that Romantic tourists could wander there without danger.

Many of these figures were—particularly by the standards of their times—nonracist and even courageously antiracist. The racial hierarchy in their thought was implied in a larger vision of the continent and its history. By contrast, an obsession with race was a primary motive in all that Madison Grant did. The thinking of other conservationists and Romantics tended more to universalism. Roosevelt admired Grant's book, but his own fixations revolved more around cultures and civilizations than around races: some rose and grew strong, like the young United States, while others faded into decadence, like China. It was no coincidence that the future lay with Roosevelt's people; but his view of history was not organized by genetic typologies and hierarchies. For John Muir and his Transcendentalist predecessors, the human qualities that wild nature vivified were higher potentials that everyone shared; they were quite blind to their cultural and, in effect, racial particularity. Muir, like other Enlightenment and Romantic figures, sometimes contradicted these universalist claims in his concrete racial attitudes, but that is very different from saying his beliefs themselves were racist. The Romantics' dominant thought was that a certain relation to nature should be American because it was true, not that American racial stock implied a right relation to nature. This idea fits a nation of conquerors and immigrants: the primary thing was less a claim to origins than a claim to destination: the indwelling potential of the American land, open to those who could claim it, was what the European colonists and their descendants had in fact claimed and made.

Precisely because of its universalist cast, environmental thinking can obscure the fact that its origins lie in a quite particular patch of the American people. Interpreting American nature, especially in a Romantic register, was the special preoccupation of educated white Protestants, especially traditional elites with roots in New England and the Upper Midwest. The early Sierra Club was a collection of academics, artists, scientists, and seekers after outdoor adventure and aesthetic delight. They saw appreciation of nature as a mark of refined sensibility that set them apart from the hurly-burly of money seeking and from utilitarian ideas of what gave life value. They constantly assured one another that their time in the high country confirmed these values. The view of nature that they helped to make popular supported the special status of a traditional elite that had lost some control over the country's economy and political institutions and felt the need for other bases of distinction and deference.

Much the same holds true for the anxious elites who gathered around the Boone and Crockett Club to worry over the loss of adventure, greatness, and manliness in American culture. They bloodied their hands on the aristocratic species of the continent—the moose, the bear, the wolf—to confirm their place as the natural aristocracy of the American nation. Historian Richard Hofstadter emphasized decades ago (too sweepingly, but still) that the entire Progressive era was shaped by the status struggles of declining American elites; this was acutely true of both Romantic and conservationist views of nature.

Privilege and nostalgia infuse these early forms of environmental imagination, and they are *someone's* privilege and nostalgia in particular. Much of the continent was interpreted, then shaped and managed, as an austere but spectacular pleasure ground that marked the refinement of those who could enjoy it. It was a public-lands equivalent of the aristocratic English gardens of the eighteenth and nineteenth centuries, which deliberately shaped parts of the landscape to show off the educated eye of their owners. What it holds up as the universal spirit of nature was also the favored bauble of a declining elite, which looked to nature for reassurance of its continued specialness.

Of course, the fact that an idea arose in a certain group, even to assert that group's privilege, need not limit its validity for others. If we disqualified ideas that began in this way, we would have to start with democracy and citizenship, which began as the special powers and rights of an overclass in the slave societies of the ancient Mediterranean and acquired their modern forms when white, male landowners' political privileges were gradually extended—through great struggle—to every citizen. The test of environmental imagination is not its origins but its uses. Yet many of those uses have been in the anti-democratic and racially exclusionary self-assertion of elites, and it is essential to keep in mind the marks they have left.

6

A WILDERNESS PASSAGE
INTO ECOLOGY

IN THE HALF-CENTURY after John Muir's death in 1917, a movement arose that was devoted to literal wilderness. The wilderness movement emerged in the 1920s from conflicts over whose ideas of nature the national parks should serve. In *Our National Parks* (1901), Muir had promised readers solitude and epiphany steps away from a railway platform running trains to San Francisco. It soon became clear that, when solitude was easy to reach from crowded places, it did not remain solitude for long. Tourism rose along with wealth, mobility, and—ironically—popular love of scenic places.

These contradictions soon crystallized as disputes over parks policy. Tourists eager to follow Muir's pilgrimage routes demanded roads to speed their way. The National Park Service, alert to the benefits of increased budgets, was generally eager to comply. In the 1920s, major parks such as Yosemite featured jazz concerts, bear circuses, and nighttime light shows dancing over the famous waterfalls. Parks officials sought funding for roads and hotels, to attract even more visitors.

These changes divided the National Parks Service. Director Stephen Mather supported opening the parks to more users. Robert

Sterling Yard, who, as noted in Chapter 4, wrote *The Book of National Parks* and gave a touchstone encomium to the parks as nature's "cathedrals," believed that commerce and entertainment profaned sacred places.[1] After a series of clashes with Mather, Yard left the Parks Service to become head of the independent National Parks Association, where he advocated for wild and primitive areas on public land. He then co-founded the Wilderness Society, which would be the center of the wilderness movement for the next forty years. The Wilderness Society attracted purists who wanted their Romantic nature undiluted by anything easy or popular. They created a new category of public land: roadless, free of built structures, and minimally shaped by human activity. This became the legal definition of "wilderness" when the activists won their biggest victory, passage of the federal Wilderness Act in 1964.

Wilderness advocates struggled to express the value of wild lands. There was little idea in early twentieth-century lands politics that a place could be valuable precisely because it remained untouched where few people would visit it. Activists had to make a language for what they treasured. The Wilderness Society's platform accordingly defined "wilderness" as "the environment of solitude."[2] The platform contrasted solitude with scenic beauty, which the parks mainly served: "scenery and solitude are intrinsically separate things."[3] The difference was that scenery, the crowd-pleasing gem of the parks, could be shared among many eyes. Solitude could not.

Solitude was more than physical isolation, although it required that. It was a state of mind, a specific way of encountering the natural world, whether in struggle or in communion. If public-lands management did not expand its purposes to include solitude, activists warned, wilderness would be "sacrificed to the mechanical invasion in its various killing forms."[4] The Wilderness Act of 1964, which was drafted by Wilderness Society leaders, commemorates the triumph of these ideas. The preamble to the statute announces its purpose—"to ensure that an increasing population, accompanied by expanding settlement and growing mechanization, does not occupy and modify all areas within the United States"[5]—and defines "wilderness areas" as offering "outstanding opportunities for solitude or a primitive and unconfined type of recreation" on "land retaining its primeval character."[6] A new movement had won acreage for a new idea, adding wilderness to the geography of American ideals.

Early efforts to establish solitude as a public value look awkward and sometimes paradoxical in hindsight, because advocates were trying to build a new public language of wilderness from within an older lexicon that brought its own constraints. The dominant way to defend national parks was to appeal to conservation: beauty and recreation yielded utilitarian benefits, so they should be managed as wisely as timber and coal. The Wilderness Society platform followed in these tracks, designating wilderness "a natural mental resource . . . a public utility . . . [and] a human need rather than a luxury or plaything."[7] But utilitarianism was an inapt vehicle for defending wilderness, which required a lot of undisturbed acreage per solitary person. Because solitude was not for sharing, wilderness could produce its benefits only if most of the public were excluded from it at any time and place.

So when Wilderness Society co-founder Bob Marshall set out to make a conservationist case for wilderness in a 1930 *Scientific Monthly* essay, he instead wrote an accidental *reductio ad absurdum* of utilitarian wilderness advocacy. The nub of the problem was how to argue that a few wilderness enthusiasts should enjoy millions of acres for their exclusive use. When Marshall's would-be utilitarian argument came to grips with this problem, it fell apart. He claimed that wilderness devotees took *so much* satisfaction from their outings that their happiness vastly outweighed that of parks visitors and timber users. This argument is implausible; everyone has about the same capacity for happiness. This is why utilitari-

anism arose as a leveling theory, a denial that some kinds of satisfactions, and some people's satisfactions, should count for more
than others. Unless wilderness enthusiasts were practically a
different species from stay-at-homers or park-goers, they could not
be orders of magnitude happier than those other, competing resource users.[8]

So, without announcing that he was changing ground, Marshall
veered away from utilitarianism to defend wilderness as an aspect
of human diversity. He quoted John Stuart Mill at length, adopting
Mill's claim from *On Liberty* that, because people find satisfaction
in diverse ways, human flourishing requires a tolerant society.
Otherwise, some would find their paths to fulfillment blocked.
Without wilderness, Marshall insisted, people like him would be
unable to flourish. Liberal tolerance required preserving wild lands.

Now, though, Marshall was caught in a fallacy. Mill's argument
was in favor of negative liberty: it advocated not banning or pun-
ishing unpopular beliefs or practices. This kind of liberty protects
religious and sexual minorities, for instance. But wilderness advocates were not asking for tolerance; they were asking for land, and
for federal money to administer it. Mill's argument for diversity
did not imply that the public must spend limited public resources
to promote some particular minority value. That, however, was
what Marshall wanted. He was arguing that public land should go
to the use that mattered most to him and his preservationist allies. His appeal to tolerance got him no further down this road than
utilitarianism had. By failing so spectacularly, both arguments
highlighted how far the wilderness program fell outside recognized
ways of valuing public land.

Marshall was a central figure in both the Wilderness Society and
public-lands administration until a heart attack killed him at age
thirty-eight. As chief of the Forest Service's Division of Recreation
and Lands, he wrote the 1940 regulations that first put the wilderness concept into legal effect and marked the path toward the 1964

Wilderness Act. He was speaking for the wilderness movement when he wrote in 1930, and his argument's failure was emblematic. Advocates for wilderness did not really care about increasing the sum of human satisfactions in a calculus that put wilderness excursions alongside railroads, circuses, and hospitals. Like their allies in the Sierra Club, they cared about special, heightened forms of consciousness. Like later environmentalists of the ecological age, they cared about the wild, tangled fabric of nature as such, just because it existed, apart from its service to human beings. These two values—human consciousness and inhuman nature—were linked for them because the consciousness they prized was precisely awareness of, and attunement to, indifferent, alien nature. They came to describe this as an attitude of "humility"—a word that connoted, in its etymology, at-homeness but also smallness and modesty, as if to say that the world is our home, but not one that we own or master in any simple or complete way. As they set out these ideas, wilderness activists became, quite unknowingly, a bridge between the Romantics of the Sierra Club, for whom encountering nature elevated consciousness, and the ecologically minded environmentalists, for whom nature was a difficult but precious home.

As early as 1935, Aldo Leopold began to make the case that wilderness was the key to a new consciousness, a fresh relation between humanity and nature. A few years before, he had sounded like Theodore Roosevelt, adapting a familiar line to argue that wilderness provided a testing ground for frontier virtues, like the former president's ranching and hunting adventures. Now Leopold was looking in a very different direction: "The Wilderness Society is, philosophically, a disclaimer of the biotic arrogance of *homo americanus*. It is one of the focal points of a new attitude—an intelligent humility toward man's place in nature."[9] Soon after World War II, Howard Zahniser, the society's longtime secretary and the editor of *Living Wilderness,* made a similar argument in response to a correspondent's accusation that wilderness advocates were elitists addicted to extreme forms of adventure: "Many [who visit the wilderness] . . . experience a better understanding of themselves in relation to the whole community of life on the earth and rather earnestly compare their civilized living with natural realities—to the improvement of their civilization."[10] The idea came from Leopold's writing, and Zahniser increasingly placed it at the center of the society's case for wilderness, suggesting that he found it the strongest of the arguments that he and his allies had crafted. He put it forward when speaking for the society, and allies in Congress and the broader conservation movement picked it up, giving it wider circulation and the beginning of touchstone status.

A signal moment came at the start of 1956, when the *Sierra Club Bulletin* ran a back-cover statement by Zahniser on "the underlying philosophy of the wilderness idea."[11] It was a time of self-definition for the preservation movement: several years of conflict over a proposed dam in Dinosaur National Monument, on the border between Colorado and Utah, had greatly increased the movement's national visibility and brought its major organizations into what Sierra Club director David Brower called a "new unity."[12] A coalition of groups would soon turn its attention to the Wilderness Act. A showcase in the flagship *Sierra Bulletin* gave Zahniser the chance to argue that wilderness should be the top priority of an increasingly coherent movement:

> We have a profound, a fundamental need for areas of wilderness—a need that is not only recreational and spiritual but also educational and scientific, and withal *essential to a true understanding of ourselves, our culture, our own natures, and our place in all nature.* The need is for *areas of the earth within which we stand without our mechanisms that make us immediate masters over our environment*—areas of wild nature in which *we sense ourselves to be, what in fact*

I believe we are, dependent members of an interdependent community of living creatures that together derive their existence from the sun . . . [ellipsis in original] *We deeply need the humility to know ourselves as the dependent members of a great community of life, and this can indeed be one of the spiritual benefits of the wilderness experience.* Without the . . . contrivances whereby men have seemed to establish among themselves an independence of nature, without these distractions, *to know the wilderness is to know a profound humility,* to recognize one's littleness.[13]

The same themes traveled from the movement's literature to congressional debate on the Wilderness Act. When supporters entered a canonical statement of wilderness values into the *Congressional Record,* they selected Zahniser's essay "Our World and Its Wilderness," which, like his *Sierra Bulletin* excerpt, was devoted mostly to the ethics of ecological awareness.[14] Encounters with wild country, he argued, would keep Americans "in touch with the fundamental reality of the universe of which we are a part," aware of their status as "dependent members of this great community of all life," and alert to "our human existence as spiritual creatures nurtured and sustained by and from the great community of life on this earth."[15] This awareness would induce "a sense of ourselves as a responsible part of a continuing community of life," and would give us "the understanding to deal wisely with all the resources of the earth."[16]

It is a curious feature of environmental politics, and wilderness advocacy in particular, that its rhetorical fidelity to the past can trick an observer into overlooking how innovative it is, and how unrecognizable its "past" would have been to those who actually lived in the past. In this respect, environmental politics resembles many religious traditions and the constitutional politics of the United States: it continuously crafted a usable past, then hurriedly covered up the signs of effort. Wilderness advocates, like other conservationists, often invoked their movement's symbolic ancestors, above all John Muir and Henry David Thoreau. This backward genuflection obscured the innovation and democratic energy that brought Romantic themes ever closer to the center of environmental public language between the 1890s and the 1970s. It also obscured how much wilderness advocates and other political ecologists recast Romantic themes through their advocacy. Muir and his allies worked hard to create the public mood that could receive Thoreau as a prophet of wilderness, rather than of the multifarious and much more psychological "wildness"—let alone as the picturesque observer of nature that his contemporary reviewers and first generation of canonizers made him out to be. It took another great exercise in imagination and persuasion to arrive where Leopold, Zahniser, and their allies led the wilderness movement: to an ecological view of nature that prized humility.

The wilderness movement shifted Muir's meaning in hindsight, as he had shifted Thoreau's. Today, Muir is probably best remembered for observing that one cannot tug at anything in nature without finding it connected to everything else—a folksy slogan of interdependence. That, however, is not the Muir whose acolytes created the Sierra Club: their Muir was a high-country pilgrim, a surveyor of nature's sublime temples, which he saw as important not because they were interdependent with lowland human habitats, but because they were radically apart. Our Muir, like our Thoreau, has been recast as part of a usable history for the age of ecology.

The ideal relation to nature here is two-sided and defined by its doubleness. We can love the world because it is intelligible, formed in an order that we can understand ever more richly. At the same time, it awes us because it is always older, stranger, and more complex than we can grasp: in every dimension, it runs beyond our reach. Ecological consciousness both enriches our understanding of what we know and attunes us to what is unknown and mysterious. The world is a web of knowable relations set amid mystery, and it repays attention by deepening our appreciation of both qualities. This was the new, ecological shape that wilderness advocates gave to the Romantic tradition of treating the politics of nature as a politics of consciousness.

The ethic of "humility" had several aspects. Humility was part of wonder: the mind, in the face of what it could not know, stilled its quest for mastery and settled into partial knowledge of a world only partially knowable. Humility admitted that a part of knowledge was to know the limits of knowledge. Humility had a practical aspect, too, which the emphasis on "dependence" captured. It was beyond the power of humans to be perfect masters of complex and fragile nature. They came from and returned to the earth, could not go on without it, and could not entirely choose the terms of their relation to it. Indeed, the very idea that humans were essentially apart from earth, sojourners or governors here, obscured the fact that they were dependent on it. Humility invited a homecoming—not to the sublime mountains, as Muir had urged, but to a sense of being entirely native to the planet at large.

According to advocates, wilderness supported these ecological values in several ways. Undeveloped land showed nature working in freedom and fullness, without the simplifications that human use imposed. The ban on development and motor transport in wilderness areas was a relinquishing of mastery. Going technologically naked into the woods was an embrace of dependence on nature.

Even though it served wilderness advocacy, the ideal of ecological humility could easily apply in other places. Wilderness was the touchstone; but humility and openness to nature might be present anywhere. These changes would bear more political fruit in the later 1960s and 1970s, when the politics of nature took a new direction. The natural world returned to the center of American self-interpretation, becoming a key to diagnosing national discontents and, for some, a way of healing those. Americans concerned with the natural world did nothing less in those years than invent something we now take for granted: the concept of *the environment*. The nascent version of environmental imagination that centered on awareness, interdependence, and humility was an important source of this invention.

In 1968, an urgent warning appeared in *Time* magazine: "The false assumption that nature exists only to serve man is at the root of an ecological crisis that ranges from the lowly litterbug to the lunacy of nuclear proliferation. At this hour, man's only choice is to live in harmony with nature, not to conquer it."[17] Two years later, the *Sierra Club Bulletin* published a faux-naïve parable, "A Fable for Our Times," which recalled the fate of "a small, beautiful, green and graceful country called Vietnam." According to the fable, Vietnam "needed to be saved," though "in later years no one could remember exactly what it needed to be saved from." A would-be heroic country called America tried to play savior.

> Sadly, America had one fatal flaw—its inhabitants were in love with technology and thought it could do no wrong. A visitor to America during the time of this story would probably have guessed its outcome after seeing how its inhabitants were treating their own country. The air was mostly foul, the water putrid, and most of the land was either covered with concrete or garbage. But Americans were never much on introspection and they didn't foresee the result of their loving embrace on the small country. They set out to save Vietnam with the same enthusiasm and determination their forefathers had displayed in conquering the frontier. They bombed. . . . Thousands of herbicide and defoliant missions

were flown before anyone seriously questioned their long-range effect on humans and animals as well as plants. By the time deformed fetuses began appearing and signs of lasting ecological damage were becoming apparent, success had been achieved. Vietnam had been saved. But the country was dead.[18]

More than forty years later, a reader may feel some impatience with *Time*'s now-clichéd warnings of "ecological crisis" and calls for "harmony with nature," and with the pious tone of the Sierra Club's fable. One decade's cliché, however, is an earlier decade's watershed. These passages announce a new way of thinking about nature and humans' place in it. We still live in this picture of the world, the ecological picture, and are still working out its meaning for ethics, economics, politics, and law. The age of ecology catches us midstream—and it is itself the stream.

What are its elements? Consider again the passage from *Time*. The magazine's editors supposed that tossing a bottle from a car window and building apocalyptic weapons were more similar than different. For that thought to make sense, the reader's mental landscape must include the idea of *ecological issues* or *environmental problems*—a category that spans the beauty of a wilderness landscape, invisible pollution in a city neighborhood, the fossil-fuel economy, the extinction of species, roadside littering, and the looming threat that life on earth might end. The list alone suggests that "the environment" is not exactly an unavoidable way to sort the world. Indeed, it is not an idea that would have occurred to members of the early Sierra Club as a way of uniting their aesthetic response to "wild" nature, their everyday consumption, any misgivings they held about the industrial economy, and their views of geopolitics. They prized the remote and spectacular over the settled and mechanical; Yosemite elevated them, and some of them disliked shops and factories (though most lived in cities). But that thread of judgment did not make factories, mountain valleys, and urban neighborhoods part of one thing: "ecology" or "the environment." The environment, the wholeness of the world, had to be named, and in some measure invented, before people could think of it as endangered and aim to save it.

The discovery or invention (of course it was some of both) of the environment was only part of this change. Consider again the Sierra Club's Vietnam fable. What makes it faux-naïve, besides its tone, is the way it leaves aside international affairs, domestic politics, and political ideology, and recounts a kind of fairy tale in which the sole wicked source of trouble is technology-loving hubris. This simplistic attitude is normal in a morality tale; here an idea of nature has become the moral master narrative, able to organize vice and virtue, hubris and comeuppance. Americans' attitude to nature, in this story, was the pivot of national destiny. Because this idea made sense to the *Bulletin*'s readers, the (anonymous) writer could recast the Vietnam War as a symptom of runaway love of technology, then ascribe an American environmental crisis to the same sin. These two quite different situations could then become part of the same deeper problem: faith in chemicals, machines, and human mastery, in ignorant defiance of nature's order, delicacy, and limits. Once invented, the environmental crisis could encompass many crises.

Earlier views of nature had also been deeply moralized. The settlers of the nineteenth-century frontier, clearing and sowing a continental garden, took to heart John Locke's insistence that "God wants us to do something" and that nature revealed the intended tasks. For the conservationists of the Progressive era, managing nature required a combination of civic spirit and administrative expertise—which were also the defining elements of their larger political program and vision of social reform. And for the Romantics who created the Sierra Club, nature's beauty was evidence that awe and admiration, not just usefulness, were parts of the human purpose. God wanted us not just to do something, but also to stand there—and look.[19]

What moral image of nature rose with the ecological age? Part of the answer is that interconnection between people and the rest of the natural world came to seem deeper and more important. Ecology studies interdependence, the interaction between organisms and their environments—including humans and the worlds we half-find, half-make. In the ecological perspective, all natural systems, including the bodies of living things, are linked and interpermeable. In Rachel Carson's *Silent Spring* (1962) toxins released into the air pass through wind, water, soil, and the flesh of animals, and finally return to human tissue. Aldo Leopold's writing worked toward a poetics of ecology, inviting readers to imagine the world as viewed by an atom that passes through many organisms, sometimes "alive" in plants and animals and sometimes "lifeless" in soil and streams, moving through the long currents of deep time. In this view, the basic fact of the world is not that we are separate, coherent entities, but rather that we are formed of common elements that join to compose us, then separate to play another part.

At the beginning of the ecological era, then, interdependence seemed both inspiring and ominous. There was widespread fear of a public-health emergency, a "poisoned world" that would sicken humans and broader ecosystems alike.[20] This threat could expand to become apocalyptic: in 1970 the *New York Times* envisioned a world "as devoid of life as the mountains of the moon," and the paper's environmental reporter warned that the world might become uninhabitable.[21] These threats were vaster by orders of magnitude than the worst environmental prospects of earlier times. For conservationists like Gifford Pinchot, the earth was a storehouse or farmer's field, and the problem was that, with poor management, it would run short. Now the earth was a kind of super-organism, and the threat was of systemic failure. The ecological idea of the earth as a living world invited the bleak thought of a lifeless planet.

Where did these ideas come from? The ecological worldview was not so much new as newly composed of mostly old elements. The term "ecology"—which, as we've seen, is a neologism deriving from the Greek *oikos,* for "household"—was the coinage of Ernst Haeckel, a nineteenth-century German naturalist and speculative "natural philosopher." The image of the world as intensely interdependent went back centuries in the Christian apologetics of the "natural theologians" and in the worried polemics of George Perkins Marsh and his followers, who understood, for instance, that felling forests denied habitat to birds that, in turn, controlled pests. Leopold, Carson, and the generation that followed them augmented Marsh's description of interdependence with the Romantic ideas that nature mattered in itself and contained lessons essential to the human spirit. Understanding the natural world, for them, gave us more than tips for prudent management: nature was a tutor in enlightened consciousness. Gifford Pinchot would have disagreed sharply, and George Perkins Marsh would have been nonplussed at best. But John Muir and, for that matter, Madison Grant would have said much the same thing. The bearers of ecological ideas combined the conservationists' description of nature with the Romantics' way of valuing it. Of course, in doing so, they intensified some parts of earlier ideas, changed others, and set some aside. Nonetheless, the ecological perspective was continuous with the older views, as well as a synthesis of the two.

The ecological perspective also responded to changes in brute material reality, changes that were impinging on American awareness in the decades after World War II. The country's resource use—its environmental footprint—was increasing at a pace like the one seen in China today. The new environmentalists were not only seeing the world through a finer lens than others had done—although writers like Rachel Carson were surely doing that; they were also documenting the result of Americans' releasing far more toxins into winds and waterways than they had ever done before.

any one of the integral parts of the planet's chemistry and "the earth will die—will become as dead as the moon." These were the themes that, twenty years later, would be suddenly ubiquitous in the national conversation: nature as an interdependent system, human power as an epochal disruptor of its harmonies, and the dangers of ecological collapse and mass extinction—even (Osborn seemed to hint) the extinction of humanity itself. Writing in the wake of World War II, Osborn called man's "destroying his own life sources . . . that other, silent world-wide 'war.'"[22]

Osborn's prescription, too, was proto-environmentalist. He regretted that "[man] has failed so far to recognize that he is a child of the earth and that, this being so, he must for his own survival work with nature in understanding rather than in conflict." Like Leopold, he urged his readers to appreciate the brief span of human civilization: the universe was vast, time was deep, and if we hoped to survive in our fragment of it, we would have to understand that "human life on this earth . . . is but an element in the great scheme of nature" and must conform to nature's standards. He shared with Leopold a great emphasis on the vital importance of soil to life and the need to preserve earth's fertility. Osborn also gave in capsule form the argument about the dangers of pesticide, specifically DDT, that Carson would later make an emblem of the ecological imagination. He explained that DDT could move through the food web, from its insect targets to birds, fishes, and reptiles, finally jeopardizing "the life scheme of the earth." If insects had to be controlled, he argued, it should be by means resembling nature's own measures, such as preserving natural predators; above all, we should bear in mind their presumed importance within "the relatedness of all living things."[23] Carson ended *Silent Spring* with a call for precisely this kind of nature-modeled insect control as an alternative to pesticides.

What distinguishes Osborn's contribution to ecological thinking is his deep pessimism about humanity, which he seems to have inherited in part from earlier theories of racial decline. *Our Plundered Planet* is very much a book about ecology. It is also, quite emphatically, a book about population. The first line of its preface is about the harmony of the "good earth," and the first line of the main text is an image of the 175,000 newborns who, according to Osborn, were coming into the world each day. As he states in his conclusion, the book's basic argument describes a pincer action between two forces: "The tide of the earth's population is rising, the reservoir of the earth's living resources is falling." This situation, Osborn insists, gives the lie to such humanitarian hopes as the Franklin Roosevelt slogan, "Freedom from Want": he declares this "an illusory hope" unless we can limit our pressure on the planet by respecting "the enduring processes of nature." One of Osborn's most striking remarks is: "It is difficult to adjust one's mind to the possibility that . . . the problem of the pressure of increasing population—perhaps the greatest problem facing humanity today—cannot be solved in a way that is consistent with the principles of humanity."[24] What other principles might be more compatible with "the enduring processes of nature" Osborn does not say, but his warnings of extinction give a clear enough picture.

It was a misanthropic sentiment, not just in its deep skepticism toward humanitarianism, but also in a certain grim eagerness to condemn human optimism in the name of the natural limits humanity had supposedly violated. Reflecting on Fairfield Osborn may remind former students of philosophy of a passage in the *Genealogy of Morals* where Friedrich Nietzsche purports to find hatred at the root of Christianity's doctrine of love—suppressed and redirected, but hatred nonetheless. Why, he asks, do Saint Thomas Aquinas and the Church Father Tertullian write with such energy of the punishments of Hell, if they are not secretly elated to see the proud, lustful, and wholly *alive* pagans wrung on the rack of the Christian God?[25] Is a similar spirit lurking in Osborn's oblique, portentous passages about how nature answers those who disregard her? Is it present in his willingness to set aside "the principles of humanity" as sentimental error?

Maybe so. In any event, it is clear that the older, eugenicist strain of disgust at disorderly, overbreeding humanity did not disappear after World War II. In 1962 Fairfield Osborn's uncle, Frederick H. Osborn, contributed to a collection of essays on the global population crisis, edited by his nephew. In his piece, Frederick Osborn remarked tellingly on the modern strategy of the "geneticist," or eugenicist. "If he is wise," Osborn wrote, today's eugenicist "will not introduce the genetic argument," because people "don't like to admit" the importance of genetic differences.[26] Instead, he should hope that "population pressures may bring about genetic reform by intensifying the problems of civilization and forcing us to seek new solutions."[27] Here is the old eugenics, gone underground in the movement to control population growth, and casting about for new allies.

The persistence of the Osborns, linking ecology genealogically to Madison Grant just as Aldo Leopold ties it to John Muir, is not an indictment but a reminder that ecological imagination carried forward two troubling strands of earlier politics. It involved, like certain moments in conservationist and Romantic thinking, a fiercely misanthropic pessimism about human beings and hints of satisfaction at the thought of their comeuppance. And, like earlier versions of environmental imagination, it simply assumed that certain kinds of Americans were specially tied to, and qualified to interpret and advocate for, the natural world. This assumption showed up in the scope of "environmental" issues. From the beginning, it seemed obvious that suburban poisonings and the loss of tourist-friendly charismatic species were both environmental problems, bound together in ecological thinking; but it took much longer for the asthma afflicting urban children to emerge as an equally serious environmental issue. For that matter, workplace chemical exposure has never commanded anything like the same "environmental" status as pollution that threatens prosperous homes. When some environmental activists and observers drew attention to the heavy and often neglected burdens on poor, working-class, and minority communities, their emphasis on "environmental justice" was unmistakably a change and challenge to a movement that was radical in some respects, but also rather comfortably mainstream in its constituency and priorities.

Ecology teaches that everything is connected, but the politics of ecology has always insisted, sometimes silently, that some things, and some connections, count more than others—among places and species, and among human beings. This particularism, with its exclusions, has been part of the American politics of nature from the beginning. As the Anthropocene radicalizes ecological awareness into a fully democratic politics of nature, the chance to question these limits in environmental imagination is as great as it has ever been. As always, the first step is to have them in view.

Opening a New Door

Left, right, and eccentric, hopeful and despairing, the secular prophets and mass-media commentators who created a popular ecology were responding to the anxieties and hopes of the time, taking energy from what people wished for and what they feared. The destruction wreaked by the Vietnam War suggested to many that technocratic mastery had become self-consuming. The threat of nuclear conflict, which had loomed so large in the 1950s and 1960s, did the same. Many Americans were newly prepared to accept a moral story in which, as *Time* put it in 1968, "technological man, master of the atom and soon the moon, is so aware of his strength that he is unaware of his weakness—the fact that his pressure on nature may provoke revenge."[28] *Time* went further two years later, describing "technological man as the personification of Faust, endlessly pursuing the unattainable."[29] To those who suspected contemporary society was basically misguided, it made sense that environmental crisis should be rooted in distorted values and identity, and that the answer would have to come on those levels. *Time* once more: "Behind the environment crisis in the U.S. are a few deeply ingrained assumptions . . . that nature exists primarily for man to conquer . . . [and] that nature is endlessly bountiful." In short, the crisis stemmed from "a dedication to infinite growth on a finite planet."[30]

The new idea of ecology also promised a unifying challenge for a divided time. In his 1970 State of the Union address, President Richard Nixon argued that environmental responsibility could unite Americans split over race and war.[31] Picking up the cue, *Time* described the environmental crisis as an attractive "problem which American skills . . . might actually solve, unlike the immensely more elusive problems of race prejudice or the war in Viet Nam."[32] From the beginning of the ecological era, some radical observers mistrusted environmentalism precisely because it seemed to promise easy consensus. It struck them as, John Schaar and Sheldon Wolin remarked, an issue "around which the hippies and the Hickels [a reference to Nixon's Secretary of the Interior, Walter Hickel] might unite . . . in common cause with the power elite."[33] Schaar and Wolin continued: "It is the kind of issue which is particularly appealing when the disappointments and abrasions of political encounters become too much, for it permits a full catharsis of moral indignation without seriously altering the structure of power or the logic of the system."[34] To these critics, environmentalism was a kind of fantasy cause, rich in seeming moral urgency, light in practical demands.

Besides the threat of disaster and diagnosis of hubris, ecology offered a familiar appeal: a path to spiritual health and clarity. In early 1970s environmentalists began asserting that "ecology [which yesterday] was a science . . . had better become something like a religion"[35] and calling for a "cultural transformation" around "personal commitment to a new philosophy and poetry of ecology."[36] The promise was that awareness of a web of ecological ties could enrich self-knowledge and one's relations to others. Buddhist popularizer Alan Watts argued that the links among all things meant that "our whole knowledge of the world is, in one sense, self-knowledge."[37] Paul Shepard wrote in *The Subversive Science,* a 1969 treatment of the politics and ethics of ecology, that "we must affirm nature's metabolism as our own" and that "the world is a being, a part of our own body."[38]

The ecological perspective, like other views of nature, bears the stamp of the time when it was born—both the hopes and anxieties of the moment, and the scientific and practical facts that seemed most urgent then. It acknowledged the perplexity of the human predicament: *homo sapiens* is at once acutely vulnerable and the most powerful actor on an interdependent planet. That perplexity is the setting of all our acts, and of our reflections on how to live in a beautiful, devastated, resilient, fragile world that nurtures and threatens, inspires and alienates us.

Ecology: From New Dawn to Chronic Crisis

Toward the end of his 1971 book, *A Theory of Justice,* the political philosopher John Rawls turned briefly to the topic of "right conduct in regard to animals and the rest of nature." *A Theory of Justice* is widely regarded as the most important work of political philosophy in the past seventy years, but Rawls's remarks here were not part of the book's general argument about "fair terms of social cooperation," which launched decades of debate about distributive justice and political legitimacy. The question of nature was about something else. What was that? Rawls asserted that "a correct conception of our relations to animals and to nature" would depend on "metaphysics," which he defined as "a theory of the natural order and our place in it."[39]

A towering figure in political philosophy, Rawls had a gift for seeing to the heart of an issue. But for all its pursuit of timeless truths, philosophy tends to distill the premises of the moment. The late 1960s and early 1970s were a peculiar cultural moment, when many people saw "environmental values" as radical on the one hand and, on the other hand, as likely points of consensus. Such ideas found expression in the law courts, academic forums, national politics, media, and social movements. Lynton Caldwell, whose proposal for a national environmental-planning regime formed the basis of the National Environmental Policy Act, presented this statute as placing an "ecological" way of thinking at the heart of U.S. law. He contrasted ecological thinking, which adjusted human purposes to honor the interdependence of life, with "economic" thinking, which "ma[d]e nature serve man's material needs."[40] (This is particularly striking today, when NEPA is regarded as an almost entirely procedural law, which requires federal agencies to produce lengthy reports before major decisions but imposes no particular values on those choices.) In another landmark argument of the time, law professor Christopher Stone proposed that natural entities such as trees, rivers, valleys, and animals should have standing—that is, the right to have lawsuits brought in their name—because it might contribute to "a radical new theory or myth . . . of man's relationships to the rest of nature . . . . [in which] we may come to regard the Earth . . . as one organism."[41] Mainstream institutions and forums were suddenly open, for the first time, to arguments that ecology must turn from a science to a civic religion, or at least a new definition of citizenship.

Environmentalists of the day were beginning to advance legal arguments that would have been very difficult to make without this impression of an emerging consensus. Take the seminal environmental-standing case, *Sierra Club v. Morton*. Here, the Supreme Court considered whether the Sierra Club could sue to oppose development in California's Mineral King Valley, and ruled that the group had standing to appear in court only if at least one of its members used the disputed area and would be personally affected by the proposed development. The case is most famous, though, for Justice William O. Douglas's animist-toned dissent, which adopted the language and spirit of proposals to recognize natural entities as legal actors: "The river as plaintiff speaks for the ecological unit of life that is part of it. . . . The voice of the inanimate object, therefore, should not be stilled."[42] Less well remembered, because less colorful, is Justice Harry Blackmun's dissent, which called for "an imaginative expansion of our traditional concepts of standing" in light of the urgency of environmental problems and the "sincere, dedicated, and established status" of the Sierra Club with respect to conservation.[43] Justice Blackmun argued for granting more or less automatic standing to groups such as the Sierra Club because, as several federal appeals courts had recently concluded, these conservation advocates were agents of the public interest.[44] Such legal opinions were possible (though their proposals failed) because there was widespread perception of a clear, definite public interest in environmental protection. Whether the courts called the representatives of that interest "the river as plaintiff" or regarded the Sierra Club as a private advocate of public values, honoring the natural world *just meant* supporting the emerging environmentalist position.

A spate of new environmental lawmaking expressed this fleeting sense of a new national consensus. The National Environmental Policy Act became law on New Year's Day 1970, the Clean Air Act later the same year (with substantial amendments in 1977), the Clean Water Act in 1972, and the Endangered Species Act in 1973. The new laws expressed both urgency and optimism: the challenge was difficult, but lawmakers and commentators agreed that the country could embrace the new ecological paradigm—not just pragmatically, but at the level of value and identity. Senator Edmund Muskie of Maine, the most prominent congressional environmentalist of the decade, compared the fight for clean air to the struggles of World War II or the Space Race; he called pollution control "a national objective more serious than either" of those earlier struggles, and warned that "Man, no less than the peregrine falcon or the mountain lion, is an endangered species."[45] Other lawmakers agreed that a complex, fragile global ecology was under dangerous assault. According to Congressman Charles Vanik of Ohio, "If we continue to allow harmful discharges and the waste of resources—even small amounts—we will continue to rapidly disrupt, in ways which we do not now understand, the natural balance of the world—a balance that evolved over billions of years and which supports all living things, including ourselves. . . . We can destroy the sea. Similarly, we can destroy the delicate balance of the world's atmosphere. That destruction is happening every hour of every day."[46] These statements from the Senate and House floor reflect all the themes that popular ecology had gathered over the previous decade: complexity, fragility, the limits of human knowledge, and the possibility that natural systems could collapse, making the world uninhabitable even for human beings.

Ecology seemed to be the key to solving problems as well as to diagnosing them. Senator Muskie called the Clean Water Act a "decision to recognize fundamental principles of ecology."[47] Senator John Sherman Cooper of Kentucky agreed, saying that the bill "asserts the primacy of the natural order, on which all, including man, depends"; he went on to argue that the "underlying theme" of the Clean Water Act was "to rely on the natural order."[48] We have already seen that claims like these were typical of the popular ecology of the time: by understanding the lessons of ecology, people could solve the same problems that ecological interconnection had created. In 1971 *Time* predicted that "by changing national values, [environmentalism] may well spur a profound advance in U.S. maturity and harmony with nature."[49] Flora Lewis, a doyenne of establishment liberal opinion, urged Americans to heed ecological lessons that were "so fundamentally new, so drastically opposed to the heritage of many centuries, they are painful to absorb."[50]

Members of Congress voiced optimism that Americans could absorb these lessons and change their lives. Senator Muskie declared, "The whole intent of [the Clean Water Act] is to make a national commitment" and warned that the Clean Air Act would "be a test of our commitment and a test of our faith . . . in the ability of Americans to rise to the challenge of ending the threat of air pollution." The Clean Air Act, he argued, would "require that the American motorist change his habits, his tastes, and driving appetites."[51] Senator Cooper went further: the Clean Air Act would "place great burdens on the people generally" and would "not succeed without a massive effort . . . [by] citizens throughout the country to make the sacrifices necessary and to pay the price of accomplishing the goals of clean air."[52] The *New York Times* editorial board agreed, writing that "New Yorkers are going to have to adjust to some possibly shocking changes in their way of life" under the Clean Air Act.[53] Some of this may seem to be just standard hortatory rhetoric, and there is something to that deflationist response to any political speech or newspaper editorial; it hardly needs saying that these are the paradigms of clichéd urgency and vague exhortation. Nonetheless, the burst of environmental lawmaking in the 1970s displays the belief, among legislators and observers, that something new was happening: not just insight into new problems that required new solutions, but also a new ethical and political spirit for a new view of the natural world.

The hope for a new and unifying American relation to nature did not last long. It gave way to a fragmented politics that remained entangled in the legacies of the past. Instead of harmonious unity, the new generation of environmental laws produced two kinds of conflict. One was internal to the workings of the laws themselves: they could not do all they promised, so a new set of hard choices came to the fore. The second kind of conflict was between the constituencies of the new ecological laws and those that remained invested in earlier American approaches to the natural world. Both kinds of conflict lent themselves to an unexpected development: the rise of cost-benefit analysis as the dominant language of environmental law and policy, and of economics as a sort of master-science for ecological management.

The laws set unreachable goals of nonpolluting, noninvasive human harmony with the natural world. The Endangered Species Act (ESA), for instance, prohibits harm to endangered species and to their "critical habitat" in a way that assumes human beings can save everything, if only we limit our incursions into ecologically important places. This proved unrealistic. The human impact on habitat is so pervasive that, in practice, the question is not how to save everything, but what to save and why, a question the ESA gives scant help in addressing. As climate change shifts habitat zones, preserving species becomes a matter of active management—for instance, moving animal populations from region to region or creating pathways for migration so that species in jeopardy can move themselves. The ESA, which works mostly by forbidding harm to species and habitats as we find them, provides few tools for this kind of work.

Other environmental laws set their own unattainable goals. The Clean Water Act required that by 1983 all United States waterways should be clean enough for fishing and swimming, and that by 1985 all water pollution should have come to an end. This extraordinary goal reflected the ideal of restoring a "natural order." Sounding a strongly moral note, Senator Muskie and Congressman Vanik announced that "streams and rivers are no longer to be considered part of the waste treatment process" and that "the use of any river, lake, stream, or ocean as a waste treatment system is unacceptable. In other words, no one has the right to pollute."[54]

It is important not to impute too much naïveté to those who wrote the new environmental laws. Congressional sponsors understood that they were setting their bar very high. They explicitly rejected trimming their goals to more feasible measures; they hoped that ambitious regulation would spur innovation, making pollution control cheaper and easier than expected. Some of this has happened, and the major environmental laws are widely seen as having cost the country much less than was expected when they passed. Just as important, though, was some lawmakers' conviction that setting a national commitment, even one that went beyond what was then feasible, would establish new values for the country, while more modest statutes would, in effect, reinforce business-as-usual. Indignantly rejecting an amendment that would have added a pollution tax to the Clean Water Act, Senator Howard Baker of Tennessee warned that economic incentives blurred the line between moral obligations and economic convenience: "I do not accept the implication . . . that the people of the United States are more willing to abide by an Internal Revenue statute than by a categorical prohibition."[55] Senator Muskie chimed in to remind the chamber of the act's moral purpose: "We cannot give anyone the option of polluting for a fee. We are saying that our aim is to have no discharge."[56] If the new laws created a right to a clean environment, as the sponsors liked to say, and recognized a moral obligation to the natural world, then these "national commitments" should not be negotiable in terms of the marginal dollar.

Soon enough, though, these considerations began to seem quixotic. Once tradeoffs became unavoidable, the statutes made easy targets for aggressive economic criticism. The Clean Air Act, for instance, required the EPA to set air pollution limits with reference to human health alone, regardless of economic cost. This proved impossible to do. Once one accepts that no unpolluted world is available, there is always a decision to define "health" at a cutoff point that implicitly balances it against other values.

Environmental economics thus became the coin of the realm. At its most abstract, economic analysis is simply the systematic consideration of tradeoffs like the one between health and the cost of air-pollution controls. As environmental law moved from legislation, which centrally involves setting national goals, to administration, which requires balancing goals that have already been established, such tradeoffs became the heart of its activity. Any priority had to be expressed in terms of how much of something else it required giving up—how much timber or coal for a park, how much economic growth for pollution control, how much farmland for endangered species habitat, and so forth. Being explicit about these inescapable choices meant thinking of the most sublime ecological commitment and the most mundane economic benefit as coins in the same currency, to be traded off against each other. Anything else seemed fatally impractical.

Economics-minded reformers tended to miss the irony: their corrections and technical improvements could get traction only because the first generation of environmental lawmakers had succeeded so well in establishing a new set of national commitments. Because environmental quality had high status as a public value, reforms that improved the laws pursuing it were presumptively important. The reformers did not have to argue for or establish their goals; they only had to show a shorter path to the goals that others had worked to put in place. The very laws that they often criticized as impractical embodied and helped to create the social valuations of nature that the reformers' economic analyses presupposed.

That reminder of how much the early environmentalist lawmakers succeeded is only half the story. They also failed dramatically to establish a new consensus on national values. At least part of the reason is that they imagined they were discovering the theme of Americans' relation to the natural world, when in fact they were revisiting it in a fourth generation. Ecology came after the managerial conservationism of the Progressives, the Romantic preservation movement, and the providential ideology of settler republicanism. Each of these had its vital legacies in the United States of the 1970s. These legacies resided in the older laws and institutions that interacted with the new environmental laws; in political constituencies attached to older visions of nature, not least by financial benefit from grazing, mining, and so forth; and in ideals and forms of identity that were tied to pre-ecological ways of imagining the natural world and the human place in it.

The environmental laws of the 1970s had a new design, founded on the ecological premise of radical interconnection, which created new kinds of conflict among constituencies. From 1785, when Congress passed the first major act to sell frontier land to settlers, through the 1964 Wilderness Act, major legislation shared a design principle: continental zoning. Those laws allocated tracts of land to private ownership or public management, the latter of these by creating parks, national forests, and wilderness areas and finally by closing the remaining public domain to further privatization. Each vision of nature claimed its acreage, and relatively little thought went into cross-border interactions among zones and their dedicated uses. (The major exception is awareness of erosion, which helped to inspire forest preservation at the headwaters of many western rivers and canal systems.)

By contrast, the new anti-pollution statutes set out to govern "media" such as air and water that connect all places—and that can carry toxins wherever they go. This meant environmental regulation of private industry and property, largely for the first time. An area of law that had mainly addressed the government's management of public lands now aimed at the environmental effects of the whole economy. The Clean Air and Clean Water acts inserted their requirements directly into industrial operations, involving federal and state officials in the running of power plants, chemical facilities, oil refineries, and a panoply of smaller-scale polluters. The Endangered Species Act and the wetlands-preservation requirements of the Clean Water Act imposed the first meaningful federal limits on property owners' right to develop their land. The Toxic Substances Control Act, laws governing processing of hazardous waste and the use of pesticides, and the battleship of a toxins cleanup law that is (un)popularly called Superfund, brought environmental law to the heart of everyday life in an industrial society. These laws aimed to control the levels of toxins that ended up in the bodies of workers and suburb-dwellers in a world with so much man-made poison that no place was pristine.

Old, influential constituencies had long profited economically from natural resources and taken identity and pride from the ways that they worked the land. Farmers, ranchers, miners, and other resource users had long been the darlings of public rhetoric, invited to believe themselves the economic and moral linchpins of the nation. These groups enjoyed access to public lands for mining, grazing, and timbering, and extensive liberty to do as they liked on private land. When they reasserted their traditional prerogatives in the first modern anti-environmental movement, the Sagebrush Rebellion of the late 1970s and 1980s, these traditional resource-users gave notice that older views of nature were not going away. Moreover, they formed alliances with business interests that had begun to resist regulation with new aggressiveness, leaving behind a relatively consensual approach that had been regnant for several decades. Anti-regulatory voices entered the heart of public debate, from lobbying and campaign contributions to litigation and think tanks, making the impression of a pro-conservation consensus impossible to maintain.

One of the spurs for the Sagebrush Rebellion, the western move-ment of the 1970s dedicated to private property-rights and local management of public lands, was the announcement that ranchers' permits for grazing cattle on federal land would be subject to review under the National Environmental Policy Act. This sharp encounter between a Progressive-era policy of regulated economic use and an ecological-era statute imposing intensive environmental oversight disrupted a long-established pattern in which the Bureau of Land Management treated grazing permits as something close to entitlements. Similar resistance has sprung up from Western farmers where the Endangered Species Act has broken up the tradi-tional pro-development and pro-agriculture priorities of the Bu-reau of Reclamation, requiring it to dedicate publicly managed water to habitat preservation rather than irrigation.

Economics' promise of objectivity is especially attractive when decision makers are seeking neutrality among competing values, because costs and benefits measured in dollars seem uncontrover-sial compared to differences in worldview and identity. So growing conflict between the constituencies of the new environmental laws and those of predecessor statutes put the appearance of neutrality at a premium for both decision makers and scholars. For those charged with administering new laws, the challenge was now to maintain legitimacy through a mode of decision making that seemed to transcend and integrate divided values: economic analysis and, in particular, cost-benefit analysis, with its attempt to tally the good and bad effects of a proposal in a single, incon-trovertible bottom line.

Intergenerational Legal Interpretation in the Ecological Age

These conflicts also presented challenges for legal interpretation. The problem for judges was to integrate different generations of environmental lawmaking, with very different premises about the natural world and the human place in it, into a single skein of law. The biggest legal legacy of settler republicanism is the private property that dominates the U.S. landscape east of the Rocky Mountains. The longstanding premise of private property was that owners could exploit it as they thought best. Other than reciprocal limits that protect neighbors from one another's intrusions, such as doctrines barring "nuisances," most environmental regulation of private property is the product of laws passed in the 1970s and later.

This tradition of broad property rights, associated with images of self-reliance and autonomy, is the legal basis, and the moral and political subtext, of much resistance to federal environmental regulation. This resistance is salient in cases decided under the Takings Clause and the Commerce Clause of the U.S. Constitution, which play out the continuing struggle between settler-republican visions of land use and those that begin from ecological interdependence. In *Lucas v. South Carolina Coastal Council,* which ruled that the government must compensate owners when environmental regulations block all economically beneficial use of their land, Justice Antonin Scalia wrote that the "erection of . . . habitable or productive improvements on . . . land" is its "essential use" and so enjoys presumptive constitutional protection.[57] As was the case throughout the long history of settler republicanism, the paradigmatic human relation to a piece of land is that people settle on it and develop it. In an echo of earlier settler resistance to federal land management, Justice Scalia referred to the Army Corps of Engineers as having the "discretion of an enlightened despot" in its control over property owners' use of their wetlands.[58] By contrast, in the same cases, dissenting justices insisted that the old ideal—an autonomous owner on a piece of land—must yield to the "constant learning and evolution—both moral and practical" that have driven modern environmental law, as "new appreciation of the significance of endangered species, the importance of wetlands, and the vulnerability of coastal lands shapes our evolving understand of property rights."[59]

The heart of these cases is the question of how far traditional legal concepts, embedded in the Constitution and throughout the law, should be reinterpreted to accommodate ecological interdependence. In *Lucas v. South Carolina Coastal Council,* the Supreme Court had to decide whether the Fifth Amendment's protection of property rights should continue to protect the development rights that an owner would have enjoyed in the later nineteenth century or whether twentieth-century legislatures could adjust the meaning of "property" in light of new ecological insights and values. This question—how far does the settler view of property remain the constitutional bedrock, and how far may ecological developments revise it?—divided the justices in that case, with Justice Scalia ruling, over adamant dissents, that owners had to be compensated when new laws wiped out traditional rights and left property without economic value.

Similarly, *Rapanos v. United States* decided whether a federal law passed under Congress's power to regulate "commerce among the several states" could stop a property owner from filling in his wetlands for development. Congress's power under the Clean Water Act extended to the "waters of the United States"—a term that, for settlers and others in the early republic, would have meant the waters that could be used as commercial highways, those places where a person could take a boat. The premise of the Clean Water Act, though, was the ecological insight that waters are interconnected in subtle and complex ways that go well beyond navigable surfaces, and environmental regulation—unlike regulation of, say, riverboat commerce—must be able to take account of this. In that case, the Supreme Court narrowly reached a pro-ecological decision, as Justice Anthony Kennedy, who provided the decisive vote, argued that the Clean Water Act applied where there was an ecological connection, such as subterranean seepage, between a wetland and a traditional "navigable water."

Settler republicanism aimed to produce an extractive republic as well as an agrarian one. Congress expressed this commitment in the General Mining Law of 1872, which entitled private individuals to stake mining claims on federal public land and, after establishing mines, to acquire ownership of both the land and the minerals beneath it. Nineteenth-century law also recognized rights to road access across federal public land: from the passage of the 1866 Mining Law to its repeal in 1976, a provision known as Revised Statute (R.S.) 2477 created public access rights wherever people developed the custom of crossing federal land, unless that land had already been reserved for some specific purpose (such as a national park). The Bureau of Land Management has estimated that there are 1.1 million mining claims on federal land, with significant environmental effects. In 2003 a pair of researchers concluded that the state of Utah and its municipalities had claimed public-access rights to upward of 10,000 roads across federal land under R.S. 2477. Mining claims can disrupt recreation or conservation. For instance, during the second George W. Bush administration, a spate of new uranium claims came very near the Grand Canyon; and even outside such dramatic conflicts, mining claims produce water pollution and bring traffic and buildings to otherwise preserved land. Road access under R.S. 2477 can make public land ineligible to become federal wilderness, because wilderness is defined as roadless and undeveloped acreage; this has made R.S. 2477 roads a tactical battleground in fights over expanding wilderness—itself a major flashpoint between partisans of Romantic nature and those committed to economic use.

In deciding whether an R.S. 2477 road exists, courts must choose where to find guidance, and this choice juxtaposes the institutions and procedures of different eras. Will the decision fall to a common-law (usually state) court employing a traditional property-law test to determine whether public use of the claimed road has been regular and extensive enough to establish a lasting easement? Or will the decision belong to the administrators of the Bureau of Land Management, with its mission of balancing competing uses, including recreation, extraction, and environmental preservation, on the model of progressive conservation? The alternatives are the paradigmatic bodies of law of two eras: property law interpreted by a judge, for settler republicanism, and a federal land-use statute administered by an official of the Executive Branch, for conservation. In the event, the appeals court for Utah ruled that the legal standard should be that of property law, and the judgment should belong to courts.[60] This decision kept the principles and institutions of settler republicanism vital in twenty-first century land-use disputes.

Similar issues arise in the interpretation of constitutional standing doctrine, which determines who may bring suit in federal court. Formally speaking, standing doctrine asks whether a plaintiff has a close enough relation to the underlying facts of a dispute for his or her suit to qualify as a "case" (the term appears in Article III of the Constitution), rather than an abstract opinion about policy. This question has had particular bite in suits to enforce environmental law. The Supreme Court has held that, in order to be heard in federal court, a plaintiff must have a concrete injury that has actually happened or is imminent, that stems from the violation of law he or she is complaining of, and that is likely to be corrected by the legal remedy being sought. The model for this standard is a traditional litigant in the world of settler republicanism: someone, for instance, whose property has been intruded upon, and who wants either to expel the intruder or to claim compensation for harm. The trouble is that environmental suits often involve either demands for the government *to regulate* a third party under a law such as the Clean Air Act, or a complaint involving a complex, widely shared, and diffuse problem such as climate change. In both cases, even an interested and informed litigant may strike the court as being too remotely related to the issue to belong in court. It may be hard to show that the would-be plaintiff's concrete, personal interests would be affected much by a court's enforcing the law that the plaintiff wishes to have enforced. This is because the post-1970 environmental statutes were responses to the recognition that many serious problems did not fit the traditional paradigm of an injury: they involved chains of cause and effect too long to trace, or statistical increases in the risk of illness, rather than a direct intrusion on a person or a tract of land. Where standing doctrine keeps the traditional plaintiff at the heart of constitutional doctrine, it can make enforcing these environmental laws much harder than enforcing traditional rights, such as rights in private property.

In *Lujan v. Defenders of Wildlife* (involving a claim under the Endangered Species Act), plaintiffs claimed they could bring suit because they had visited the region where the species at issue lived and hoped to return there in the future, though they had no specific plans. The Supreme Court denied standing and belittled plaintiffs' attempts to expand standing in an ecological fashion to include any plaintiff who worked with members of a given species or with any part of the ecosystem where the species' critical habitat occurred. In *Massachusetts v. EPA,* a suit to enforce the Clean Air Act against greenhouse-gas emissions from new cars, the Court found standing for the state of Massachusetts but did not decide whether any plaintiff that was not a sovereign state could also seek to have a federal court restrict greenhouse gases.[61] Much of the dispute between the five justices who found standing and the four who signed a vehement dissent by Chief Justice John Roberts pivoted on whether climate change, the paradigmatic problem of ecological interdependence, could ever be the basis of standing. Roberts argued that climate change is so diffuse, complex, and uncertain, and draws such a long and tortuous thread between any emission of greenhouse gas and an injury from coastal flooding or changed weather, that it defies two of the core requirements of standing: proof that a plaintiff's injury is traceable to some specific violation of law, and proof that it is likely to be redressed by a remedy a court can provide.

These cases adjudicate between paradigms of the human relation to nature. The controversial standing claims rested on problems that were paradigms for the ecological lawmaking of the 1970s: preserving species that people might not care about or ever see, and addressing the long-distance and complex effects of pollution. By contrast, the conceptions of injury, causation, and redressability that stood in the way of standing rested on an image of the most traditional interests in nature: that of an owner trying to make economic use of his land. Justice Scalia has argued that the purpose of standing doctrine is to honor such plaintiffs, who seek to resist regulatory action in defense of their own personal interests, and to distinguish these from plaintiffs who seek to make the government enforce environmental laws against someone else.[62] This distinction excludes from court the model subject of ecological lawmaking, whose claim rests on interdependence with, or moral and aesthetic investment in, a faraway part of nature. The heart of lawmaking under the ecological paradigm has been the assertion that such interests should not be less legally substantial just because their bases are more abstract and remote than traditional interests. To the contrary, standing doctrine so far has tended to hold that these interests are less weighty than the traditional sort.

One might look at the example of standing in either of two ways. It might seem, on the one hand, to be an exercise in intergenerational synthesis. Courts often labor to integrate the premises of different eras or episodes of lawmaking, producing partial reconciliations that sacrifice aspects of each source of law and often generate approaches not precisely present in any one source. The disputes in these standing cases arise from the sharpness of the break that ecological lawmaking marked from earlier periods. It should not be surprising, then, that when justices weighed the new statutes against traditional ideas about what made a claim justiciable, some found it necessary to trim the courts' role in environmental enforcement to keep standing close to its pre-ecological concepts of injury, causation, and redress.

By contrast, these cases might instead seem a more straightforward political defeat for the premises of ecological interdependence. On this view, the restrictive standing doctrine of *Lujan* is not necessary to preserve any essential part of the judicial role. Rather, federal adjudication is quite compatible with the premises of ecological interdependence—or would be, if not for standing decisions that effectively limit the enforceability of environmental law.

Whichever view one takes, the standing cases and other disputes highlight the layered character of environmental law and of the environmental imagination that law expresses and shapes. Providential republicanism, Romanticism, conservation, and ecology: all four ways of approaching the natural world remain active in the age of ecology, in statutes and doctrines, in constituencies, and in the landscapes that are governed under these overlapping and competing ideas of nature and the human place in it.

The age of ecology, then, has not replaced what came before, but has deepened and complicated the palimpsest of American environmental imagination, law, and politics. Making things even more complicated, the idea of ecology has itself been not one, but several. In the 1960s and early 1970s, ecological imagination was invested in a sharp contrast between natural order (good) and human order (suspect), even though the insights of ecology itself should have cast doubt on this opposition between humanity and the natural world. In the ecological imagination, unspoiled nature was as inspiring as any Romantic landscape, but also reassuring and harmonious, a kind of ecological pastoral. The danger from toxic pollution that traveled across ecological systems was the poisonous fruit of humanity's disconnection from and misuse of nature. But the trouble did not seem irredeemable: a return to "harmony with nature" promised to stem the crisis. Even in the face of apocalyptic warnings about a "poisoned planet" and the end of life on earth, there was hopefulness, even optimism, about getting back on the one true path.

By the 1980s, the tone of the early ecological era had given way to a new mood—of a crisis that was not acute but chronic. Environmental apocalypse had not come. New laws had rolled back the terrifying incidents of wildlife poisonings and burning rivers that had sparked the sense of crisis in the 1960s, and no larger disaster emerged. For most people, life in nature continued much as it had before the crisis was declared. A sense of urgency, a hint of the end times, could not last in the face of unrelenting normality. The mood of crisis receded.

At the same time, many crises came—none apocalyptic, most lingering unresolved: continuing extinctions, the erosion of the ozone layer, the logging of rain forests, and the seemingly endless meanderings of "garbage barges" off the Atlantic coast of the United States, to name just a few signal episodes.[63] Together, these events implied that, while the world was not going to end, neither it nor human life on it would be healed. Crisis, but that crisis had become the normal state of affairs—a low-grade and dispersed crisis, too modest for apocalypse, too disruptive for any pastoral to survive.

So we now find ourselves in a world very different from the one that the age of ecology seemed to open around 1970. Neither the melodrama of ecological apocalypse nor the appeal to ecological harmony is really plausible in a mixed-up, fallen world where pristineness and pollution, ecological connection and technological alienation, are blended and are matters of degree. Paradoxes are common: nature may be as alienating as the fear of Lyme disease, while technology is as integrating as Google Earth. To envision the unified world at many scales simultaneously is an old hope of environmental imagination, but nothing has brought it nearer in practice than satellite imagery and computing—which are also the emblematic technologies of mastery over the planet and of abstraction from any particular place on it. That very abstraction, it turns out, can help us to understand our place on the globe, perhaps more vividly than when we crash through a thicket, then pause, unsure where we are, to check our bare arms and legs for tiny ticks. Paradox, partiality, and the mixed-up character of everything have come after the grasp at wholeness that began the ecological age.

7

ENVIRONMENTAL LAW
IN THE ANTHROPOCENE

RECALL JAMES WILSON'S 1788 INDEPENDENCE DAY speech on freedom, progress, and landscape. Wilson was describing a program of economic development for North America, a program infused with moral and aesthetic value. In his telling, prosperity would arise alongside the virtue and knowledge of citizens and the beauty of the land, as labor and reason drew out the fertile promise of the continent. The economy Wilson envisioned was also a form of life—a way for people to live together in free collaboration, rather than bound by arrogant command on one side and servile obedience on the other. It should foster a certain kind of person: intelligent, curious, ready to take the initiative, neither belligerent nor fearful but steady and competent. Such people could be citizens of a republic, responsible for both personal and public affairs. The earth itself would testify to these good qualities in its orderly, productive fields and orchards.

Delivering his speech at a time when slavery existed in most of the North as well as the South, Wilson was plainly not speaking for all Americans, nor did he have encouraging words for Native Americans who were fighting losing wars for their land; but his images were real for those he addressed. As we have seen, he did not imagine that his ideal American landscape would emerge sponta-neously. It was a national project, ordered by politics and law, that rooted human freedom and discipline in nature's beauty and fer-tility. Wilson's version of the American landscape was thoroughly moralized, as well as thoroughly politicized: he appealed to nature to show how Americans ought to live, and also argued for actively shaping the natural world to achieve the right kind of national life.

This is the circuit of environmental imagination. Ways of valuing and inhabiting the natural world have been woven together from the material stuff of land and resources and from the imagi-native devices of religion, aesthetics, and rhetoric. Law is the warp and weft that binds the two, shaping the material landscape, guiding human action on it, by translating ideal images of people and nature into concrete regimes of power. This is not to say, of course, that law is an idealistic enterprise in any straightforward way. Frequently, what law translates is the strength of material interests: the engines of change are land speculators, miners, ranchers, railroads, elite tourists, suburban voters panicked by a poisoning scare. But even those interests are made partly out of ideals: the dignity of the rancher, the sublime experience of the tourist, the ecological picture of nature that helps the suburbanite see a tie between the soil in her backyard and the industrial regu-lation of the Clean Air Act. Interests are formed by interpretation as much as by brute fact, and so they are shot through with ideals. Environmental imagination has always been a blend of the two.

Moreover, the range of interests one can pursue forcefully and effectively in politics has much to do with the specific ideals the public culture has embraced. An intense rhetorical and imagina-tive commitment to developing the continent lent authority to a century of self-interested calls to privatize the frontier. The national commitment to development also formed the uphill slope that the Sierra Club and Progressive reformers had to climb when they called for limiting privatization and preserving public land.

It sometimes may seem that the element of imagination recedes as technical calculations replace choices of value. This is an illusion, though, which we fall into when we focus on the official activity of environmental law, which these days stems more from agency regulation than from legislation. In fact, the time is rife with contests over environmental imagination. On the one hand, the political settlements that the lawmaking of the 1970s seemed to put in place are under assault in the United States from anti-regulatory populism that has adapted the themes of settler providence to new circumstances. On the other hand, environmental imagination is flowering in areas (such as agriculture) that long seemed marginal to environmental concerns, and in problems that confound familiar environmental thinking, especially the slow crisis of climate change.

Food, the treatment of animals, and climate change are paradigmatic Anthropocene problems, immensely frustrating and also potentially fruitful. All three pose quandaries: in them, people are uncertain what to make of key encounters with the natural world and are experimenting in the face of that uncertainty. Such experiments can change ethical vocabularies; in some measure, they already have. These three problems, then, present three changes, or beginnings of change, in the relationship between humans and nature.

One of these changes is the shift from wilderness preservation to food production as a model environmental issue—from the notion that wild land should ideally remain untouched by human hands to the notion that labor connects people with the land and animals that they unavoidably use. The second change is the way that beauty and sublimity, the old aesthetic touchstones, have been supplanted by a response to nature that makes room for the uncanny—the unsettling perception that we do not know, maybe cannot know, the ethical status, meaning, or experience of another living thing that stands in front of us. The third change is the transition from saving nature and solving environmental problems to living with problems that are our new and permanent conditions.

From Wilderness to Cultivation:
Food, Agriculture, and the Value of Work

As the Romantic strain of environmental imagination took hold, farmers, who animated James Wilson's flourishing American landscape, became figures of plodding, spiritless labor instead. Thoreau portrayed his neighbors as slaves to their land, labors, and conventional ideas. Emerson complained that he could not enjoy contemplating a landscape when farmers were working on it.[1] When Thoreau famously reflected on hoeing weeds in his bean-field at Walden Pond, he concluded that his next harvest should be left entirely for the birds. As for eating, the most ascetic and self-castigating passages of *Walden* concern the body's need for food.[2] John Muir condescendingly described a dirty shepherd who could not feel the wonder of the Sierra Nevada.[3] Legally protected wilderness, the signal achievement of Romantic environmentalism, provides exalted scenery and strenuous recreation—opportunities for admiring the landscape and powering one's own way across it—to the exclusion of getting food. The wilderness movement worked to preserve elemental human bonds with nature, but left eating out of the picture. It assigned food production to the farms and factories whose canned goods trekkers carried into the back county. Wilderness became a place where there was much life but nothing to eat.

Today, a new appreciation is emerging for worked and inhabited landscapes, fertile terrains of responsible labor. This is the landscape of what one might call the food movement. It is not providential but ecological. Working there converts ecological consciousness into concrete activity, as surely as John Muir's walking guides did for Romantic ways of seeing. This new appreciation for agriculture has begun to heal the rift between environmental imagination and work, specifically the dignity and value of work, which mainly belonged to the legacy of settler providentialism.

I trust readers will recognize what I am calling the food movement, though it swirls around diverse ideas and has no organizational center. It shows up as an interest in where food comes from, who grows food and how, and the way food travels from farm to plate. It is evident in consumer fads and high-end restaurants, local economies that have been rebuilt around community-supported agriculture and farmers markets, and people's renewed eagerness to put their own hands in the dirt. Altogether, it hints at a new picture of people and nature. In this picture, the physical labor of growing, gathering, and cooking food is a source of satisfaction, enriched by knowledge of the ecological, chemical, and other processes that the work engages.

This movement aims at a kind of farming that preserves, even enhances, natural processes, rather than exhausting them. The ideal, "integrated" food system returns crop and animal waste to the soil to preserve a circle of fertility. In contrast, "industrial" farming makes animal waste a pollutant even as it replaces soil fertility with chemical fertilizers that must be separately manufactured, and in some cases mined, and that run off from fields to pollute rivers and groundwater. These images of two kinds of farming, integrated and industrial, are also moralized images of two kinds of system: one that maintains a resilient cycle of life, and another that builds up unsustainable ecological debt by drawing down natural fertility and producing pollution.

As a cultural matter, the food movement offers a way to make abstract ecological values concretely one's own. It poses an answer to a puzzle in post-1970 environmental thought, a puzzle present in any effort to think ecologically. An environmental ethic that people can live by must tap into basic motives, and there are two familiar ways to do this. On the one hand, an environmental ethic can meld its values to practices and commitments already in place. Following this model, the conservation politics of Theodore Roosevelt and Gifford Pinchot made patriotic concern for the long-term well-being of the whole country into an ally of public-lands conservation by arguing that, without such conservation, the United States would exhaust its wealth and decline in power. On the other hand, an environmental ethic can offer a new practice and identity—a new way of interacting with the natural world and a new image of one's self in that encounter. This was the achievement of the settler ethic on the one hand, and, on the other, of the wild-lands pilgrimages favored by the Sierra Club and its successors in the wilderness movement.

The post-1970 wave of environmental ideas and lawmaking took the first path: it presented industrial pollution as a public-health crisis and a threat stemming from runaway technology—hazards that the country knew how to fear and, in some measure, how to manage. The new environmental laws did little to secure new modes of personal practice. Working at the scale of the industrial economy—power plant emissions, automobile efficiency standards, pre-use review of toxins, and ambient pollution standards—these laws made their changes invisible from the point of view of anyone outside the regulated industries. Although there was great popular appetite for "ecological" values, the new laws did little to bring such values alive in personal life.

The more affirmative values that many commentators linked to ecological consciousness, though, were elusively abstract—interdependence, integration, humility. How did one build these into an economy, into a way of life? Ecological consciousness stood to change everything and nothing. The emerging conviction that knowledgeable, sustainable work can be a source of personal satisfaction offers a more concrete change: an ecological practice that invites being woven into the identity of the person doing the work.

This ecological image of food presents different values from those of the standard environmental approach to agriculture. Conventional cost-benefit analysis of farm policy concentrates on the polluting side-effects of fertilizers, pesticides, and fossil fuels. It sets out the ways federal subsidies, especially for corn and soybean production, shape farming practice and the national diet, with cascading health costs and environmental harms. These well-established complaints are among the food movement's claims, but they are not all, nor are they even at the heart. The ecological ideal that I have been describing makes knowledgeable, sustainable work, with natural processes, into a freestanding value, a reason to pursue a food economy that fosters such work.

What does this perspective mean for the law? Law thoroughly shapes the food economy. A large share of corn and soybean subsidies goes to very large producers, discouraging the smaller-scale farming that makes personal, physical engagement viable, and where integrated, multi-crop operations have some chance of surviving competition with industrial agriculture. Lax anti-pollution laws give an advantage to large operations whose feedlots and warehouses of cattle, pigs, and chickens produce lagoons of semi-liquid waste that pollutes both air and water. Regulations permit use of low ("sub-therapeutic") doses of antibiotics to enable dense animal populations to survive without epidemics, even though the practice risks breeding antibiotic-resistant strains of diseases that will afflict not only animals but humans. Small farmers face interlinked logistical and regulatory problems: slaughtering facilities are often far from farms, necessitating travel, fuel use, and animal stress at the last stage of raising meat.[4] This bottleneck is difficult to open partly because of the small number of federal health-and-safety inspectors, whose limited ranks reflect the fact that they have long been expected to cover only a few, industrial-scale slaughtering facilities.

Are these reasons to make the law friendlier to eco-pastoral farming? It depends. But on what? According to standard cost-benefit analysis, it depends on the bottom line. Various defenses of industrial agriculture vindicate one aspect or another as being less resource-intensive than the smaller and more participatory farming that the food movement embraces. Even when industrial produce travels halfway around the world, economies of scale may make it more energy-efficient than small, local production.

If one starts from the ecological ideal, then thinking of agriculture solely in standard cost-benefit terms seems misguided—much the way privatizing and developing wilderness came to seem in the early twentieth century, in light of then-new movements for national parks and other public recreational land. The older perspective, with its emphasis on development, lost force once many Americans accepted that Romantic engagement with nature was worth promoting through federal policy. If farming offers its own experiential value, the case for reversing the law's bias toward large and specialized production stands on its own, rather than depending on standard cost-benefit analysis. This does not mean that the ecological ideal should always prevail, of course; but its grounds are its own, not derived from other values. On this view, agricultural policy is, in a serious sense, cultural policy, like establishing national parks. Parks policy is an investment in a relation to nature that generates thinking about humanity's place in the world. Similarly, agricultural policy that supported small-scale, participatory food-raising would be an investment in developing environmental ethics out of the very practices the policy fostered.

Ecological farming's roots tap the writing of Aldo Leopold, the seminal wilderness advocate whose ecological preoccupations brought him to a deep interest in restoring worn-out farmland. In the realms of both wilderness and farming, Leopold asked how people could participate in the natural world with full awareness of its processes and with the aim of improving what he called its "beauty, stability, integrity." He deplored "clean farming . . . aimed solely at economic profit and purged of all non-conforming links" and argued instead for an ecological view of agriculture that would "harmonize the wild and the tame."[5] The point of the wild had been to contradict the tame, to be its opposite. Leopold suggested that the wild and the tame, which had long seemed to be antagonistic principles in nature, belonged together within a single province comprising both humans and nature.

Wendell Berry took up the same themes almost three decades after Leopold's untimely death. Berry, a novelist, poet, and essayist who became a muse of the food movement, argued in 1977 that "the ecological crisis" was also "a crisis of agriculture" because the move from integrated to extractive farming, and from producing food to consuming it, marked a larger divorce from sustainable interaction with the natural world. In this divorce, an extractive and quantifying attitude replaced a preservative and qualitative one.[6] Berry's argument could seem nostalgic if one assessed it simply as history, but he made a lasting contribution by proposing a set of contrasts in value. He cast different approaches to farming and food as emblems of different ways of living on earth. One way treated the soil's productive power as an industrial resource, to be engineered for maximum production. The other, which Berry embraced, treated working the land as a relationship on which other relationships rest—an ecological interaction that shapes the health of people and the health of land and animals, the kinds of rural communities people can inhabit, and the kind of labor they can choose to do.

This approach to agriculture belongs to a style of environmental thinking that eschews hard lines between protected places, where aesthetic and spiritual values flourish, and ordinary places that are treated as industrial reserves. No one has to reject the special experience of wilderness, but one does have to recognize its incompleteness. Attention to food offers the Anthropocene a picture of humans with their hands in the dirt, engaged in a metabolic bond with what sustains them. Like other organisms, human beings destroy in order to live, and transform their environment by this sustaining destruction. The abstention from use that wilderness represents deserves a place in Anthropocene environmental imagination, but it cannot be at the center. An Anthropocene attitude must also take account of the work that people do, the landscapes they create by living, and the things that they destroy.

Integrating human work into an ecological vision has a broader potential, which is to refigure the relationship between the natural world and the human economy. Ecology is the only possible home of an economy; an ecology and an economy must share some of the same shape, and must rise or fall together. Recognizing this, neoliberal environmentalists today portray the world as "natural capital," a productive form of wealth that rewards prudent investment. The metaphor of capital makes the natural world visible in economic thinking, where it has often been invisible—think of generations of ignored greenhouse gases and lost topsoil in service of narrowly defined profit—and in this way the metaphor is useful. But it also implies a nature that needs to be managed by investment bankers: nature's God as venture capitalist. This is no surprise in this age of capital, just as it is no surprise that Theodore Roosevelt's nature needed strong-willed, expert bureaucrats, or that the nature cleared by frontier Americans demanded pioneer settlers to complete it. Each version of nature has its economy, and each economy has its nature. The wild and scenic nature that popular environmentalism inherited from the Romantics is in many ways the nature that accords with a consumer economy: its devotees ingest it in recreational activities far from their working lives, which they return to unchanged. Talking about the earth as "natural capital" is, among other things, a bid to overcome this consumerist image by recognizing that the natural world is the ground of every productive part of the economy. It brings nature fully into political economy, but a specifically neoliberal political economy, committed to the perspective of capital.

An alternative would be to think of nature not as providing capital but as doing work, work in which human labor collaborates.[7] The human and natural systems in which we are all involved are, among other things, systems of labor. Although the politics of labor is often associated with the industrial economy, whose Blakean "dark, satanic mills" seemed the archetypal opposite of nature, it also has agrarian versions, from the English Diggers of the 1640s to the American Populists of the 1890s. In these movements, the labor that is the great human equalizer had, as its central image, working on and with the land. (The providential view that informed much of Populist politics and the nineteenth-century American vision of land generally portrayed people collaborating with the natural world even as it showed them overcoming it, precisely because providentialism insisted that nature bent of its own accord toward pastoral development.) In this tradition and in modern ecology, there is potential to realize that work is not only industry, the productive action that transforms the world, but also reproduction, the work of remaking life with each year and generation. Seeing nature's work in this light would align environmental politics with the key feminist insight that much socially necessary work is ignored or devalued as "caregiving," a gendered afterthought to the real dynamos of the economy, when in reality no shared life could do without it. This approach would also have the potential to align environmental politics with a labor movement of caregivers in an economy where an increasing amount of the work done by human beings (rather than machines) is the work of social reproduction: nursing, teaching, parenting—all the things today's technology cannot step in to do.

The nature we might imagine in this way would not be the Bankers' Nature of "natural capital," or the Backpackers' Nature of the Wilderness Society. It would be a Mother Nature for a post-gender caring economy (a Parent Nature, then?) and also a Sister, Brother, or even Comrade Nature—a collaborator in the given and necessary work of carrying on living. The food economy and the atmosphere, urban gardens and national parks, would all be part of a world, no longer natural but never wholly artificial, in which the foundational work is to go on living.

Animals and the Ethics of Encounters across Species

People destroy animals to survive. We also create them to survive, producing breeds for human use and fabricating the environments, from pastures to factory farms, where they pass their truncated lives. If you accept the ethical arguments against factory farming and meat eating, you have to agree that many Americans get their meals through a massive violation of basic morality.

Two prominent approaches to this issue have very different lessons for eating. The first is abolitionist, concluding that there is no moral defense for most of the ways people use animals, and that we should stop taking their flesh, hides, and lives. The second approach is reformist: it seeks to renovate human relations with animals without giving up domestication or meat eating. The most visible recent reformist proposal comes from the journalist Michael Pollan. In *The Omnivore's Dilemma,* Pollan argues for an animal husbandry that frees animals to move around and use their bodies, eat grass and enjoy sunshine, and generally live something like the "natural" lives of their species (albeit shorter versions) until they go to slaughter.[8]

One important strut of this argument is that most domesticated species would not exist at all in a world without farming. Therefore, the argument goes, it would be paradoxical to say that we should abolish farming out of concern for domestic species, since they would then not exist at all. Any ethical standard must thus be compatible with extensive domestication and use of animals.

This approach has several problems. Why should the fact that these species depend on us for their survival entitle us to use them for food? Why not say instead, just as logically, that we are responsible for what we have made? This part of the argument resembles the bad habit of calling "natural" whatever is already happening, including the very thing we set out to assess: if we co-evolved with cattle and pigs through exploitation, does that make exploitation immune to ethical scrutiny? Surely not, any more than pervasive social practices such as slavery and gender segregation should be immune because they are widespread in human history.

There are other difficulties. Even if one accepts Pollan's standard in the abstract, does it make sense to say that an animal has lived a fitting life when it faces slaughter at a fraction of its natural lifespan? Castration of most males forecloses certain activity, even though it leaves steers, capons, barrows, and geldings free to enjoy sunshine and grass. The obvious appeal of Pollan's position is its promise to reconcile persistent and opposite impulses: to continue our basic relations to other animals, while checking some of the palpable enormities of those relations. Whether it succeeds is less clear. Surely it would be simpler just to stop the killing?

Maybe so. My point here, though, is not to decide between reform and abolition. Rather, it is to point out something that the two share, which points toward a third approach. Both reformism and abolitionism confidently declare the moral significance of animals. An abolitionist might find astonishing—to put it charitably—Pollan's confident judgment about what it means to be a pig; but the abolitionist, too, has a definite view about the meaning of pigness. Each side has judged a question that—as the continuing dispute among thoughtful people shows—is not settled in the larger ethical, political, and legal argument. The continuing dispute reflects the difficulty of interpreting animal experience, which we cannot know except through speculation and which likely is very different from ours.

Genuinely difficult problems like this one can give rise to ethical development. The problem of animals' experience conjures up uncanniness, the bewilderment that comes with not knowing another's consciousness, or even whether another consciousness is present at all. To experience uncanniness in the presence of an animal is to be right up against a question—what is this other creature's experience?—that will not resolve itself into one clear answer. In that position, we might hope to learn from our acknowledged confusion.

Law might make this problem more palpable, and so, perhaps, more ethically generative. The public argument around factory farming is stunted, partly because the practice itself is concealed. Access to confined animal feeding operations (CAFOs) and slaughterhouses is severely restricted, and those who seek it (including me) report that access policies are even stricter in action than on paper. This enforced invisibility indulges the tendency to avoid what is unpleasant or difficult. There is every self-interested reason for livestock operations to keep out the curious, especially those with cameras and plans to tell their stories. Today, just as when Upton Sinclair wrote *The Jungle,* debates about meat tend to arise from triumphs of muckraking.[9] Even Peter Singer's landmark philosophical treatise, *Animal Liberation,* uses vivid reportage to argue for the ethical importance of animal suffering.[10] Reflection in this area seems to arise, in important part, from our being confronted with what we had managed to avoid. Whoever favors things as they are thus has a strong interest in concealment and avoidance.

Concealment has a legal infrastructure: it rests on the owners' power to keep others out. Recent laws pile extra penalties on whoever records and reports what happens in slaughterhouses. The most straightforward way to foster reflection on how we use

animals would be to reverse this trend toward greater concealment by creating a right to know the sources of one's food. This
could mean a right of public access, under controlled conditions,
to industrial food operations. Physical access would not be necessary; video technology should be enough. Slaughterhouses might
be required to admit independent film crews producing publicly
available documentaries (one thinks optimistically of the use
Werner Herzog made of strictly limited access to the ancient cave
paintings of Chauvet, France, in his *Cave of Forgotten Dreams*), or
simply to install web cameras. Labeling requirements for meat
could include web addresses where buyers could look inside the
facilities where the animal was raised and slaughtered.

Such public-access rights would resemble transparency requirements in other areas of law. For example, the Toxics Release
Inventory, which requires industrial facilities to make their toxic-
pollution records public, has mostly been celebrated for seeding
public pressure to drive down emissions. The big difference is that
the information that came out of the slaughterhouses would be
useful for more than pursuing established goals, such as profit or
a certain level of clean air. Instead, whatever insight can come from
inside a slaughterhouse would feed back into the development of
values. A public right to know would be a kind of cultural policy:
support for ethical development informed by experience.

This proposal is connected with the uncanny because it aims to
make concrete the enigma of another animal's experience, suffering, and death. Meeting that enigma firsthand is one help in
thinking about how to treat other species. Encounters with everyday violence might help viewers to assess the things we already
do but tend not to see.

Uncanniness is different from the time-honored aesthetic responses to nature—beauty and sublimity—in that the latter pair
express definite ideas of nature's significance: they are instances of
something the viewer already knows, whether about beauty's har-

mony and usefulness or about sublimity's inhuman power and scale. By contrast, uncanniness expresses an uncertainty at the heart of the Anthropocene. The meaning that we find in nature is meaning that we help to produce by preparing ourselves to encounter it, creating vocabularies in which to share it, and so making it part of cultural life. But that meaning is not just a human invention; it arises from a real encounter with other beings. The gap of mystery that divides us from them does not swallow all continuity and interconnection. Commonality and mystery, well-founded intuition and utter uncertainty: both sides of these pairs form the human relation to the living world, and uncanniness responds to the uncertainty that pulses between them, though it cannot perfectly bridge them.

Embracing uncanniness need not mean abandoning the aesthetic legacies of beauty and sublimity. Uncanniness offers an ethics of uncertainty, a pause before judgment. It expresses recognition that, in interpreting nonhuman species and other parts of nature, no judgment can be entirely confident and stable. The hesitation of uncanniness can inflect the experience of beauty and sublimity, reminding the observer that a beautiful, regular, fertile landscape is not "there for us," any more than an awe-inspiring sublime landscape has the "purpose" of thrilling or morally instructing the person who sees it. Beauty and sublimity bring the viewer into a definite relation to a place because they imbue the place with a purpose, a meaning, that addresses the person who sees. Uncanniness is a reminder that these meanings are partly human things, not simple readings of an indwelling mind in nature, and that we are not sure what, if anything, is looking back at us.

Beauty and sublimity do express genuine relations, ways of identifying with and, in a sense, becoming a part of a place. They may also motivate more thoroughgoing relations with that place: a farmer's, forager's, or walker's knowledge of what lives there, its seasons and habits; a climber's or painter's assiduous attention to dangerous or overwhelming terrain. But beauty and sublimity should be marked by the uncertainty that uncanniness cultivates. Uncanniness has priority because, once we recognize that the "meaning" of nature has always been a way of talking about human life and purposes, all our relations to the nonhuman world must be touched by the uncanny. We simply do not know what is behind another pair of eyes, and what is projection from behind our own.

This returns us to the question of animals, but that question can now stand for the larger issue of how to see nature. *Seeing* means finding value and meaning—not just perceiving the object, but interpreting it as part of a world we share with it. Uncanniness starts from admitting that we don't know what an animal's life means, to it or to us, and that the answer we give can only be some blend of discernment and projection. We only ever see through a mirror darkly.

That is why at least a part of the law relating to animals should be a law made for ethical discovery, a law that makes it harder to keep unresolved questions out of sight. A public right to see into slaughterhouses would confront us with our effect on the non-human world, and so with the question of what sense we can make of it. We might think in a similar way of disclosing other human effects beyond those of slaughterhouses. The energy economy, for instance, tends to look as abstract and superficially clean as in-dustrially produced meat did to supermarket buyers fifteen years ago. It would be a change to link energy use, in the eye and the mind, with Appalachian strip mines. Ruined mountains, choked streams, and buried valleys are as much a part of how we power our laptops as the killing bolt is of the steak, and usually just as invisible. Being aware of what we do is the first part of making sense of it.

The sustained, deliberately tentative attention that uncanniness encourages might be a bridge to other parts of Anthropocene aes-thetics and ethics. We might develop, for instance, ways of appre-ciating landscapes that we know are permanently changed, damaged, in some ways even ruined. We are going to have to live with such landscapes; we already do, mainly by trying to avoid and ignore them. An aesthetics of damage, a way of living with harm and not disowning the place that is harmed, might someday become its own version of beauty. Uncanniness might be the door to that new way of seeing.

This is easy to say. What it might mean would be considerably more complicated. I write at a time when the aesthetic of post-industrial ruins is everywhere, to the point that it sometimes feels as if every old factory, library, and opera house in Detroit and similarly blown-out cities has been photographed through every known filter. The art world is full, too, of images of strip mines and pit mines, desalination plants and sewage ponds, of everything that seeps and festers and rusts. The surprise of such images originally had something to teach about how much our standard ideas of beauty and sublimity leave out, and how arbitrary we often are in what we admire.

But sometimes the aesthetic charge obscures more than it reveals about the damaged place. Mountaintop removal and massive pit mines produce landscapes with the geometric shock of Futurism and the alien scale of Romantic sublimity. They are something to see. The fact remains, though, that when they are done the streams that ran there have been buried, the springs and underground reservoirs wrecked. Trees will hardly grow again. An aesthetic response misleads when it overlooks the ways that the place is dead, its death feeding the inexpensive vitality of coal-powered electricity and the false cleanness of the tools that it runs.

Aesthetics does not need to be ethical, and when artists try to make it do ethical or political work, the result is often to do no good. But let us say we want another way to see the energy economy whole, as the food movement has been teaching us to see the overall food economy. That project might benefit from what the food movement has helped to create: an aesthetics that responds to resilience, health, and mutuality among species and ecosystems. That new aesthetics in agriculture is now part of the cultural basis for a new politics and a possible new period of law reform around the food economy. The energy economy has no such thing. Much of it remains invisible and, mainly, unimagined.

A beginning would be to imagine the world's possible energy futures as alternative landscapes, alternative economies, alternative ways of living in the full sense of a political economy that is also an ecology. A coal economy implies a form of landscape and a kind of life. So does a petroleum economy—a fact that has become newly vivid as fracking has taken natural-gas drilling into regions that had previously not seen much of it, unsettling the feeling of immunity that had prevailed there. As with coal and oil, so with wind and solar energy. Each has its own versions of destruction, its own kinds of beauty, and its own forms of human work. Some of these are familiar, and some are strange. Whoever wants to contribute to an Anthropocene politics had better start developing ways of imagining them all, and of bending our work toward some of them.

That takes us to the question of climate change, and of exactly how big the world's biggest problem is.

Climate Change:
From Failure to New Standards of Success

A good deal of intellectual energy has gone into the question of whether doing anything about climate change is possible, and, more pointedly, whether various specific efforts have any chance of making a difference. The implicit idea is that we have a standard of success, that we might "solve" or "prevent" climate change by keeping total levels of heat-trapping greenhouse gases below some threshold—commonly the equivalent of 350 parts per million (ppm) of carbon. One admirable organization, 350.org, has made this goal its touchstone and namesake. In 2013 it declared that building a proposed pipeline to transport oil from Canadian tar sands across the United States would mean "game over for the climate." The whole logic here is that success and failure are the possible outcomes, that climate-regulating efforts can either win or lose.

When the problem is viewed in light of these alternatives, there is plenty of reason to expect failure. Scholars and commentators usually express the reasons for pessimism in terms of the problems rational people encounter when trying to solve problems together. This rational-actor theory, which assumes that individuals and collective entities such as countries act to advance their own interests, has been a keystone of refined pessimism. Because the forces that drive climate change are terribly complex and work over a very long time, the benefits of doing anything to stop it are hard to forecast and, in any event, will mostly help people far away and far in the future. The costs of doing something about it, by contrast, tend to come quickly, be fairly concrete, and affect the people trying to solve the problem. For a country like the United States, with a bit less than 5 percent of the world's population, taking on the cost of retooling the national economy to reduce greenhouse-gas emissions would have the fiscal logic of foreign aid: 95 percent of the benefits would go to non-Americans.

Moreover, most of the benefits would go to non-Americans who haven't even been born yet. In some ways, this is the worse problem. Countries can get together to solve shared problems, though often with difficulty, because their governments can all come to the same table. If we imagined generations, however, as if they were negotiators in climate talks, we would discover that the only one actually present at the table is always the present generation—the one that will bear all the costs of doing something about the problem, and receive almost none of the benefits. Understood in the narrow terms of self-interest, it can always look rational for the living to sell out their descendants. In the language of rational-actor theory, climate change produces spatial and temporal externalities large enough to swamp internalized effects: it threatens to become the collective-action problem that ate the planet.

As greenhouse-gas levels have rapidly passed 350 ppm (recently reaching 400) without major public action to control emissions, a predictable response has emerged: the claim that there is no alternative to geo-engineering, a catch-all term for technologies that do not reduce emissions but instead directly adjust global warming. Geo-engineering technologies may reduce the solar energy entering the atmosphere (for instance, with orbiting mirrors or sun-blocking particulates in the upper atmosphere); or consume carbon (by spurring carbon-eating algae blooms in the ocean, for example); or intervene in other aspects of climate change (for instance, by using alkaline chemicals to counter the gradual acidification of the oceans). It does seem likely that such technologies will end up as part of the response to climate change, along with a great deal of more conventional adaptation, such as building seawalls. For the moment, though, the move to embrace geo-engineering is much too easy. It starts from fatalism—*of course* we haven't done anything to control emissions, and *of course* we wouldn't, because we are rationally incapable of collective self-restraint—and leaps from fatalism to hubris: we can better handle the problem as one of planetary engineering than of collective self-restraint, anyway. This last-minute burst of optimism is, to say the least, striking. If any process would seem to require collective self-restraint, it is the intentional use of planet-altering technologies that geo-engineering envisages.

Ironically, both the pessimism and the hubris take comfort from the same starting point: that if we fail to "prevent" climate change or "save" the planet from it, then all bets are off; we have failed, the game is up, and it's time for drastic measures. As long as we approach the problem that way, forecasts of "failure" will seem powerful, and the next step will be the "try anything—now!" attitude of geo-engineering. Both attitudes manage to avoid the thought that collective self-restraint should be part of our response, perhaps including refraining from geo-engineering: the pessimism avoids that thought by demonstrating, or assuming, that self-restraint would be irrational and therefore must be impossible; and the hubris avoids it by announcing that although self-restraint has failed (as it had to fail, "rationally" speaking), it was unnecessary all along anyway.

I would like to propose a different way of looking at it. It is true that climate change, so far, has outrun the human capacity for self-restraint. As greenhouse-gas levels rise and the earth's systems shift, climate change has also begun to overwhelm the very idea that there is a "nature" to be saved or preserved. If success means keeping things as they are, we have already failed, probably irrevocably. This is why climate change is the emblematic problem of the Anthropocene: it is both a driver and a symbol of a thoroughly transformed world.

We need new standards for shaping, managing, and living well in a transformed world. Familiar ideas of environmental failure and success will not reliably serve anymore. We should ask, of efforts to address climate change, not just whether they are likely to "succeed" at solving the problem, but whether they are promising experiments—workable approaches to valuing a world that we have everywhere changed, and to thinking about how we will change it next. Climate change gives us a model of how familiar approaches to environmental problems can break down, and how the problems that disintegrate those familiar approaches can become the seedbed of new approaches. The old adage was never truer or more relevant: we make the road by walking.

The Breakdown of Familiar Ideas

How do familiar ethical frameworks run aground on climate change? Begin with pollution, the paradigmatic problem for much of modern environmental law. In the pollution paradigm, a harmful, alien agent enters an otherwise healthy system, sickening animals and people and weakening the underlying system. This narrative recurs throughout Rachel Carson's *Silent Spring,* taproot of the environmental imagination in the age of anti-pollution statutes. It captures the public discussion around those statutes: human effluents were seen as violating the order of a clean world, making it unhealthful and unsafe.[11]

The pollutants of classic environmental problems are either man-made or at least a rupture when they enter ecosystems in large amounts. Moreover, they are generally toxic or otherwise harmful to the human body (particulates may not be poison, but they can ruin a set of lungs). In these ways, pollution resembles familiar injuries and wrongs. Like hitting a person, it violates a vivid baseline condition—clean water or clean air in the case of pollution, nonviolence and bodily integrity in the case of a person. Like hitting a person, pollution also involves fairly direct harm to individuals, even if, as with many toxins, the harm takes a long time to manifest itself. Finally, classic pollution is "unnatural": it introduces foreign elements into a world that one can imagine as having been pristine before the pollution was introduced.

Climate change is different. Greenhouse gases do not resemble "pollution" in the sense that has traditionally triggered moral responses. The major greenhouse gases, notably those that are carbon-based, are elements in planetary cycles integral to life as we know it. They are the very opposite of "unnatural." Nor are they toxic. Moreover, because the climate system is always changing and because human-caused disturbances interact with underlying natural dynamics, there is no stable "baseline" of an undisturbed world, a baseline analogous to, say, a river without pollution.

Little wonder, then, that climate change often stirs no felt sense that people are doing harm, no impulse to stay the hand that flips on the light switch or turns the car key. Greenhouse-gas emissions by billions of people over the past several centuries produce a globally dispersed, systemic change that intensifies certain atmospheric processes in a terrifically complex global phenomenon, all against a naturally unstable baseline. These are not the kinds of facts that trigger a classic sense of having caused harm, with the accompanying sense of responsibility. Ethical appeals that have worked to organize our sense of other environmental problems are less effective here.

If modern environmental law has taken shape around the pollution paradigm, it has also defined itself by the mission of saving a charismatic species or special place. Again and again, calls for preserving large natural areas and systems were anchored on exemplary places, whether Yosemite Valley, the neighboring (now inundated) Hetch Hetchy, or Dinosaur Monument, the site of the Sierra Club's defining post–World War II preservation fight and occasion of a great increase in the club's membership and in national attention to its agenda. The same appeals drove passage of the Endangered Species Act. Although the statute's terms protect biodiversity generally, Congress passed it overwhelmingly thanks to enthusiasm for the eagles, bears, and wolves that environmentalists have learned to call, with one eyebrow arched, "charismatic megafauna."

Climate change confounds this paradigm, too. When advocates try to anchor climate politics on the fate of individual species, notably the polar bear, they are striving to trigger the moral responses that have served in the past. If a polar bear cub can stand in for the global atmosphere, the thought goes, maybe it can make climate change morally compelling. Although it is early days yet, this tactic seems not to have worked. Both the attempt and the failure reinforce the thought that climate change ties deed and result together by threads that are too numerous, long, tangled, and obscure to fit familiar ideas of victim, harm, and responsibility that have been central to the ecological era of environmental lawmaking.

Respect for Failure

Precisely because addressing climate change means making new values or adapting old ones, efforts to do something about the problem can make essential contributions even if they prove futile in every immediate sense. Asking simply whether a new approach to climate change will succeed as a lawmaking or regulatory strategy is too narrow. For instance, municipal efforts to address greenhouse-gas emissions and community-level attempts to define a personal ethics of low-carbon living, although palpably ineffective in one way—they will not directly contribute much to reducing global emissions—may nonetheless turn out to be effective in somewhat the way Sierra Club excursions were: they could be efforts to find new ways of experiencing climate change as important, and to devise new shared vocabularies for expressing and living out its importance. Law and lawmaking are forums where cultural and imaginative innovation happens, innovation that will help to lay the foundation of any future legal regime for climate change. Environmental politics does not just solve problems or fail to do so: even in "failure," it is a forum for questions that we cannot yet resolve, but can at least give more definite shape.[12] The culture that these political efforts help to shape might yet shape ecological concepts and motives for the Anthropocene.

Consider a few ways that the continuing ferment over climate might rework familiar ideas. Aesthetic response has organized environmental values by gathering together many qualities of the human-natural world into a single powerful assessment. To find beauty in a landscape has meant admiring its regularity, fertility, gentleness; experiencing a sense that it fits the human scale; feeling gratitude for a habitable world. Sublimity, by contrast, emerges from inhuman scale, great power, a sense of danger, and difficulty grasping the dimensions of the sublime thing—a general overwhelming of the human power to cope and comprehend. These responses acknowledge value and meaning in the things that stir them. To find a thing beautiful or sublime is to prize it and, often, to want to preserve the qualities in it that move the observer. Nothing in aesthetic response depends on a stable "natural" baseline that precedes human intervention. Nothing in it is confounded by complexity. Aesthetic response arises out of an interaction between human observers and an always-complex natural world.

One might imagine, then, learning to see the global atmospheric system, the interwoven patterns of currents and winds, seasons and climatic regions, as something beautiful. It makes a world suited for human life, a world in which we have learned to live. It is the condition of all our homelands and home landscapes: the seasons we knew as children, the crops that show up in local markets, the wild animals glimpsed at the edge of a yard or during a hike. The question to ask about greenhouse gases, in this light, would be not whether they move the planet off a natural baseline, let alone whether they pollute it, but whether they tend to mar the beauty of a system that, for all its inherent perturbations, describes a set of rough balances that we have come to find beautiful. Alternatively, but not incompatibly, the global atmosphere might come to seem sublime: a brooding, powerful source of threat, beyond our complete understanding, out of the scale of our control, able to disrupt our familiar worlds and make us aware of human smallness and fragility. In fact, it seems right to see it in both ways: it is the condition of a climate-changed world that the global atmosphere undergirds the welcoming stability of beauty and the alienating threat of sublimity, all at once. Both treasuring beauty and feeling awe at sublimity are ways of respecting an order of things, and of valuing motives to act so as to uphold it, to recognize the limits it might enforce.

One might also think of virtue ethics as a little-tapped source in climate politics. Networks of individuals and communities are now trying to achieve models of low-carbon living, with some even driving their carbon emissions close to zero. These efforts are sure to fail in one sense: they are eminently susceptible to classic rational-actor problems. Something that is "irrational" for a country to do—shoulder the costs of a marginal reduction in greenhouse gases that, if it makes a difference, will mostly benefit others—is vastly more irrational for a person. The point, however, may be that virtuous action is worth doing because, to a person with the right set of dispositions, it just is the fitting response to a situation. For such a person, the fact that reducing one's own emissions will not make much global difference, and will help others rather than one's self, might be exactly the sort of thing one should not take into account in acting.

Much of life is organized by this sort of disposition. From choices of transport to conduct toward friends and family members, from how we dispose of trash to how we comport ourselves in the workplace, we do not usually act either on pure and reasoned principle or on sheer self-interest; rather, we act according to a sense of fit, of rough propriety, that weaves together how we see a situation and how we are motivated to act in it. These dispositions are weak, though, in the context of climate and other complex environmental problems; in part, it may be because they are so weak that small-scale rational-actor problems seem to have special force. We can hope to develop a set of Anthropocene virtues, oriented to action in a world that we are constantly shaping, and to which we are constantly vulnerable. Those who "irrationally" try to address climate change in their own lives and communities may be shaping the dispositions that the future will regard as its essential virtues.

It may also turn out that solidarity, the collective meaning of national identity and similar groupings (such as language and religion) will matter for climate politics. So far, not much has come of desultory efforts to identify climate change with the Apollo Project or World War II—supposed moments of American unity and common purpose. These, however, have not been much better than hortatory attempts to will—or wish—shared conviction into being. They are of little value as tests of the possibility.

Maybe a global problem will have to be translated into many national and other idioms before it can touch the ethical lives that people live together. It may be, for instance, that in fifty years there will be a U.S. politics and ethics of climate change, another version in Europe (or in countries or regions of Europe), and cognates in India, China, Brazil, and elsewhere, with overlaps, parallels, and outright divergences. This would not be so different from what happens when any other complex, identity-touching idea travels from setting to setting: democracy, liberalism, feminism, Islam, and individualism, to name a few broad themes of the global twenty-first century, are recognizable from place to place, but not identical. To matter motivationally, climate, too, may have to be worked into other identities, integrated with other dispositions and commitments.

It would be quite mistaken to imagine that climate change is exceptional because it confounds ethical and political responses that have succeeded brilliantly elsewhere in motivating and organizing environmental politics. It would be more accurate to say that it is exceptional because it exemplifies some of the problems that have stood in the way of environmental success across the board. Continuing mass extinctions, growing toxicity in many global systems, and intense pressure on habitat diversity are all reminders that environmental politics is as much an ongoing failure as it is a success. Environmental problems are complex, involve ambiguous effects, and are far too easy to ignore. For all such problems, the question might be how to learn from, and what to do with, our substantial and continuing failure. Climate change is the exemplary permanent crisis for an age of many permanent crises. Responding to it with despair because it induces so many forms of failure is exactly wrong. Answering the failures it induces by trying to learn from, live with, and improve upon our panoply of failures is the only right response available to us.

8

WHAT KIND OF DEMOCRACY?

DEMOCRACY HAS NOT BEEN DOING WELL. For this reason, now is an awkward time to argue that it must be the fulcrum of the Anthropocene. In the United States and Europe, democracies have rushed into foolish wars and stumbled in the face of economic crises—or created those crises. At the time of writing, the North Atlantic democracies are splitting into elite technocrats, who wish they could govern without consulting the masses, and angry populists, who would like to liquidate the technocrats. Nondemocratic governments openly disdain democratic pieties. Official Chinese voices even suggest that American failures prove the future does not belong to democracies.

Democratic failures are often failures to impose self-restraint, and self-restraint is exactly what environmental politics needs. In the past fifteen years, democracies have failed to pay their burgeoning debts and have started wars that turned out to have little credible rationale and no decent ending. Climate change looks like another unsustainable deficit that is going to keep growing, a burden on future generations to pay for today's convenience. The preferred responses to climate change, too, have an aspect of militarized fantasy: satellite mirrors to deflect solar energy from the earth, and other sci-fi technologies. These climate failures are part of a broader environmental failure. Although there have been important successes, notably anti-pollution laws, resource use and environmental impact continue to accelerate in the world's richest democracies, and all the more in fast-growing poorer countries. Water shortage, soil health, toxicity, and loss of biodiversity are all looming sources of future crises.

In recent decades, too, a basic change in the terms of government has narrowed the scope of democratic rule. Independent central banks, supra-national organizations like the World Trade Organization and the European Union, and constitutional limitations on taxation and spending have all taken economic governance out of the hands of popular majorities and placed it with technocrats and judges. The ideas behind these moves are twofold: first, that democracies are not to be trusted with their own most basic affairs, and, second, that there is one right way to organize economic life, which experts know and administer and everyone else must accept. These ideas coincide with a broader exhaustion in the rich modern tradition of political economy. In the last Gilded Age and in earlier economic crises, many alternative visions of economic life competed for popular attention: some of these influenced anti-trust law, labor legislation, unionization, and the New Deal. In the past decade, economic crises and suffering, even widespread discontent with the way our market capitalism is working, have inspired mainly austerity in Europe and gridlock in the United States. Democratic citizens' capacity to rework their own common lives has been hollowed out in overt and explicit ways, and eroded by a decline in political imagination.

At the same time, the power of organized money in politics has only increased. It is a common—and fair—complaint that the U.S. government is distorted through and through by the political power of wealth. In environmental matters, the problem is even worse. Wealth is produced and sustained by an economy that effectively subsidizes fossil fuels (by treating greenhouse-gas emissions as costless) and industrial agriculture (through explicit subsidies to big producers and regulatory tolerance of massive feedlots and slaughterhouses), along with every individual decision to buy from those industries. It's as if the Constitution gave three votes to everyone who wants to keep things as they are, and only one vote to those who seek to change them.

Real environmental reform is a matter of political economy. That is, it requires engaging the foundations of economic life: what kind of wealth an economy produces, how it distributes that wealth, what kind of freedom and equality it promotes, and what provision it makes for the future. These are political questions whose answers must be worked out through economic institutions. But the politics of modern democracies has become less able to engage such questions, even as the questions have become harder and more urgent. This is the crux of the difficulty.

The problem is not entirely new. In the 1970s, some environmentalists took democratic failures as reason to hope that nondemocratic governments would save the natural world. Such arguments were motivated by the hope that state socialism could avoid capitalism's demands for economic growth. The environmental record of the Soviet bloc established that, on the contrary, the pressure for economic growth was just as powerful there as in the West. Worse, those nondemocratic systems gave ordinary people no way to resist environmental destruction: while environmental politics was emerging in its modern form in the West, the heavy industry of the Eastern bloc created some of the worst disasters of the century, from the Chernobyl reactor meltdown to the death of the Aral Sea. Nonetheless, today there are resurgent fantasies of green authoritarianism, this time hung on China, with its state-led investment in solar cells. Where older hopes for an authoritarian savior expressed discontent with capitalism, today's attraction to China is rooted in weariness of sclerotic democracy. China's overall environmental record, though, is hardly better than the Soviet

Union's was, and its economic growth has massively increased the human impact on the planet. The lesson of the past fifty years is that humanity itself is the challenge. No political system has succeeded by contradicting the demand for more: more energy, more calories, more technology, and so more pressure on natural resources of all kinds.

It is not surprising, then, that many people hope technology will save the world. The greatest optimism rests on clean and renewable energy sources, carbon-eating organisms, and other fixes that could reduce human pressure on natural systems as thoroughly as steam power and internal combustion lightened the economy's demands on human muscles. Those technologies freed people from exhausting labor and early deaths. Mightn't the next wave of technology free the planet from some of the more crushing human demands? A weaker form of optimism looks to technology as the key to managing a continuing crisis: geo-engineering will not free the planet, but it may make a carbon-dense atmosphere more livable by reducing its effect on temperature and climate.

Maybe technological optimism will prove apt. Any environmentally responsible future would become much more likely if technology lessened the conflict between human flourishing and ecological health. There are, however, two reasons to doubt that technology alone could do the job. First, the environmental impact of innovation has always been a double-edged sword. With one edge, new technologies have made resource use much more efficient; for instance, the so-called carbon density of advanced economies, their carbon production per unit of economic activity, is much lower than in developing countries. This is a benefit of efficient energy production and use. The other edge of the sword, though, is a vast increase in overall resource use. As China has developed, for instance, its carbon density has dropped, but its overall carbon emissions have exploded, so that it in 2007 it surpassed the United States as the world's largest emitter. This example captures the general pattern: as human powers increase, each individual puts more pressure on the natural world. The second limit on technology's power to stem environmental crisis is that no technology can tell its users how to use it, or how to shape the earth with it. But those questions will need answers. Whatever innovation brings, people will continue to shape the earth by inhabiting it, changing everything from its atmospheric cycles to its soils and habitats. It is much too late to imagine that any technology could enable humanity to "stop disturbing" the earth. Instead, every technology will become part of the joint human-natural system in which we make and remake the world just by living here.

Technology, then, brings efficiency, but it brings neither restraint nor purpose. People need both in engaging the planet. Understandably, then, many look for environmental hope in culture and consciousness. These, after all, are where individuals, families, and communities find both restraint and purpose. At some point, many meditations on environmental questions conclude that consciousness must change, or nothing will change. People must learn to make more modest choices, find satisfactions that exact a smaller toll on the natural world. After all, technology and democratic politics channel the values and priorities of individuals, families, and communities. In some way, these are always the local roots of a national failure of self-restraint and purpose.

The emphasis on culture and consciousness, then, cannot be wrong. But is it helpful? History suggests that changes in consciousness are a necessary precondition for big and material changes in the human relation to the natural world, but also that they are not enough. By themselves, changes in personal values make differences on the margins of, say, buying decisions, or even choices of career, but they do little to change the larger systems that organize the relationship between humans and nature. Say that 60 percent of Americans come to value sustainably raised food and low-energy commutes enough to spend money on them. As most U.S. readers will realize on the basis of experience, the effect of this change will be to make sustainable food and urban housing into luxuries, inducing more production of these things, but also pushing the less wealthy into exurbs and utilitarian supermarkets. Some environmentally beneficial changes can follow from shifts in consciousness alone, but the biggest material changes happen through changes in the legal and economic infrastructure that guide human energies and activity. So long as the economy treats greenhouse-gas emissions and soil exhaustion as free and the legal system permits the mass feeding operations and slaughterhouses of industrial agriculture, a good deal of changed consciousness will mean no more than shuffling furniture between the first-class and second-class cabins of the *Titanic*.

Ecological Economics

With this in mind, many hope that economics will be the force that saves the world. The ideal of much of the U.S. policy elite is an economy in which every environmental effect of an action is expressed in monetary terms as a cost or a reward. Buy gasoline for your car, or burn coal in your power plant, and you should pay a premium that captures the effect of carbon emissions on climate change. On the reward side, farm in a way that preserves topsoil or wetlands, supporting soil fertility and clean waterways, and you should receive a payment or tax credit. If every act has consequences, the logic goes, let every consequence have a price. Such pricing would drive down use of fossil fuels and other harmful technologies, and encourage environmentally friendly alternatives. It would also spur research in alternative energy and soil-preserving technology. With a green hue tingeing every decision, the whole economy would tilt toward sustainability.

This is a sort of eco-utopian economics. In its ideal form, it would harmonize the ecological effects of human activity with the rewards and penalties of the economy by building complete eco-logical information into every choice. It offers a "corrected" market as a neutral framework to reconcile our appetite for the world's re-sources with the earth's finitude and fragility.

This market vision has a special affinity with ecology: both are ways of engaging the world's complexity. "Neoclassical" economics praises markets for solving the insufficient-knowledge problem: that the information relevant to economic choices is too diverse and widely dispersed for any decision maker to know it all. Mar-kets gather this information through as many small, locally in-formed decisions as there are human actions in a day. When you decide between copper and ceramic tile, the price tag summarizes a huge amount of information: orders from factories in China, a recession in Europe that drives down copper use there, and wor-ries over political instability in copper-producing countries. You don't need to know any of this: the higher price of copper "tells" you enough to coordinate your choice with everyone else's.

This image of social life as too complex to be managed from any one perspective resembles the picture of the natural world that ecology introduced: everything is connected to everything else, often in subtle and hidden ways, and any attempt to master the whole from a single standpoint is hubris and likely to turn out badly. We live in the age of complexity, in both economic and ecological terms. The ecological revolution has thus become an invitation to recast environmental regulation economically, as an ecological market, able to gather and integrate the complex, dis-persed facts of the natural world through millions of individual decisions, organized into a single system by the price mecha-nism, the universal translator, which makes it possible to measure any choice—what to use, what to save, what to waste—in terms of all possible others.

The ideal of an ecological economy also grows out of the prom-inence of cost-benefit analysis. Whether one sees it as desecration of precious incomparables such as life and health, or as simple rationality in a world of inevitable tradeoffs, the upshot of such analysis is that all values can be expressed as prices—and, to be useful in decision making, should be so expressed. The ecological-utopian economy would combine this ambition to price everything with the neoclassical embrace of complexity, the reliance on dispersed, individual choices rather than on a central regulator.

By combining economic means with ecological ends, eco-utopian economics gives the appearance of marrying hard-headed realism to charismatic radicalism, at once making environmentalism mentally tough and helping economics to become spiritually deep. But the idea that "getting the prices right" can produce a neutral architecture for environmental choice is a fantasy. Economics depends on political—which should be democratic—judgments about nature's value. Without these, it is both conceptually incoherent and useless in practice.

A scheme relying on ecological economics depends on "getting the prices right" so that individual decisions entail appropriate penalties and rewards. Ordinary economic activity—not the eco-utopian kind—produces prices automatically: gasoline prices rise and fall with summer demand, changes in car use by the Chinese, and political vicissitudes in the Middle East. By contrast, in ecological economics, prices arise only through regulation; in fact, the starting point for all economic study of environmental problems is the insight that markets do not spontaneously produce prices for resources that nobody owns, such as clean air or a stable atmosphere. The result is that markets effectively treat these resources as "free," and in consequence they are used wastefully. The starting point of eco-utopian economics is to create prices deliberately where none arise spontaneously. But how, then, to decide what the prices should be? The answers can only come from political judgments.[1]

Economists try to generate prices by measuring individual preferences for unpriced environmental goods—basically, how much people value air, water, biodiversity, etc.—but to do so they must choose tools for measurement, and it turns out that their choice of tools makes a big difference in the "facts" about preferences that they end up "finding." The act of measuring itself does a lot to produce the reality it aims to discern. Moreover, individuals' environmental attitudes do not spring fully formed from their heads, but are themselves the products of previous policy judgments. People learn to value nature by interacting with the world in which they are born and grow up. When that world includes national parks and other public lands, intact forests and charismatic species, these become treasures. Otherwise, like the giant ground sloth and dire wolf of ancient North America, they fade until not even a sense of loss remains.

Moreover, just as we are products of past judgments, so our judgments today shape the experiences and values of the future. In making a world, we also contribute to making those who live in it. This may not be a welcome burden, but it is not optional. Environmental policy making is a choice among futures.

Other questions that masquerade as technical are really ethical and political. How much should future interests—a life in 2100, for example—count in calculations today? Again, there is no merely technical answer. Cost-benefit analysis of decisions whose repercussions extend across many decades must consider effects on people not yet born. All standard methods give those future interests less weight than present ones. This "discounting" of future interests began as an accounting convention: in decisions about expenditure and investment, it is assumed that a dollar of returns in the future is equivalent to the smaller amount that would have to be invested today to reap that future income. Discounting persists for a variety of ethical and practical reasons, which people have debated intensively. The point here is not to assess those arguments, but to make a more basic point: this is another choice among values that must come before the technical procedure.

These considerations show that, although markets and economic analysis are valuable tools for coordinating choices and implementing collective commitments, they cannot substitute for those commitments. Economic analysis depends on political judgments, past, present, and future, about how to value the natural world. In shaping the world, we shape ourselves and future generations, as we are shaped in turn by the world that past generations made. This is the Anthropocene reality. Political judgment must precede economic pricing—not because politics is always morally superior, but because the valuations that economic analysis and market-creating policy require simply cannot come from economic analysis itself. With respect to the natural world, that analysis is necessarily incomplete, and political decisions about how to put cultural values to work are what fills that gap.

Economic analysis aims at a kind of neutrality and objectivity: ideally, it does not say what people should value—it only measures what they do value. Appealing to it is a way of avoiding divisive political and cultural conflict. Unfortunately, however, it depends on noneconomic values, and trying to impose "economic answers" on ethical and political questions is a form of ideological question-begging. The limitations of economics are particularly acute in connection with the natural world. Aiming at economics-style neutrality may, ironically, degrade the quality of decisions by diminishing the capacity to reflect on and argue over basic values and disagreements. Reflection and argument take effort and practice, and when people are embarrassed to express commitments that seem "subjective" or "culturally relative," they lose practice and slacken effort. A part of what we need to do—it's not enough, but necessary—is just to be bold in voicing the visions of the natural world that we carry and the ways they matter to us. The benefits could be greater understanding of what matters most to any one person or group, a clearer sense of what unites us, and a sharper image of our divisions. A critical part of environmental politics is what philosopher Charles Taylor calls an ethics of articulacy—the work of saying what we mean, finding words for what we see and feel. There is no way around this kind of work, so we might as well get better at it.

Political judgment, then, makes an economy, and an economy goes far toward making a world. Politics is the fulcrum, not because it is attractive or easy, but because the questions about what kind of world to make cannot be answered without collective choice.

Democracy and Post-Humanism

This brings us to democracy. Today democratic consent is the only widely accepted way to make political power legitimate, and for very good reasons. It expresses two critically important ideas: that power should not be exercised over people without their consent, and that all individuals should have equal voice in the question of consent—in saying yes or no to a law or a government. But democracy's standing is less secure than this quick summary suggests. Widespread acceptance of democracy as the standard of political legitimacy can be thin and nominal: it is effectively universal, but not because of deep commitment. In fact, as noted at the beginning of this chapter, pieties about democracy are now under pressure from, and sometimes yielding to, technocratic government at the heart of the historically democratic world, such as Europe, and assertive authoritarianism in countries such as Russia and China. This newly evident fragility is a reminder that much of democracy's seemingly universal triumph came from the failure and decline of alternatives, rather than from affirmative democratic success. Moreover, even democracy's thin universality is novel, a mere wrinkle in history. Less than a century ago, it was common to say that democracies were weak, enervating, feckless, and that stronger, more demanding forms of government must rise to replace them.

The romance of authoritarianism was a major theme of the twentieth century, with fascism being only the most indelible instance, and it would be complacent to suppose that the romance will not return. Not all of its variants are revolutionary; indeed, some of the most important today are technocratic and distinctly conservative in their relation to the existing order of power and authority.

Disgust with democracy grows where democracy palpably fails, and failure has recently seemed to be its specialty. Here we return to the irony that opened this chapter: the awkwardness of calling for more democracy when democracy seems a formula for failure. Today's American voters, the country's political parties, and the government they form are unlikely to strike anyone as the source of attractive answers to the question: What kind of world shall we make together? In fact, their answer is already visible in the world we are making, and its drawbacks are evident. Whatever else it means, a call for deepened democracy had better not amount to "More of this, please!"

It will not do to raise pious calls for democracy just because democracy is abstractly a good thing. The Anthropocene question—what kind of world to make together—should be taken as a challenge to democracy. The test is whether citizens can form the kind of democracy that can address the Anthropocene question, the question of what kind of world to make. A democracy that cannot do this will have marked itself as inadequate to its most basic problems.

A commitment to democracy must not be a pious test of faith in a failing system. It must be a commitment to producing democratic politics that can meet these challenges, that can achieve strength and decisiveness of the most delicate kind: in favor of self-restraint.

To ask the question, "What kind of democracy?" means asking both "What kind of democracy could address the Anthropocene question?" and "What kind of democracy should we be trying to build?" The heart of the answer must be this: a democracy capable of self-restraint. But, ironically, democratic self-restraint can come only from democratic self-assertion: a political community must be able to act effectively and decisively on hard questions in order to commit to accepting certain limitations. The ultimate political challenge is to limit, together and legitimately, the scope of human appetites, so that we do not exhaust and undo the living world. Our demands must have their boundaries. The ultimate boundary, of course, is the survival of humankind; but that limit remains remote, in time and in imagination. Closer questions form the heart of the Anthropocene problem: the need for the limits that give the world some definite shape, some stability in its climate and seasons, some diversity in species and habitats and landscapes.

It is important to emphasize that no one really knows what a democracy on the scale of Anthropocene challenges—global in scope and deep in the reach of its unavoidably shaping relationship to the living world—would look like. To write of a "we," a polity that could inhabit and constitute such a democracy, in the absence of the institutions and shared identities that would make it real, is to write fiction, imaginative literature. And such literature is unavoidably written from the perspective of someone in particular, who, with the leisure to step back and imagine a world that is nowhere near existing, is not very representative of the people who might eventually make up that polity. So a purblind fiction is the best one can do here. The thing is to hope that it is a productive fiction.

The way to make it productive is not to attempt a utopian blueprint of global Anthropocene democracy, but to name some attitudes that would bend toward it, while always keeping at the center of awareness the vast gap between the ideal of Anthropocene democracy and the very different present realities. Here are three of those attitudes. First is skepticism toward all those political approaches to the Anthropocene that patently flout a democratic future, that replace political and ethical judgment with expert technique, such as cost-benefit analysis, that conceals its political and ethical judgments and tends to hollow out, rather than expand, the ambition to make the choice of Anthropocene futures democratic. The same suspicion should be aimed at any way of shaping the planetary future that imposes one group's vision willy-nilly on another, whether through explicit unilateralism (say, a program of geo-engineering launched from the United States or India) or by guiding decisions through a mechanism that gives vastly different world-shaping power to different populations. The neoliberal approach to the Anthropocene, which defines the regulation and shaping of nature as an economic problem best handled by markets, has just this problem: the currency it uses to select futures is the literal, and unequal, currency of economic wealth, rather than the adamantly equal currency of voting. None of this means that there may not be reason to accept and participate in environmental measures that have these limitations; but it is essential to insist that they are limitations, which cast doubt on the legitimacy of the world they produce, and to aim at overcoming them.

The second attitude is more active and constructive: to keep in view a picture, however loose-knit and utopian, of a world in which Anthropocene questions would be genuinely democratic. In that world, self-aware, collective engagement with the question of what kinds of landscapes, what kind of atmosphere and climate, and what kind of world-shaping habitation to pursue would all be parts of the repertoire of self-governance. Moral and political learning, or at least persuasion, would happen through decisions about future worlds and, in turn, the experience of living in those worlds. Even to write this feels utopian, in the pejorative sense, at a time when questions such as the very reality of climate change have become partisan footballs; but perhaps it is helpful to consider contrasting areas, such as gay rights in the United States, or recent historical moments, such as the emergence of modern environmental politics in the early 1970s, for examples of this kind of shared, world-changing progress. The need for this kind of progress is not in the least a guarantee of achieving it, of course; but it is the only alternative to half-conscious impositions of futures on one another and on our descendants. The result of an undemocratic Anthropocene is an inhumane world built on unfair terms. That would be nothing new, but the prospect of it is a reason to try to do better.

The third attitude is a bridging one, which seeks to connect the present state of things with the ideal of a democratic Anthropocene. This is an attitude of intense interest in every effort that brings some people, or many people, closer to a shared identity or compatible and overlapping identities, to a sense of solidarity, and to the political and institutional resources needed for directing that sense toward shaping future worlds. These efforts may be as concrete and political as climate activism or as concrete and personal as efforts to live a carbon-neutral life in concert with neighbors doing the same. They may be aesthetic efforts to imagine the beauty of the global atmosphere and see the qualities in a transformed landscape that can inspire attachment and stewardship. They may be theoretical efforts to specify ideas of a democratic Anthropocene more rigorously and exactly. All are as likely as not to be washed away, or at least transformed, by the flow of events, sidelong surprises, unforeseen initiatives and irruptions; but if they have inspired or provoked the latter, they will at least have lent something to the direction of change. The three focal points for Anthropocene environmental law that I considered in the previous chapter are meant as examples of how this kind of interest might lead to seeing new kinds of potential in problems or initiatives that we had thought we understood.

These are all ways to make the imaginative literature of an Anthropocene democracy serve as a productive fiction, and they are what I mean when I refer to "democracy" here. So, what kind of democracy? Part of the answer is a democracy less beholden to money than the current American one. To repeat: the role that money plays in American politics gives, in effect, louder voices and more votes to those who benefit from the present economy, with all its ecological harms, than to those who seek to change it. Reducing the power of money would ease—but only ease—the grip that the current, reckless economy has on politics.

The next version of the question, "What kind of democracy?" is more radical: How human-centered should democracy be? Recent political thought presents a series of calls to turn away from "humanism," toward something we might called "post-humanism," "ecocentrism," a "new animism," or a "politics of nature"—ways of thinking and acting in the world that would give a place to the nonhuman. One call is for leveling the hierarchical divide between human and nonhuman by blurring that boundary. We are less distinct from the rest of nature than we often imagine, the argument goes, and it rests on important and often-neglected facts. Much of our weight and metabolism is formed of other creatures, bacteria above all; we are not entities but ecologies. We are animals like others: bodily, appetitive, susceptible to pain. We are embedded in the technological ecologies we have made: we are cyborgs, acting through silicon and data, seeing through plastic or glass, moving like cells through transport networks, gleaning our meme-y thoughts from our cultures like the bacteria in our guts sharing DNA. Whether we think our way to the larger scale or the smaller one, whether we emphasize our organic composition or our artificial environments, the familiar human scale gives way easily, and so does the familiar thought that a human being is a solid, self-contained entity, unique in the world.[2]

The post-humanist tendency sometimes roots human value in a more basic ontology. From this perspective, all of life, or even all of physical reality, is self-organizing matter, sometimes called *autopoesis.* Life reproduces itself by drawing and shaping "mere matter" into distinctive forms, whether trees, algae, viruses, or human bodies. From some post-humanist perspectives that call themselves ecocentric, or biocentric, autopoesis is the basis of value: all things that share this quality have an interest in perpetuating their form of being, the order they draw out of randomly existing atoms and molecules. Human consciousness, language, and culture are complex forms of autopoesis, emergent orders among other emergent orders. They do not make us unique; they only make us distinctive. We share our value with other living things—and maybe even with nonliving phenomena such as atmospheric processes. In this view, the consciousness, intentions, and personalities that humanism treats as our sources of moral importance are nothing more than special instances of the general structure of value that we share with other elements of an autopoetic universe.[3]

Post-humanism is sometimes allied with what we can call *new animism,* the suggestion that we should not think of the natural world as inert matter moved by mute physical laws, but as *acting* upon us. Political theorist Jane Bennett suggests that when micronutrients produce health or disease, storms and droughts trigger political crisis, and mountains stir the feeling of sublimity, these things are *actants:* they are not agents, in the intentional and self-aware way that humans are and some other species seem to be, but they act upon us, and upon one another. Animals, too, are actants, though the character of their intent and their consciousness is controversial. And human beings are actants, in thinking and speaking, but also in the aggregate effects of the technological and economic orders that we inhabit—in, for instance, our shared contribution to climate change. Thinking of people as actants on the scale of the species helps to make sense of a provocative claim by Bruno Latour, a sociologist and philosopher of science, to the effect that we are all climate skeptics: regardless of our thoughts and intentions, we all act as if climate change were not real or not a threat, because we act within economic and political systems that proceed as if it were not. The new animism is a kind of leveling, but also a shift of ground, like that of ecocentrism, to concentrate on what we share with the rest of nature (we *act*), rather than what distinguishes us from it (we *intend, deliberate,* and *speak*).[4]

Bennett suggests that adopting a new animism—not exactly as metaphysics, but as a moral attitude and mode of experience—might alert people to the dangers afoot in a disrupted world (climate change as a Pandora's box of actants). It also might dignify the widespread sense that *things* matter: mountains move us; the atmosphere is healthy or unwell. We know that, if these perceptions are to move us in the Anthropocene, when everything has changed, we must admit that what moves or frightens us is partly what we have created: the timeless mountain and the unchanging atmosphere are myths that we have lost and temples that we have broken. In the Anthropocene, if we are to deepen our relations to these places and processes, we will have to find a new way of grasping how they matter.

Post-humanist thinkers tend to assert that all forms of life have equal value in principle. This theoretical equality gives way in practice to the survival of one's own species; but that priority is always under principled pressure, and it might be cut back at any number of points. Maybe there should be fewer people? Maybe people should all be vegetarians? Maybe industrial agriculture is an intolerable subjection of other forms of life? Equality reasserts itself in these limits on the preference for human beings. Despite their willingness to curtail the special claims of their species, self-identified post-humanists tend to embrace human equality across lines of gender, language, culture, and sometimes even class. One might find this strange, since human equality is a core *humanist* principle, but the post-humanists propose to improve on it. The thought here is that humanism's legacy is haunted by the ghost of its founding epitome, the white and privileged male, and by his crimes. On this account, imperialism, racism, and gender hierarchy all came from the same arrogance that led to the humanist subjection of the living world, and post-humanism is the way to overcome them all.

The call to post-humanism is worth taking seriously for at least two reasons. First, it is an effort to understand the ethical complacency that enables humans to remake and destroy the nonhuman world, turning species into industrial food reserves and landscapes into fuel, mostly without more than a blink of hesitation. Post-humanists propose that these things are easy for us to do because of a worldview that puts people and our interests squarely at the center. Nudging humans away from their special place at the center of the world might be a productive response, a Copernican revolution in ethical imagination. One historical parallel, imperfect but useful, is the way that democracy itself used to presuppose intense kinds of exclusion: equal citizenship was for propertied white men, or for white men but not other races, or for men but not women. Each of those versions of political equality carried a whole ethical worldview: tolerance of slavery, of domestic violence and women's subordination, and so forth. Each worldview had to be broken apart, and the figure at its center dislodged, to deepen democracy. Maybe the next step is to dislodge humanity itself.

Second, the call for post-humanism is true, in important ways, to the forms of environmental imagination that have found so much value in the nonhuman world. From a human-centered perspective, in which only people have interests and value, the meanings we find in the rest of the world are merely projection, and treating them as more than human fancies would be fallacious sentimentalism. This exclusively human-centered outlook would wipe out a great swath of the experience, perception, and relationships—to places, other living things, and practices such as wilderness pilgrimages and eco-pastoral farming—that have formed environmental imagination. That obliteration would take away, make unsayable, much of what has mattered in powering environmental politics, and seems likely to matter just as much or more in Anthropocene politics. The basis of this obliteration would be a humanist judgment about what is real—human interests, human projects—and what is not: relations with the nonhuman world, a sense that parts and places of that world have their own values and purposes. The opposite hope is that a post-humanist attitude would open space for experiences and relationships that cross the boundary between human and nonhuman, as so much of environmental imagination has done.

Post-humanism, then, is a chapter in the long dispute over whether, and in what ways, the natural world contains meaning, value, and order that humans can grasp and acknowledge. What may seem at first glance to be just a fad in the humanities, then, is better understood as a new expression of an old and persistent impulse in philosophy, one rooted in an equally persistent circuit between people and the natural world: we do, over and again, find meaning and value in that world. To repurpose Galileo's apocryphal murmur of defiance *(eppur si muove):* for all the denials, nevertheless it does move us.

So, what kind of democracy? Should we seek a biologically egalitarian democracy, a polity of all beings, or of all actants, to govern a world that is at once natural and artificial? A forceful *No!* comes from the tradition of John Stuart Mill, echoed today in the liberal humanism of philosopher Jürgen Habermas. In this tradition, what defines human beings morally and politically is precisely what marks the impassable barrier between us and the rest of the world. This is the marriage of self-awareness and language that means humans can abstract from and reflect upon our own experience; consider our motives and choose among possible actions; deliberately adopt a value as our own; and make a commitment, then hold

ourselves to it as a matter of intentional consistency. These capacities add up to what is sometimes called *reason* and sometimes
freedom: the power to author our acts and lives, according to patterns we can establish, name, consider, and revise—patterns that
are not our acts and lives themselves, but ideals, principles, or commitments that we follow as things distinct from what we happen
to do. To different degrees and in different ways, thinkers in this
tradition insist that what I have just described as reason or freedom
is what makes human beings morally important. It is what we value
in one another—the basis of our dignity, as Habermas puts it—
which we do not share, so far as we know, with anything else on
earth.

According to this approach, post-humanism is a dangerous
mistake. When we level down, thinking of people as assemblages
of bacteria, raw matter, and technology, linked by the same bodily
needs and pains that affect dogs and reptiles, we elide the thing that
matters most: the reason that is the basis of our dignity. When we
level up, highlighting the ways that other forms of life share autopoesis and affection, when we observe that even weather systems
seem to "act," we make a bad analogy, because once again we are
ignoring the freedom that sets us apart from these other things and
that imparts specifically *human* dignity. These mistakes are dangerous, according to the humanist position, because they misread
history. Humanism was not the handmaiden of such hierarchical
abuses as slavery, imperialism, and twentieth-century genocides.
Those crimes were *failures of humanism,* failures to appreciate its
force and follow through on its principles. Instead of acknowledging the common core of humanity that they shared with their
victims, the authors of those crimes treated others as parts of nature: as animals to be exploited or raw resources to be developed.
In the case of the Nazis' fascism, the abuses involved understanding
all of humanity as a "natural" phenomenon—leveling down—and
aiming to make one's own people a world-historical biological

success. By contrast, the slow and partial progress of human equality comes from recognizing what we have in common, the universal qualities of language, reason, and freedom that unite people across race, sex, and nationality—and divide them, essentially, from the rest of the world, whether natural or artificial. Treating gut bacteria and cyborg communication as morally important misses the point, and opens space for forgetting the special dignity of human beings. Because history shows how fragile that dignity is, this philosophical mistake is not a casual matter. Democracy is the form of government that tries to take seriously the moral value of each *human* participant. Whatever people make of the natural world, they should never imagine the democratic enterprise as post-humanist. So goes the humanist riposte.

What kind of democracy, then? I would like to resist the choice between the post-humanist position and the humanist riposte, and instead adopt both, but each for a different sort of work. Each names truths that are important but incomplete. Both sides are unconvincing when they blame the other for historical wrongs and warn that adopting those ideas will make such crimes more likely today. Taken together, this should mean that one can learn from both, without being too troubled by dire warnings against stumbling onto the wrong side of history.

First to the most powerful part of the traditional humanist position: the special place of human choice, judgment, and value. Nature does not teach us how to live. Equality, whether among people, cultures, or species, never follows from any set of facts. No share of human body weight that comes from bacteria, or of DNA in common with roundworms, can imply respect or sympathy for other forms of life. Nor do these facts about nature imply any view of equality among human beings: facts about gut bacteria and DNA may mean that a twenty-first-century American man has to imagine himself somewhat differently from the average British imperial administrator in 1815, but that does not mean he will be any more respectful of other cultures or races, or of women. The bases of that respect lie elsewhere.

Post-humanism treasures equality, among species and life forms as well as (usually) among kinds of human beings; but equality is not a fact. It is a principle. As such, it is thoroughly artificial. It is created through abstraction—the recognition that, for all their palpable differences, people share a common core of qualities, and the assertion that we should value those commonalities above the differences. ("Diversity," with its embrace of "difference," is not a counterexample, but simply an instance of valuing people's experiences, cultures, etc. *because they are people* and hence presumptively morally equal.) Equality is established through language: by naming it, we place it in the common world of artificial principle, where all may see it, call on it, and fight over its meaning. Equality takes force from the ultimate artificiality, legal pronouncement, such as the U.S. Constitution's guarantee of "equal protection of the laws." Indeed, if I were to make a list of actants in the history of the United States, I would place the phrase "all men are created equal" somewhere in the vicinity of the Union Army and the fertile soil of the Midwest. Moreover, to treat this efflorescence of language and principle as just another form of autopoesis would miss its uniqueness: such material makes an artificial world—of language, culture, politics, and law—where an artificial principle such as equality can acquire reality and become a shared reference point for fights over its meaning. It is only in this artificial world that autopoetic creatures turn back to examine their own self-replicating orders and change them, deliberately and reflectively, in keeping with standards such as equality, which they created themselves but nonetheless experience as having a reality independent of their creators.

Law and politics, those houses of rule and principle, are where the humanist case is most powerful. They are artificial—they have to be, because they exist only where people make them—and they are the only possible houses for precious values such as equality. They rest squarely on those qualities that distinguish people from everything else. We are, to be sure, fleshy animals and autopoetic like trees, and we are teched-up cyborgs, too. But none of these leveling observations, which tie us to the rest of the post-natural world, quite touches the core of what makes us citizens. It is as citizens—as participants in and authors of politics and law—that we make and live by principles. It is also as citizens that we deliberately and collectively shift our autopoesis, building a different kind of home for ourselves in the living world.

These points mean that calls for inter-species egalitarianism and for a politics based in councils of all beings can only be metaphors. The artificial worlds of principle and of politics are built from language and abstraction; without language and abstraction, one cannot enter these worlds. Whatever values have weight in those artificial realms must be ones that humans can grasp. Because we cannot know the perspective, if there is one, of a tree or a termite colony, we cannot represent them in our councils, any more than we can negotiate respectfully with actants such as a changing global atmosphere. The bounds of our knowledge and imagination are the bounds of our possible politics. The most that humans can do here is to know what we cannot know, and recognize the uncanniness that is both the boundary marker and the psychic weather of the borderlands.

Moreover, there is something to protect in our artificiality. Thinking of ourselves as all-too-natural has often provided excuses for exercising power while avoiding ethical and political challenges. Treating humanity as just "part of nature" has fostered racism, imperialism, and fascism, which imagined social life through a corrupted Darwinian triumphalism. Today the danger is different. A twenty-first-century celebration of autopoesis as a "natural" social form can all too easily conjure up the capitalist market. Markets are relentlessly praised as forms of spontaneous order, in contrast to politics. Economist and social theorist Friedrich Hayek's influential praise of markets rests on exactly this distinction, and has won acolytes from Silicon Valley to the anti-government populist right. And markets, whatever their other virtues as instruments of policy, are the greatest vehicles of inequality today, driving growing differences in wealth, opportunity, and income across much of the world. In a subtler way, market participants view one another instrumentally: they approach one another as resources, occasions for profit or some other satisfaction. While they may also be connected by other kinds of relationships, these come under relentless pressure from market logic, which always asks what others have to offer one's own projects and preferences. The abstract logic of equality gives way to concrete differences in bargaining power and in people's usefulness to one another. In practice, this steady rhythm of self-interest and advantage taking, and not the enslavement or conquest of the past, is the way that people today treat one another as mere parts of nature, mere resources. Although declared post-humanists are generally academics of the left, and thus ideologically skeptical of markets, their ideas have affinities with the autopoetic, anti-political markets of Hayek. Whatever they intend, this will be part of the meaning of their ideas in a time that already celebrates markets for their alleged spontaneous order and mistrusts the artificial equality of politics.

Now, however, consider the other side. Although the signal human achievements are artificial, that is not because we are artificial creatures. We are natural creatures. A great deal of our experience is formed out of what we share, or seem to share, with other living things. We are, as the post-humanists say, bodily, emotional, even bacterial animals. Our formal approach to one another, as political and legal equals, is palpably artificial—a fact that has been the starting point for generations of criticism directed at liberal society and legalistic culture. According to this criticism, the society of rights and equality is thin and superficial in the connections it draws among people, remote from the intimate and powerful resonances of identity and experience.

So it is. Knowing one another through the public language and legal forms of modern liberalism is a poor sort of knowledge. Compare such language to liturgies, intimate jokes, the old catchphrases of family and nation, even the slurs that mark your people off from their neighbors: this second kind of language, exactly because it is exclusionary and unequal, touches a different chord.

Language itself can be a poor thing, as anyone knows who has relied on it too much. Compare explaining yourself to another with being terrified, then relieved, together; with giving or receiving care in a time of sickness or suffering; with working together or waking up together; or just with touching someone. Any of these can leave people strangers, of course, but they can also produce a degree of mutual knowledge that language often fails to approach. They are experiences that draw on our resemblance to other animals, not our difference from them. But in us, all of these experiences come with interpretations, meanings, and it will be language that carries those beyond what is intimately shared and makes them common.

When interpretations of our natural, emotional, and bodily experience enter politics, they add depth and texture, and even accrete to build new principles that anchor future reasoning. To say that the considerations that guide human decisions must be intelligible to humans, and that public expressions of them must be in language, does not at all mean that their sources must be restricted to our uniquely rational and linguistic qualities. Much of environmental imagination and public language have developed through accounts of intimate, strange, sensual, and aesthetic encounters with the natural world, and the ways those helped people like Thoreau, Muir, Leopold, and Carson to reimagine their humanity. The history of environmental lawmaking is evidence that we need this kind of language, experience, and motivation, even at the very heart of the artificial and distinctive achievements of humanity, politics, and law. To be fully human, we need the parts of us that are not uniquely human. They, too, are part of the identities, insights, and attachments that we bring to the table of our artificial and common worlds.

What kind of democracy, then? At least in part, a democracy open to the strange intuitions of post-humanism: intuitions of ethical affinity with other species, of the moral importance of landscapes and climates, of the permeable line between humans and the rest of the living world.

Exclusion and Misanthropy

What should we make of the fact that much of the history of environmental imagination is pessimistic, misanthropic, and too much the special property of privileged groups? The answer to the last question, about the elite sources of environmental imagination, is the simplest. Undue privilege is not intrinsic in environmental imagination; it is just the product of broader inequalities that have marked all the politics of the modern world, including the politics of nature. This is a legacy to be overcome. Saying that the Anthropocene should take its standard from democracy means that everyone must have a voice in shaping the world. Bringing the question of the nonhuman world fully into politics is as inclusive or exclusionary as the politics itself.

But the problems of pessimism and misanthropy remain. American environmental imagination is deeply involved in a set of reactions against strands of the modern world: from Thoreau's shopkeepers to Muir's lowlands, from Roosevelt's unhealthful cities to the tourists the Wilderness Society struggled to keep out of its shrines, the involvement with nature has been a way to stand apart from the ordinary human situation, with all its compromises, indignities, and petty satisfactions. A disgust at much of humanity shows up again and again, and aligning with nature has often meant disowning ordinary humanity, or at least exempting oneself from it.

There is also pessimism. Aldo Leopold rejected human mastery of the world as "biotic arrogance," while Fairfield Osborn saw it pitting humanity mortally against nature, with humanity bound to lose, but only after a spurious (because unsustainable) victory. Although Rachel Carson was careful to insist that there were many safe and scientifically sound ways to engineer nature and control pests, critics have accused her of pessimistic fearmongering in her categorical denunciation of pesticides as technologies of hubris and self-destruction. Consider, by contrast, John Stuart Mill's argument that our duty toward nature is simply to transform it to promote human security and freedom. Mill's formula distills centuries of humanitarian hopes of making the world more humane by mastering it. The stronger an environmentalist's pessimism about technology, the more easily he or she writes off that hope as hubris. This pessimism sometimes joins with an indictment against humanity for disrupting the natural order by raising our needs above those of the rest of the living world. Then the complaint is not just that controlling nature is likely to fail—the basic pessimistic claim—but that success would itself be a kind of moral failure.

Environmental historian William Cronon has gathered these criticisms, especially disgust at humanity, into a charge that environmentalism as a whole suffers from what he calls "the trouble with wilderness." The trouble is that American environmentalists imagine wild nature as diametrically opposed to the lowlands of society, technology, and politics—a view that enables nature's devotees to divide their loyalties in a too-convenient copout. When in the lowlands of everyday life, they are not entirely of it, because they hold apart the most essential portion of themselves. In wild nature, they cultivate a (supposedly) higher part of the self, but assume that this, the best in them, cannot thrive where they spend most of their time and energy. The best and highest, what they live for, is elsewhere for most of their lives. This divided attitude, according to Cronon, is an excuse to neglect and disrespect the places where environmentalists actually live and the people they live among. This attitude ironically also fails to take seriously the "higher" values of nature, because it reserves those values for rare occasions in faraway places, rather than working to bring them into everyday life.[5]

To assess this charge, it helps to ask an impolitic question: whether, in some versions, pessimism and misanthropy can be helpful. The impulse to treat them as self-evidently bad reveals something about the premises of our time, premises that might be worth challenging. Our public ideas encourage accepting—at least nominally—the equal value of every individual's perspective and denying that anyone has any business telling others how to live. Although we do rather poorly at actually showing respect to each person, we happily knock others off their high horses. American politics accepts enormous economic inequality, so long as it comes with cultural equality. A billionaire mayor has his democratic credentials questioned not when he buys elections but when he presumes to prohibit New Yorkers from drinking giant sodas—as if he, and medical science, knew better. American tax rebellions are more likely to aim at cutting funds for public institutions that can be colored as elitist, such as public broadcasting or state universities, than at raising rates for the wealthy. This style of equality helps to power the disdain for so-called elitism and misanthropy. What makes backcountry skis better than a snowmobile, a wilderness better than a scenic highway, solitude better than a mall or nightclub? And who has any business saying so? "Nothing" and "nobody" are today's habitual answers.

Our present age is also committed to boundless economic growth. The survival of any western government, and probably the very legitimacy of states such as China, depend on it. In our politics, it is suicide to ask whether mandatory economic optimism points not to real prospects, but only to a convenient illusion.

Environmental ideas sometimes loosen the hold of these premises in productive ways. Take the prejudice against judgment, the assertion that no one is entitled to assess another's life. Because environmental lawmaking dedicates acreage and resources to visions of nature's value and our place in it, it unavoidably engages questions about what is valuable and how to live. Being committed to one version of nature's value and willing to argue and fight for it can indeed seem judgmental, and, in certain events, elitist. The unavoidable clash between many environmental ideas and our highways and strip malls can seem misanthropic. But that is what it means to argue for a view of nature's value that lacks the support of a present majority or a cost-benefit report. This conflict between things-as-they-are and an urgent account of how they might be is intrinsic to the prophetic strain of environmental politics, which has always been a part of its power, and is more important than ever today.

The anti-judgmental, live-and-let-live attitude, for all its good points, is too superficial to get a hold on many environmental problems. Sometimes neutrality about values is spurious. Any environmental regime—like any economic order, like any legal order at all—tilts power, resources, and everyday experience toward one version of how to live together, and those who see things differently have no choice but to argue democratically about the direction of the tilt. In this way, arguments about nature's value ask a democratic country to recognize the questions it is already unavoidably answering. Withholding judgment, though it may seem egalitarian, ironically simply benefits those whom the present system privileges, because it leaves their privilege undisturbed.

A dissenter must be able to address a majority by criticizing, even denouncing it. Citizens must understand that, in environmental politics as elsewhere, their government is choosing among values, in the face of disagreement, and that such choice is unavoidable. A democratic people should be able to hope that, over time, it is improving—not just getting richer, but understanding more of how it intends to live and coming closer to that ideal. For this to make sense, its members must be able to step outside the familiar present and call on a better version of the country. They will call on familiar strands of dissent, of course—religious prophecy, constitutional ideals, practices of civil disobedience—to show that they are addressing the present from a possible, imagined future. A democratic culture gives its members the means to speak to one another in this way. Calling on nature is one of the ways such speech is possible in American politics. It troubles our simpler premises—neutrality and nonjudgment—but strengthens essential democratic powers: to criticize, exhort, and change ourselves.

This is where taking responsibility for nature and taking responsibility for democracy come together. The democratic responsibility is the responsibility of making a world, a responsibility that, for much of human experience, has fallen to the imagined legislation of gods. This goes for both the political and the natural world. Always bound together in imagination, in the Anthropocene these two are inseparable in fact.

Pessimism, criticism, and the social wariness that misanthropy cultivates all draw attention to basic questions: What are we doing? What shall we do next? They remind us that no providence is overseeing our burning through the planet's storehouses of energy and fertility—for they were not created as storehouses at all. They remind us that our cultural and political drift is not all we can or might wish it to be, even when a majority of us go along with it, whether comfortably or anxiously. They call us back to questions we cannot help answering, if only implicitly or passively, and which we would therefore do well to address by name, even if our questions are discomfiting and confusing. Appeals to nature are part of our repertoire for asking uncomfortable and necessary questions of one another. Calling on nature serves the most rational human power—criticism in service of clear choice; and it sometimes uses the tools and spurs of misanthropy and pessimism to do so. So understood, it does not step out of the democratic project, but presses deeper into it.

The misanthropic worry is sometimes well-founded. Environmental ideas can be, and frequently have been, braided together with bigotry, narrowness, obtuse privilege and nostalgia, and indifference to careful argument. Both history and reflection suggest that these connections are more than bad luck, that environmental ideas have some affinity with such unpleasant attitudes. Environmental thought bears the marks of the Romantic revolt against narrow forms of reason, and shares its tendency to celebrate irrationality as insight and freedom. Nature, mute and sometimes beautiful, invites the narcissistic projections of nostalgia. Environmentalism often begins in response to harm that humans have done, and in "taking nature's side" it can slide into dislike of humanity, and for this reason it attracts and amplifies misanthropy.

When environmental thought has not been parochial or immature, however, its relation to these issues has been constructive. It has pressed at the seams of the same modern commitments it has been accused of betraying—democracy, humanitarianism, technological mastery, reason. The problems it poses are reminders that democracy is not just the stripping away of old hierarchies; it means making the world together, including taking responsibility for our mutually shaping interaction with nature. Arguments about how to live can grow richer when citizens feel the power to draw apart from the present and imagine the future, to escape—temporarily—from familiar human entanglements into a sense of their place in the larger living world. This is part of the cultural, and democratic, benefit of the complicated ambition to align oneself with nature.

It becomes even more relevant, if also more complicated, in a post-natural world.

Trying to build a peaceful and humane world means finding a way to live peaceably with nature, not just mining it for our convenience. Environmentalism, taken in its best light, is a reminder that our dominant versions of democracy, reason, and progress are still superficial, especially because they rely on ignoring or recklessly exploiting nature, and that, for these values to be sustainable, we must give them a sustainable relation to the larger living world.

A democracy open to post-human encounters with the living world would be more likely to find ways to restrain its demands and stop short of exhausting the planet. The history of environmental lawmaking suggests that people are best able to change their ways when they find two things at once in nature: something to fear, a threat they must avoid, and also something to love, a quality they can admire or respect, and which they can do their best to honor. The first impulse, of fear, can be rendered in purely human-centered terms, as a matter of avoiding environmental crisis. The second impulse, of love, engages animist intuitions and carries us toward post-humanism, which is perhaps just another name for an enriched humanism. Either impulse can stay the human hand, but the first stops it just short of being burnt or broken. The second keeps the hand poised, extended in greeting or in an offer of peace. This gesture is the beginning of collaboration, among people but also beyond us, in building our next home.

NOTES

ACKNOWLEDGMENTS

INDEX

NOTES

PROLOGUE

1. Roy Scranton, "Learning How to Die in the Anthropocene," *New York Times*, Opinionator: The Stone (November 10, 2013).
2. William Bradford, "A Hideous and Desolate Wilderness," in *Environment: An Interdisciplinary Anthology*, ed. Glenn Adelson et al. (New Haven: Yale University Press, 2008), 283.

INTRODUCTION

1. William Wordsworth, "The Tables Turned," in *Selected Poems and Prefaces*, ed. Jack Stillinger (Boston: Houghton Mifflin, 1965), 107.
2. Jean-Jacques Rousseau, *Emile; or, On Education*, trans. Allan Bloom (New York: Basic Books, 1979), 47.
3. Ibid. at 37, 39.
4. John Evelyn, *The History of Religion: A Rational Account of the True Religion*, vol. 1 (London: Henry Colburn, 1850); John Ray, *The Wisdom of God Manifested in the Works of Creation*, 7th ed. (London: Printed by R. Harbin for William Innys, 1717), 375.
5. John Locke, "Second Treatise of Government," in Locke, *The Treatises of Government*, student ed., ed. Peter Laslett (Cambridge: Cambridge University Press, 2004), bk. 5.
6. Edmund Burke, "Letter from the New to the Old Whigs," in *The Works of the Right Honourable Edmund Burke*, vol. 4 (London: John C. Nimmo, 1887), 176.
7. John Stuart Mill, "Nature," in Mill, *Three Essays on Religion* (London: Longmans, Green, Brader, and Dyer, 1874), 64.

8. Thomas Piketty, *Capital in the Twenty-First Century* (Cambridge, Mass.: Harvard University Press, 2014), 1–39, 336–376.

9. See John Muir, *My First Summer in the Sierra* (Boston: Houghton Mifflin, 1911), 129, 124.

10. Robert Sterling Yard, *The Book of National Parks* (New York: Scribner's, 1919).

11. Frederick Jackson Turner, *The Significance of the Frontier in American History* (1893; rpt. New York: Henry Holt, 1931), 38.

12. Ibid., 12.

13. Ibid., 293.

14. Ibid., 246.

15. Ibid., 319.

16. Ibid., 280.

17. Abraham Lincoln, "Address to the Wisconsin Agricultural Society" (Milwaukee, September 30, 1859).

18. William Gilpin, *Mission of the North American People, Geographical, Social, and Political*, 2nd ed. (Philadelphia: Lippincott, 1874), 69–70 and passim.

19. Mencken's comment about Theodore Roosevelt is quoted in Eric Foner, *The Story of American Freedom* (New York: Norton, 1999), 154–155.

20. Robert Underwood Johnson, "John Muir as I Knew Him," *Sierra Club Bulletin* 10:2 (1916), 2–3.

21. "Fighting to Save the Earth from Man," *Time* (February 2, 1970), 56.

22. Amartya Sen, *Development as Freedom* (New York: Knopf, 1999), 152–153.

1. AN UNEQUAL TERRAIN

1. President Thomas Jefferson, "First Inaugural Address" (Washington, D.C., March 4, 1801).

2. William Gilpin, *Mission of the North American People: Geographical, Social, and Political,* 2nd ed. (Philadelphia: Lippincott, 1874), 188–189.

3. For example, President John Tyler praised "our fellow citizens who press forward into the wilderness and are the pioneers in the work of its reclamation" ("Third Annual Message to Congress," December 5, 1843), and James Buchanan described the task of territorial settlement as "generally to reclaim the wilderness" ("Second Annual Message to Congress," December 6, 1858).

4. William Cronon, "The Trouble with Wilderness," in *Uncommon Ground: Rethinking the Human Place in Nature* (New York: Norton, 1995), 69–90.

5. John Winthrop, *Winthrop's Journal "History of New England,"* vol. 1, ed. James Kendall Hosmer (New York: Scribner's, 1908), 83–84.

6. Ibid., 55.

7. Ibid., 103–104.

8. Ibid., 97.

9. Ibid., 64.

10. Ibid., 120–121.

11. Ibid., 53.

12. William Bradford, *History of the Plymouth Plantation, 1620–1647*, ed. Worthington Chauncey Ford (Boston: Houghton Mifflin, 1912), 237.

13. Ibid., 239, 240.

14. Ibid., 239; Judges 16:23; 1 Samuel 5:3–7.

15. John Evelyn, *The Diary of John Evelyn*, ed. William Bray (New York: M. Walter Dunne, 1901), 91.

16. Ibid., 179.

17. Ibid., 181.

18. Henry David Thoreau, *Walden and Other Writings* (New York: Barnes and Noble Classics, 1993), 53.

19. John Evelyn, *The History of Religion: A Rational Account of the True Religion*, vol. 1 (London: Henry Colburn, 1850), xvii–xxxiii (preface).

20. Henry More, "Psychozoia," in *The Complete Poems of Dr. Henry More, 1614–1687*, vo. 9, ed. Alexander Balloch Grosart (Edinburgh: Edinburgh University Press, 1878), 31.

21. Donald Worster, *Nature's Economy: A History of Ecological Ideas* (Cambridge: Cambridge University Press, 1985), 26–55.

22. Evelyn, *Diary*, 67–68.

23. Ibid., 69, 18.

24. John Ray, *The Wisdom of God Manifested in the Works of Creation*, 7th ed. (London: Printed by R. Harbin for William Innys, 1717), 375.

25. Ibid., 404.

26. Jonathan Edwards, "Sinners in the Hands of an Angry God," July 8, 1741, Enfield, Massachusetts (now Connecticut).

27. Quoted in Andrew D. Williams, "The Literature of the 1727 New England Earthquake," *Early American Literature* 7:3 (1973), 281.

28. Thomas Prince, "A Sermon on Earthquakes," in *The Puritan Sermon in America, 1630–1750*, ed. Ronald Bosco (New York: Scholars' Facsimiles and Reprints, 1978), 141.

29. Ibid.

30. This history is set out in vivid and accessible form in Stephen Greenblatt, *The Swerve: How the World Became Modern* (New York: Norton, 2011).

31. The eclipse of England's Civil War radicalism is explored in Christopher Hill, *The Experience of Defeat: Milton and Some Contemporaries* (Chicago: Bookmarks, 1994).

32. Max Weber, *Essays in Sociology,* in M. Weber, H. Gerth, and C. W. Mills, eds., *From Max Weber* (New York: Oxford University Press, 1958), 280.

33. See Edmund S. Morgan, *American Slavery, American Freedom* (New York: Norton, 1975), for this argument.

34. Hugh Henry Brackenridge, *Modern Chivalry,* ed. Claude M. Newlin (New York: Hafner, 1962), 135.

2. GOD'S AVID GARDENERS

1. James Wilson, "Oration Delivered at the Procession at Philadelphia" (July 4, 1788).

2. Ibid.

3. See Thomas Jefferson, "First Inaugural Address" (Washington, D.C., March 4, 1801).

4. See Gordon S. Wood, *Empire of Liberty: A History of the Early Republic* (Oxford: Oxford University Press, 2009), 357–399 (on the Jeffersonian program of western settlement); Drew R. McCoy, *The Elusive Republic: Political Economy in Jeffersonian America* (New York: Norton, 1980), 48–100, 185–208 (describing the "republican" conception of proprietor-based freedom and virtue, and the role of frontier settlement in promoting it); Eric Foner, *Free Soil, Free Labor, Free Men: The Ideology of the Republican Party before the Civil War* (Oxford: Oxford University Press, 1970), 1–37 (describing the interlaced premises of free-labor thought and the program of frontier settlement).

5. Wood, *Empire of Liberty,* 347–356 (on the revaluation of labor); Foner, *Free Labor,* 1–72 (on the dignity of labor).

6. John Locke, "Second Treatise of Government," in Locke, *The Treatises of Government,* student edition, ed. Peter Laslett (Cambridge: Cambridge University Press, 2004), bk. 5, para. 27, 287–288.

7. Ibid., bk. 5, para 49, 301; bk. 2, 269–278.

8. Ibid., para. 45, 299.

9. Ibid., para. 37 and 38, 292–295.

10. John Quincy Adams, "An Oration Delivered at Plymouth" (Plymouth, Massachusetts, December 22, 1802).

11. James Kent, *Commentaries on American Law*, 3:387 (14th ed., 1896).

12. Ibid.

13. Ibid.

14. Kent, *Commentaries on American Law*, 4:307; *Johnson v. M'Intosh*, 21 US 543 (1823).

15. *Johnson v. M'Intosh*, 21 US at 572 (declining to base opinion "solely on . . . principles of abstract justice"), 588 (declining to decide on "abstract principles" whether cultivators can displace noncultivators).

16. Ibid., 591, 573.

17. Thomas Morton, *The New English Canaan of Thomas Morton*, ed. Charles Francis Adams (Boston: Printed by John Wilson and Son, 1883), 114.

18. Ibid., 212, 209, 209.

19. Ibid., 179, 182–187, 198–199.

20. Ibid., 188, 205, 206.

21. Thomas Paine, "Letter Concerning *The Age of Reason*," in *The Writings of Thomas Paine*, ed. Moncure Daniel Conway, 4 vols. (New York: Putnam's, 1894), 4:196.

22. Paine, "The American Crisis," ibid., 1:268.

23. Paine, "The Forester Letters No. IV," ibid., 1:154–155.

24. Paine, "The American Crisis II," ibid., 1:180.

25. Paine, "Forester's Letters," ibid., 1:138–139.

26. Paine, "Peace, and the Newfoundland Fisheries," ibid., 2:17–18.

27. Paine, "African Slavery in America," ibid., 1:8.

3. NATURE AS TEACHER

1. Alexis de Tocqueville, *Journey to America*, trans. George Lawrence, ed. J. P. Mayer (New Haven: Yale University Press, 1960), 335.

2. Ibid.

3. Ibid., 337.

4. Ibid., 339.

5. Ibid., 340.

6. Thomas Jefferson, *Notes on the State of Virginia*, 1, in *The Writings of Thomas Jefferson*, vol. 2, ed. Albert Ellery Bergh (Washington, D.C.: Thomas Jefferson Memorial Association, 1907), 31–32.

7. Lewis, quoted in Charles Henry Carey, *A History of Oregon* (Chicago: The Pioneer Publishing Company, 1922), 175.

8. Timothy Dwight, *Travels in New England and New York,* vol. 1 (New Haven: self-published, 1821), vii–viii, 83.

9. Freneau, "On Mr. Paine's Rights of Man," in *Poems of Freneau,* ed. Harry Hayden Clark (New York: Harcourt, Brace, 1929), 124–125.

10. Freneau, "America Independent," ibid., 24, 32.

11. Freneau, "On the Uniformity and Perfection of Nature," ibid., 423–424.

12. Freneau, "On the Religion of Nature," ibid., 424.

13. Ibid., 425.

14. Freneau, "The Indian Burying Ground," in *Poems of Freneau,* 355–356.

15. Ibid., 92–93.

16. Ibid., 355–356.

17. John Quincy Adams, "Society and Civilization," *American Review* (July 1845), 82.

18. Ibid., 83.

19. Ibid., 84.

20. Ibid., 87.

21. Ibid., 87–88.

22. James Wilson, "Lectures on Law," in *The Works of the Honourable James Wilson, L.L.D.,* ed. Bird Wilson, Esq. (Philadelphia: Lorenzo Press, 1804), 55.

23. Ibid., 36–37.

24. Anonymous, "California," *American Review* (April 1849), 331, 338.

25. This discussion is indebted to Angela Miller's extremely interesting and illuminating study, *The Empire of the Eye* (Ithaca: Cornell University Press, 1993).

26. Asher Durand, "Introductory," in *The Crayon,* vol. 1, no. 1 (January 3, 1855), 1.

27. Thomas Cole, "Essay on American Scenery," *American Monthly Magazine,* 1 (January 1835).

28. Durand, "Introductory," 1.

29. Cole, "Essay."

30. Durand, "Introductory."

31. Cole, "Essay."

4. NATURAL UTOPIAS

1. John Muir, "A Wind-Storm in the Forests," in *American Earth: Environmental Writing since Thoreau,* ed. Bill McKibben (New York: Literary Classics of the United States, 2008), 89–97.

2. Henry David Thoreau, "Paradise (To Be) Regained," in *The Writings of Henry David Thoreau,* vol. 10 (Cambridge, Mass.: Riverside Press, 1894), 39.

3. Ibid.

4. Ibid., 62, 66, 67, 68.

5. Francis Bacon, "New Atlantis," in *Three Early Modern Utopias: Utopia, New Atlantis, The Isle of Pines,* ed. Susan Bruce (New York: Oxford University Press, 1999), 149–186.

6. *Congressional Record* 107, 18365 (1961).

7. Ibid.

8. Ralph Waldo Emerson, "Nature," in *The Essential Writings of Ralph Waldo Emerson,* ed. Brooks Atkinson (New York: Modern Library, 2000), 37.

9. Henry Stephens Salt, *The Life of Henry David Thoreau* (London: Richard Bentley and Son, 1890), 221.

10. Henry David Thoreau, *Walden and Other Writings* (New York: Barnes and Noble Classics, 1993), 237.

11. Ibid., 439.

12. Thoreau, "Paradise," 64.

13. Thoreau, *Walden,* 426.

14. This discussion is indebted to Lawrence Buell's treatment of the same themes in Buell, *The Environmental Imagination: Thoreau, Nature Writing, and the Formation of American Culture* (Cambridge, Mass.: Harvard University Press, 1995).

15. John Muir, *Our National Parks* (Boston: Houghton Mifflin, 1901), 3–5.

16. John Muir, *My First Summer in the Sierra* (Boston: Houghton Mifflin, 1911), 115–116.

17. Ibid., 131.

18. William James, *The Varieties of Religious Experience* (New York: Modern Library, 1994), 210–239.

19. Muir, *My First Summer,* 129, 128, 124.

20. William Frederic Bade, "To Higher Sierras," *Sierra Club Bulletin* 10 (1916–1919), 38, 40 (counting Muir among the "prophets and interpreters of nature"); "John Muir, Doctor of Laws, University of California (Honorary Degree)," reprinted in *Sierra Club Bulletin* 10 (1916–1919), 24 (calling Muir "uniquely gifted to interpret unto other men [nature's] mind and ways").

21. "Notable Books in Brief Review: John Muir's Account of His Historic Thousand-Mile Walk to the Gulf, and Other Recent Publications," *New York Times* (January 21, 1917), BR4.

22. Bade, "To Higher Sierras."

23. Muir, *Our National Parks*, 135–136.

24. Helen M. Gompertz, "A Tramp to Mt. Lyell," *Sierra Club Bulletin* 1 (1893–1896), 136, 141.

25. John R. Glascock, "A California Outing," *Sierra Club Bulletin* 1 (1893–1896), 147, 161.

26. Marion Randall, "Some Aspects of a Sierra Club Outing," *Sierra Club Bulletin* 5 (1904–1905), 221, 227–228.

27. Glascock, "A California Outing."

28. Randall, "Some Aspects of a Sierra Club Outing."

29. Muir, *Our National Parks,* 5.

30. Muir, *My First Summer,* 131.

31. Muir, "A Wind-Storm," 89, 95, 97.

32. See Joseph LeConte, *Religion and Science* (New York: Appleton, 1884), 269–281 (divinity expresses itself throughout nature, with increasing individuation, culminating in human consciousness).

33. Ibid., 281.

34. Joseph LeConte, *Evolution and Its Relation to Religious Thought* (New York: Appleton, 1888), 282–283 (emphasis in original).

35. Ibid., 285, 306.

36. LeConte, *Religion and Science,* 143.

37. *Congressional Record* 4, 3453, 3488 (1883) (Statement of Senator Ingalls).

38. *Congressional Globe,* 38th Cong., 1st Sess., 2300 (1864) (Statement of Senator Conness).

39. *Congressional Record* 4, 3487 (1883) (Statement of Senator Vest). The phrase comes from Epistle Four of Alexander Pope's *Essay on Man*, where Pope declares, "Worth makes the man, and want of the fellow; the rest is all but leather or prunella"—in other words, apparel rather than substance; prunella is a good-quality cloth once used to dress scholars, clerics, and lawyers. Ironically, Vest seems to misunderstood the phrase as referring to economic worthlessness.

40. George Perkins Marsh, *Man and Nature; or, Physical Geography as Modified by Human Action,* ed. David Lowenthal (Seattle: University of Washington Press, 1864), 290, 253.

41. See, e.g., F. E. Olmsted, "Fire and the Forest: The Theory of 'Light Burning,'" *Sierra Club Bulletin* 8 (1911), 43–47 (discussing methods of fire control on public lands); J. Horace McFarland, "Are National Parks Worth While?"

Sierra Club Bulletin 8 (1911), 236–239 (praising the parks as balm for "times when the tired spirit seeks a wider space for change and rest," but lamenting the absence of any unified policy or federal body devoted to management of the parks).

42. See *Sierra Club Bulletin* 8 (1911), 217–239 (collecting various updates on parks management, funding, and prospects for legislation establishing a unified management system).

43. See "Editorials," *Sierra Club Bulletin* 8 (1911), 205–207.

44. "Sierra Club Statement Submitted to Presidential Conference on the Conservation of Natural Resources," reprinted in *Sierra Club Bulletin* 6 (1908), 318.

45. Robert Sterling Yard, *The Book of National Parks* (New York: Scribner's, 1919), 20–21.

46. Muir, *Our National Parks,* 78.

47. Donald Worster, *A Passion for Nature: The Life of John Muir* (Oxford: Oxford University Press, 2008), 319.

48. Thoreau, "Walking," in *Walden and Other Writings,* ed. Brooks Atkinson (New York: Modern Library, 2000), 627.

49. Thoreau, *Walden,* ed. Atkinson, 254.

50. Ibid., 182, 184, 254, 255.

51. Ibid., 160, 164.

52. W. B. Yeats, "The Circus Animals' Desertion," *The Collected Poems of W. B. Yeats* (New York: Knopf, 1971), 335–336.

53. Thoreau, *Walden,* ed. Atkinson, 131.

54. Ibid., 151, 164.

55. Wallace Stevens, "Poems of Our Climate," *The Collected Poems of Wallace Stevens* (New York: Knopf, 1971), 193–194.

5. A CONSERVATIONIST EMPIRE

1. Albert J. Beveridge, "For the Greater Republic, Not for Imperialism" (Speech Delivered at Union Hall, Philadelphia, February 15, 1899), reprinted in *Six Famous American Statesmen and Orators, Past and Present,* ed. Alexander Kelly McClure and Byron Andrews (New York: Lovell, 1902), 6–7.

2. Ibid., 5.

3. Beveridge, "Institutional Law," ibid., 113.

4. Ibid., 4.

5. Ibid., 6.

6. Beveridge, "The Star of Empire," 118.

7. Ibid., 129.

8. Ibid., 130.

9. Ibid., 133.

10. Beveridge, "Our Philippine Policy," in *The Meaning of the Times*, 84.

11. Beveridge, "Positive and Negative in Politics," ibid., 210.

12. Beveridge, "Institutional Law," ibid., 113.

13. See Paul Wallace Gates, *History of Public Land Law Development* (Rockville, Md.: Zenger, 1968), 548 (describing Marsh's influence on timbering enforcement).

14. *Congressional Record* 7, 1722 (1878), Statement of Senator Blaine: "I know nothing in the world to parallel it except that great assertion in our immortal Declaration of Independence that the King of England 'has erected a multitude of new offices, and sent hither swarms of officers to harass our people, and eat out their substance.'"

15. Ibid., 1861 (Statement of Senator Blaine).

16. Ibid., 1867 (Statements of Senator Sargent). They also insisted that, because earlier waves of settlers in the East and Midwest had enjoyed freedom to cut timber, regulating Western cutting would deny the latest pioneers equal citizenship. Ibid., 1722, Statement of Senator Teller: "I claim that nothing is demanded by the people in the Territories now that has not been conceded to all settlers in the new Territories."

17. Albert J. Beveridge, "The National Forest Service," in *The Meaning of the Times*, 382, 375–376, 382–383.

18. Beveridge, "Greater Republic," 8.

19. Beveridge, "The National Forest Service," 403.

20. Beveridge, "Progressive Liberty," in *The Meaning of the Times*, 262.

21. Beveridge, "The March of the Flag," ibid., 48. Roosevelt had warned in his famous speech "The Strenuous Life" (Chicago, April 10, 1899) that the United States must "play the part of China, and be content to rot by inches, in ignoble ease, within our borders."

22. Albert J. Beveridge, *The Young Man and the World* (New York: Appleton, 1905), 295.

23. Ibid., 309. Emphasis in the original.

24. Before the creation of Yellowstone National Park in 1872, land not retained as military bases was in steady process of allocation to states, settlers, and industrial interests (such as railroads) under a variety of ongoing and one-off

statutes. The president first acquired the power to create federal forest reserves in 1891, by way of a scrap of language inserted into the Civil Service Act and discussed mainly after its passage, in the fierce controversy that followed President Harrison's exercise of the authority.

25. 16 U.S.C. sec. 475.

26. 16 U.S.C. sec. 1.

27. See, e.g., Roderick Nash, *Wilderness and the American Mind,* 3rd ed. (New Haven: Yale University Press, 1982), 161–181 (describing the Hetch Hetchy dispute as a signal battle between wilderness-oriented "preservationists" and development-minded "conservationists").

28. See Gifford Pinchot, *The Fight for Conservation* (New York: Doubleday, Page, 1910), 48–49: "The conservation idea covers a wider range than the field of natural resources alone. Conservation means the greatest good to the greatest number for the longest time. . . . Conservation advocates the use of foresight, thrift, and intelligence in dealing with public matters. . . . It proclaims the right and duty of the people to act for the benefit of the people. Conservation demands the application of common-sense to the common problems for the common good."

29. Ibid., 49–50.

30. See ibid., 44 (giving a definition of conservation by its antithesis: "conservation stands for the prevention of waste").

31. Ibid., 4–5 (lamenting "waste" in cases where resources are left undeveloped, as with unmined coal, and in cases where they are inefficiently consumed); 7–8 (objecting to "waste" of renewable resources such as soil fertility as well as nonrenewable resources such as coal); 43 (failure to develop a resource can be as much a source of waste as poor use of it); 45–46 (proper understanding of "waste" has at last made possible human mastery over uses of resources). For applications of the concept of *waste* to human rather than natural resources, see, e.g., Woodrow Wilson, "First Inaugural Address" (Washington, D.C., March 4, 1913); and Irving Fisher, *A Report on National Vitality: Its Wastes and Conservation,* prepared for the National Conservation Commission (Washington, D.C.: Government Printing Office, 1909), 2.

32. See *Congressional Record* 2,537 (March 22, 1890).

33. *Report of the Secretary of the Interior to Congress* 1:13–14 (1891).

34. Theodore Roosevelt, "The New Nationalism," speech delivered at Osawatomie, Kansas, August 30, 1910.

35. See Charles van Hise, *Conservation of Our National Resources,* 2nd ed., based on *The Conservation of Natural Resources in the United States* (New York: Macmillan, 1930), 514–523.

36. Fisher, *Report on National Vitality,* 2.

37. See Frederick Law Olmsted, "The Yosemite Valley and Mariposa Big Tree Grove," in *America's National Parks System: The Essential Documents,* ed. Larry M. Dilsaver (Lanham, Md.: Rowman and Littlefield, 1994), 12, 20–22.

38. Wilson, "First Inaugural Address."

39. Ibid.

40. George Perkins Marsh, *Man and Nature; or, Physical Geography as Modified by Human Action,* ed. David Lowenthal (Seattle: University of Washington Press, 1864), 43–44.

41. Ibid., 44.

42. Ibid., 36, 37, 39, 41, 36.

43. Ibid., 38.

44. Ibid., 135.

45. Ibid., 5, 6.

46. Ibid., 5–7.

47. Ibid., 63.

48. Gates, *History of Public Land Law Development.*

49. Pinchot, *Conservation,* 173, 180, 88, 95.

50. See Robert H. Wiebe, *The Search for Order* (New York: Hill and Wang, 1967), 56–66 (describing anxiety over loss of imagined "purity" and "unity," and the wish to reclaim them); Richard Hofstadter, *The Age of Reform: From Bryan to FDR* (New York: Vintage, 1956), 196–212 (on the perception of pervasive selfishness, corruption, and indifference to ideals and the public interest).

51. See Pinchot, *Conservation,* 17–20 (on the threat of national decline from heedless consumption).

52. See Theodore Roosevelt, "Fellow-Feeling as a Political Factor," in *The Works of Theodore Roosevelt: The Strenuous Life* (New York: Collier, 1901), 74–75, 78 (on class and occupational segregation as a source civic division).

53. Theodore Roosevelt, "The Strenuous Life" (speech delivered in Chicago, April 10, 1899).

54. Ibid.

55. See William James, "The Moral Equivalent of War" (speech delivered in San Francisco, 1906).

56. Chauncy Hamlin, "Introduction," in *Report of the National Conference on Outdoor Recreation* (Washington, D.C.: U.S. Government Printing Office, 1928), 1–5.

57. Ibid., 2–3.

58. Roosevelt, "Fellow-Feeling as a Political Factor," 78.

59. See ibid., 79–80: "The only way to avoid the growth of these evils [class conflict] is . . . the creation of conditions which will permit mutual understanding and fellow-feeling between the members of the different classes. . . . If the men can be mixed together in some way that will loosen the class or caste bonds and put each on his merits as an individual man, there is certain to be a regrouping independent of caste lines."

60. Ibid.

61. Roosevelt, "The New Nationalism." He also wrote that "conservation is the great fundamental basis for national efficiency." Theodore Roosevelt, "Special Message of the President," in *Report of the National Conservation Commission* (Washington, D.C.: Government Printing Office, 1909), 1–9, 4. In the same document, he explained, "National efficiency is the result of natural resources well handled, of freedom of opportunity for every man, and of the inherent capacity, trained ability, knowledge, and will, collectively and individually, to use that opportunity."

62. Roosevelt, "Special Message," 3.

63. Ibid.

64. Ibid. See Roosevelt, "The New Nationalism." In his 1901 State of the Union address, Roosevelt declared: "The chief factor in the success of each man—wage-worker, farmer, and capitalist alike—must ever be the sum of his own individual qualities and abilities." In his "Special Message," he proposed: "The man who serves the community greatly should be greatly rewarded by the community; as there is a great inequality of service, so there must be great inequality of reward; but no man and no set of men should be allowed to play the game of competition with loaded dice" (Roosevelt, "Special Message," 3).

65. Theodore Roosevelt, "First Annual Message" (Washington, D.C., December 3, 1901).

66. See Eric Foner, *Reconstruction: America Unfinished Revolution, 1863–1877* (New York: Norton, 1988), 469–480 (discussing role of the idea of public interest among Progressive reformers); Samuel P. Hays, *Conservation and the Gospel of Efficiency: The Progressive Conservation Movement, 1890–1920*

(Pittsburgh: University of Pittsburgh Press, 1979), 261–276 (discussing the role of natural resources in the Progressive ideal of public interest).

67. See, e.g., Morton Keller, *Regulating a New Economy: Public Policy and Economic Change in America, 1900–1933* (Cambridge, Mass.: Harvard University Press, 1990), 7–19 (discussing competing ideas of the nature of the industrial economy and the appropriate role of government in its management); Robert J. Steinfeld, *Coercion, Contract, and Free Labor in the Nineteenth Century* (Cambridge: Cambridge University Press, 2001) (on the persistent normative complexity and ambiguity in legal regulation of the labor market).

68. Quoted in Eric Foner, *The Story of American Freedom* (New York: Norton, 1999), 154.

69. Ibid., 146–147.

70. Walter Weyl, *The New Democracy* (New York: Macmillan, 1927), 23.

71. Ibid.

72. Ibid., 321. Weyl also wrote of his social vision, "the democracy," that "the most elemental phase of this social policy is conservation" (ibid., 320); and "The conservation of human resources is a step towards to equalization of the chances of life and health of the citizens" (ibid., 326). Weyl, unlike some Progressives, was skeptical of the concept's value, arguing that it took currency from "the vogue of the analogous policy of the conservation of natural resources," but was too narrow to describe social policy's goal of improving the population (ibid., 320).

73. Weyl wrote acidly of the time when "the struggle for money and land waxed fiercer and fiercer . . . and men wasted and garnered and laughed and fought, as the continent was conquered" (ibid., 29).

74. Ibid., 279.

75. Ibid.

76. Ibid., 323.

77. Letter to Secretary of the Interior Roy O. West, January 16, 1929, quoted in Peter Jonathan Spiro, *Defending the Master Race: Conservation, Eugenics, and the Legacy of Madison Grant* (Lebanon, N.H.: University of Vermont Press, 2001), 71.

78. Spiro, *Defending the Master Race,* 158.

79. Ibid., 357.

80. Madison Grant, *The Passing of the Great Race; or, The Racial Basis of European History,* 2nd ed. (New York: Scribner's, 1918), 91.

81. Ibid., 227.

82. Ibid., 209.

83. Madison Grant, *Conquest of a Continent* (New York: Scribner's, 1933), 285.

84. Ibid., 91.

85. Spiro, *Defending the Master Race*, 272.

86. Madison Grant, "The Vanishing Moose and Their Extermination in the Adirondacks," *The Century* 47:3 (1894), 345–356.

87. See Garland E. Allen, "'Culling the Herd': Eugenics and the Conservation Movement in the United States, 1900–1940," *Journal of the History of Biology* 46:1 (February 2013), 31–72. Online at DOI 10.1007/s10739-011-9317-1.

6. A WILDERNESS PASSAGE INTO ECOLOGY

1. Robert Sterling Yard, *The Book of National Parks* (New York: Scribner's, 1919).

2. "A Summons to Save the Wilderness," *Living Wilderness* (September 1935), 1.

3. Ibid.

4. Ibid.

5. 16 U.S.C. sec. 1131(a).

6. 16 U.S.C. sec. 1331(c)(1)–(2).

7. "A Summons to Save the Wilderness."

8. Robert Marshall, "The Problem of the Wilderness," Scientific Monthly 30 (1930), 141.

9. Aldo Leopold, "Why the Wilderness Society?" *Living Wilderness* 1 (September 1935), 6.

10. Frederick S. Baker and Howard Zahniser, "We Certainly Need a Sound Philosophy: An Exchange of Letters," *Living Wilderness* (Winter 1947–1948), 1.

11. Howard Zahniser, "What's Behind the Wilderness Idea?" *Sierra Club Bulletin* (January 1956), 32.

12. David Brower, "The Sierra Club on the National Scene," *Sierra Club Bulletin* (January 1956), 3.

13. Zahniser, "What's Behind the Wilderness Idea?" (emphasis added).

14. See *Congressional Record* 18355–18356 (September 6, 1961).

15. Ibid., 18356.

16. Ibid.

17. "The Age of Effluence," *Time* (May 10, 1968), 52, 53.

18. "A Fable for Our Times," *Sierra Club Bulletin* 55 (1970), 16–18.

19. John Locke, "Second Treatise of Government," in Locke, *The Treatises of Government,* student ed., ed. Peter Laslett (Cambridge: Cambridge University Press, 2004) bk. 5, para. 27, 287–288.

20. "Fighting to Save the Earth from Man," *Time* (February 2, 1970), 56.

21. "Earth Day and Space Day," *New York Times* (April 19, 1970), 174; "Gladwin Hill, Activity Ranges from Oratory to Legislation," *New York Times* (April 23, 1970), 1 (referring to "ecological problems, which many scientists say urgently require action if the earth is to remain habitable").

22. Henry Fairfield Osborn Jr., *Our Plundered Planet* (New York: Little, Brown, 1948), ix.

23. Ibid., 4–5, 5–10, 67–86, 61, 60.

24. Ibid., iv, 3, 201, 201, 40–41.

25. Friedrich Nietzsche, *On the Genealogy of Morals,* trans. Walter Kaufmann and R. J. Hollingdale (New York: Vintage, 1989), 48–52.

26. Frederick H. Osborn, "Overpopulation and Genetic Selection," in *Our Crowded Planet,* ed. Henry Fairfield Osborn Jr. (New York: Doubleday, 1962), 51, 60.

27. Ibid., 67.

28. "Age of Effluence," 52.

29. "Fighting to Save the Earth from Man," 62.

30. Ibid., 62–63.

31. Richard Nixon, "State of the Union Address" (Washington, D.C., January 22, 1970).

32. "Issue of the Year: The Environment," *Time* (January 21, 1971), 21.

33. John H. Schaar and Sheldon S. Wolin, "Where We Are Now?" *New York Review of Books* (May 7, 1970).

34. Ibid.

35. Elizabeth Rogers, "Protest!" *Sierra Club Bulletin* 54 (December 1969), 11, 20.

36. Connie Flatboe, "Environmental Teach-In," *Sierra Club Bulletin* 55 (March 1970), 14, 15.

37. Alan Watts, "The World Is Your Body," in *The Ecological Conscience,* ed. Robert Disch (Englewood Cliffs, N.J.: Prentice-Hall, 1970), 181, 188.

38. Paul Shepard, "Ecology and Man: A Viewpoint, in *The Subversive Science,*" ibid., 56, 59.

39. John Rawls, *A Theory of Justice,* 2nd ed. (Cambridge, Mass.: Harvard University Press, 1999), 448.

40. Lynton K. Caldwell, *Environment: A Challenge for Modern Society* (Garden City, N.Y.: Natural History Press, 1970), 238.

41. See Christopher Stone, "Should Trees Have Standing? Toward Legal Rights for Natural Objects," *South California Law Review* 45 (1972), 450, 480. Holly Doremus also picks out Stone's article as an emblem of a moment of plasticity in environmental values. See Holly Doremus, "Symposium Introduction," *U.C. Davis Law Review* 37 (2003), 1–7.

42. *Sierra Club v. Morton,* 405 U.S. 727, 743, 749 (1972).

43. Ibid., 758.

44. Ibid., 760.

45. Edmund Muskie, 116 *Congressional Record* 32,904 (1970); 117 *Congressional Record* 38,801 (1971).

46. Charles Vanik, 118 *Congressional Record* 10,261 (1972).

47. Edmund Muskie, 117 *Congressional Record* 38,800 (1971).

48. John Sherman Cooper, 117 *Congressional Record* 38,819 (1971).

49. "Issue of the Year: The Environment," *Time* (January 21, 1971), 21.

50. Flora Lewis, "Instant Mass-Movement," *L.A. Times* (April 29, 1970), B27.

51. Edmund Muskie, 118 *Congressional Record* 36,874 (1972); 116 *Congressional Record* 36,033 (1970); 116 *Congressional Record* 33,906 (1970).

52. John Sherman Cooper, 116 *Congressional Record* 42,394 (1970); 116 *Congressional Record* 32,918 (1970).

53. Editorial, "Clean Air and Autos," *New York Times* (February 12, 1973), 26.

54. 118 *Congressional Record* 36,873 (1972) (Statement of Senator Muskie); 118 *Congressional Record* 10,259 (1972) (Statement of Representative Vanik).

55. Howard Baker, 117 *Congressional Record* 38,833 (1971).

56. Edmund Muskie, 117 *Congressional Record* 38,829 (1971).

57. *Lucas v. S.C. Coastal Council,* 505 U.S. 1003, 1031 (1992).

58. *Rapanos v. United States,* 547 U.S. 715, 721 (2006).

59. *Lucas v. S.C. Coastal Council,* 1069–1070 (Stevens, J., dissenting).

60. See *Southern Utah Wilderness Alliance v. BLM,* 425 F.3d 735 (10th Cir. 2005).

61. *Massachusetts v. EPA,* 549 U.S. 497 (2007).

62. See *Lujan v. Defenders of Wildlife,* 504 US 555, 561–562 (1992) (distinguishing between the easy case in which a plaintiff is "himself" the object of regulation, and the disfavored case, where the plaintiff complains of the government's failure to regulate a third party). See also Antonin Scalia, "The Doctrine of Standing as an Essential Element of the Separation of Powers, *Suffolk*

University Law Review 17 (1983), 881 (arguing that the central judicial responsibility is to protect the rights of individuals against government action,
with protection of property rights being paradigmatic).

63. Michael Winerip, "The Big Stories Then in the Clear Light of Now" (retrospec-
tive report on the 1987 "garbage barge" episode), *New York Times,* May 6, 2013.

7. ENVIRONMENTAL LAW IN THE ANTHROPOCENE

1. See Henry David Thoreau, *Walden and Other Writings,* ed. Brooks Atkinson
(New York: Modern Library, 2000), 4–11; Ralph Waldo Emerson, "Nature,"
in *The Essential Writings of Ralph Waldo Emerson,* ed. Brooks Atkinson
(London: Random House, 2009), 33–34 (farming "may show us what discord
is between man and nature, for you cannot freely admire a noble landscape
if laborers are digging in the field hard by").

2. See Thoreau, *Walden,* 146–157 (on raising beans as a reflective experience, not
a source of nutriment or income); 203–207 (deploring sensuality in eating,
as in other appetites, and calling for self-purification).

3. See John Muir, *My First Summer in the Sierra* (Boston: Houghton Mifflin,
1911), 129–131 (contrasting the divinity-infused landscape of the Sierra Nevada
with the filthy and uncomprehending shepherd who accompanies him there).

4. For discussions of regulatory and infrastructure bottlenecks that impede
small and unconventional farmers, and of possible reforms, see Neil D. Ham-
ilton, "Moving toward Food Democracy: Better Food, New Farmers, and
the Myth of Feeding the World," *Drake Journal of Agricultural Law* 16 (2011),
117; Michael Pollan, "An Open Letter to the Next Farmer-in-Chief," *New York
Times* (October 12, 2008), MM62.

5. Aldo Leopold, "The Round River," in Aldo Leopold, *A Sand County Almanac*
(New York: Ballantine, 1966), 188–199.

6. See Wendell Berry, *The Unsettling of America: Culture and Agriculture* (New
York: Avon, 1978), 43–48 (agricultural practice and cultural value are indis-
solubly linked).

7. I am indebted for this thought to Alyssa Battistoni, who has advanced it in
an unpublished paper and in her essay "Alive in the Sunshine," *Jacobin* 13
(January 2014), 20–28.

8. See Michael Pollan, *The Omnivore's Dilemma* (New York: Penguin, 2006),
304–333 (arguing for an Aristotelian approach to the treatment of domestic
animals).

9. See Eric Schlosser, *Fast Food Nation: The Dark Side of the All-American Meal* (New York: Houghton Mifflin, 2012), 169–178 (describing a slaughterhouse); Upton Sinclair, *The Jungle* (New York: Harper, 1906) (portraying the lives of immigrant laborers in the meat industry).

10. See Peter Singer, *Animal Liberation* (New York: HarperCollins, 2002), 95–158 (describing practices on factory farms).

11. See, generally, Rachel Carson, *Silent Spring* (Boston: Houghton Mifflin, 1994); see also "The Age of Effluence," *Time* (May 10, 1968), 52.

12. See Benjamin Ewing and Douglas A. Kysar, "Prods and Pleas: Limited Government in an Era of Unlimited Liability," *Yale Law Journal* 121 (2011), 350 (arguing for seeing law's processes, such as tort suits on climate change, as moves in a cultural and political debate over basic values).

8. WHAT KIND OF DEMOCRACY?

1. Douglas Kysar, *Regulating from Nowhere: Environmental Law and the Search for Objectivity* (New Haven: Yale University Press, 2010); Dale Jamieson, *Reason in a Dark Time: Why the Struggle against Climate Change Failed—and What It Means for Our Future* (New York: Oxford University Press, 2014).

2. Rosi Baidrotti, *The Posthuman* (Malden, Mass.: Polity, 2013), 55–104.

3. Robyn Eckersley, *Environmentalism and Political Theory: Toward an Ecocentric Approach* (Albany: State University Press of New York, 1992), 49–74.

4. Jane Bennett, *Vibrant Matter: A Political Ecology of Things* (Durham, N.C.: Duke University Press, 2010); Bruno Latour, *Facing Gaia: Six Lectures on the Political Theology of Nature,* Gifford Lectures, Edinburgh (February 18–28, 2013).

5. William Cronon, "The Trouble with Wilderness; or, Getting Back to the Wrong Nature," in Cronon, ed., *Uncommon Ground: Toward Reinventing Nature* (New York: Norton, 1995), 69–90.

ACKNOWLEDGMENTS

I have wanted to write this book since at least 1996, when Robin Kelsey, then a graduate student in Art History at Harvard, encouraged me to pursue it. I finally settled on doing it almost fourteen years later, over lunch on a gorgeously bright spring day in Cambridge, when my editor, John Kulka, invited me to submit a proposal.

Much of the thinking and research behind this book took place in seminars on environmental law and politics that I taught at the law schools at Duke, Georgetown, Harvard, Tel Aviv, Virginia, and Yale. I benefited from presenting early drafts of material at all of those schools and also Berkeley Law School, Columbia Law School, Texas Law School, the UCLA Law School, and the Geography Department at the University of North Carolina at Chapel Hill. I also presented several chapters at the annual Workshop on New Thinking in Environmental Law at the University of Colorado, Boulder. I am especially indebted to a set of colleagues who spent a day with me working through the manuscript in the winter of 2014: Lynne Feeley, David Grewal, Michael Hardt, Aziz Rana, and Priscilla Wald. Their careful feedback was invaluable and resulted in great improvements in the manuscript at every scale.

I am grateful to some other readers who looked very carefully at parts of the manuscript and gave me valuable responses: Bruce Ackerman, Matthew Adler, Jamie Boyle, Peter Byrne, Jonathan

Cannon, Sara Dewey, Lisa Heinzerling, Sarah Krakoff, Doug Kysar, Rose Lambert-Sluter, Daniel Markovits, Sarah Mesle, Ralf Michaels, Robert Post, Hannah Purdy, Jim Salzman, Michelle Wilde Anderson. I benefited from the research assistance of Elly Benson, Karen Grohman, Margaret Rozen, and Brantley Webb.

John Kulka is a wonderful editor—of the old school in the best sense. He masterfully corralled the insightful but divergent views of three anonymous readers and maintained his own editorial vision, which I came to trust entirely.

INDEX